To Dad,

Merry Christmas

with love

Angela

1999.

THE FASTEST MEN ON EARTH

Pete Holthusen

Capt. Malcolm Campbell
breaks World's Record at
206·95 Miles per Hour!

Using

Castrol

DAYTONA BEACH. FEB. 19th, 1928. CAPT. MALCOLM CAMPBELL. NAPIER-CAMPBELL "BLUE BIRD" BREAKING WORLD'S MILE RECORD AT 206·95 M.P.H.

THE FASTEST MEN ON EARTH

100 YEARS OF THE LAND SPEED RECORD

PETER J.R. HOLTHUSEN

FOREWORD BY ART ARFONS

SUTTON PUBLISHING

First published in 1999 by
Sutton Publishing Limited · Phoenix Mill
Thrupp · Stroud · Gloucestershire · GL5 2BU

British Library Cataloguing in Publication Data
A catalogue record for this book is available from the British Library

ISBN 0-7509-2203-6

Title page: *Thrust SSC*, see pages 190–9. (Castrol International)
Frontispiece: Castrol has been involved in record breaking since Charles Cheers Wakefield first introduced his Wakefield Castor Motor Oil in 1906. (Castrol International)
Half-title page: Art Arfons and the *Green Monster* at Bonneville, see page 119. (Author's collection)

> # *For Rosemary,*
> # *born from a dream*

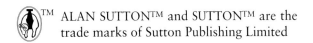

Typeset in 10/13pt Sabon.
Typesetting and origination by
Sutton Publishing Limited.
Printed in Great Britain by
Butler & Tanner, Frome, Somerset.

CONTENTS

FOREWORD

The land speed record for me has always been the ultimate endeavour. My interest in it was first piqued when I read about George Eyston and John Cobb. They were my heroes. I couldn't imagine how they felt attaining such speeds in their time. Little did I know that I would be fortunate enough to attain greater speeds in my time.

I guess speed has always been in control of my life. I can't explain my desire to attempt the land speed record. The closest I can come is in relation to music. When you listen to fine classical music, and the violinist is striving to hit that ever so high note, you hold your breath in expectation – and he hits it! That is what the record feels like to me. The car is riding and handling rough at one point, and then you cross the 400mph point and things smooth out. The car is gliding across the salt and the engine is just a distant hum. It is just you and your destiny.

Most people want to reach the top in their chosen field. This was the top for me. I've spent many a sleepless night before I run; but once I get in the car and fire it up, I lose my butterflies. I think most race drivers feel the same way.

Having survived a 600mph crash – the world's fastest – I count myself among the luckiest men alive.

Among us land speed record drivers, Peter Holthusen's first book was known as 'The Bible' – I know there is no man alive today who has a greater knowledge of the subject. Over the past twenty-five years he has earned the respect and confidence of us all as the leading authority on the land speed record.

This outstanding new book on the complete history of man's quest for ultimate speed on land will fill a much needed void. It gives me great pleasure to write the foreword to this detailed work on our sport from Peter Holthusen's pen.

Art Arfons, 1999

ACKNOWLEDGEMENTS

The preparation of this book, and the compilation of facts and figures, would have been an impossible task without the help and assistance given by numerous individuals, organizations and companies throughout the world.

Foremost, I wish to thank Jamie Dunn at Castrol International, who has always afforded me his complete support in my research. I would particularly like to express my appreciation to Art and Dusty Arfons, Craig Breedlove, Marc Samson, Peter Brock, Hal Needham, Stan Barrett and Brigadier General Charles E. 'Chuck' Yeager.

Special mention must be made of Michael Roberts who has consistently placed great faith in the project, both as a friend and through cyber contact with the Internet.

Also, my devoted wife, Rosemary, is to be congratulated for her patience, tolerance and practical support that did much to preserve a modicum of sanity during the preparation of this book, and whose love and resolute confidence provided me with the will to succeed.

To my family, Sarah, Graham, Daniella and Emmie, I offer my deepest appreciation for their love and faith in my ability to deliver. To Emmie and John whose love, kindness and country solace proved limitless. To Tamara and Dylan I am especially indebted for their love and acceptance, and to Carla for her love, kindness and most humble appreciation of life.

For her skilful translation of French to English I especially acknowledge Jodie Leahey.

For moral and other support over the years that this book has been in preparation, I wish to acknowledge encouragement from many friends, associates and colleagues, in particular Margaret Roberts, Sue and Bob, Pat, Dave and James Balcombe, and Dave and Gilly Sibley.

I would also like to thank Rupert Harding, Rebecca Nicholls, Sarah Moore and Olwen Greany at Sutton Publishing, whose skill and excellence seemingly knows no bounds.

Finally, I wish to remember one very dear person, my later father E.R. Peter Holthusen, who once told me – 'Optimism is a faith that leads to success.'

Without you all this book would not have been possible.

HUMBLE BEGINNINGS

There is no sure way of knowing where to start our story. If we did know, it would fit the historians' penchant for dates but the very beginning is just a bare strand in the fabric of history. Nevertheless, that trace thread has left an imprint sufficiently visible for a chronology banded by decades rather than specific years. It would be useful to be able to define the concept of land speed, but that too is complicated by traditional thoughts of acceleration and terminal velocity. However, the scene for the genesis of the automobile speed record can be fairly placed on the European continent.

Reporting on the Paris–Rouen reliability run of 22 July 1894, Gerald Rose in his classic *A Record of Motor Racing 1894–1908*, notes that,'many now well-known people were present at the start, among them Mr James Gordon-Bennett, the wealthy proprietor of the *New York Herald*, who sent a special reporter on a bicycle to follow the race through to Rouen'. We quibble with the otherwise impeccable Mr Rose on two counts – his use of 'race' (no doubt he tired of writing 'trials', the term used most often in describing this first of all automobile contests) and the superfluous hyphen in Gordon Bennett.

Le Petit Journal, the newspaper that sponsored the Paris–Rouen trials, considered them an unequivocal success. A large crowd saw the start on the Boulevard Maillot. Reports in the archives of the Automobile Club de France indicate that the lunch stop at Nantes was enjoyed by both the townspeople and participants and a remarkable seventeen of the twenty-one starters completed the 78.75 mile run and hill climb.

Encouraged by the reception given the trials, a group of French enthusiasts, led by the Baron de Zuylen of Belgium and Count de Dion, asked *Le Petit Journal* to lend its support to a more testing event in the summer of 1895, perhaps an all-out race of 700 or 800 miles! After showing initial interest, the paper regretfully withdrew its support, fearing that its competitors would call the *Journal* irresponsible for encouraging a speed contest. Not easily discouraged, on 2 November 1894, the enterprising Count de Dion called a meeting at his home. The committee, which one year later was to form the Automobile Club de France (ACF), eventually decided to hold a race in 1895, from Paris to Bordeaux and back, a distance of 732 miles. The winner was to be the first automobile to finish which had seats for more than two passengers. Thus did our racing forefathers help placate their critics by demonstrating that if speed were motor racing's only objective, the regulations would have been written to permit the faster two-seaters to be eligible for awards.

By the time Gordon Bennett became interested in automobile racing he was known as a successful, albeit flamboyant, newspaper publisher and an

IT BEGAN WITH THE GORDON BENNETT RACES

The popular Belgian sportsman, Baron Pierre de Caters in the 11.9-litre, 90hp Gordon Bennett-type road racing Mercedes with which he set the record at 97.25mph (156.941kph) on 25 May 1904, on the Ostend to Nieuport road. (Author's collection)

The first auto races were competitive versions of motor tours, starting in one city and ending in another. Thus were they known: Paris–Bordeaux–Paris, Paris–Berlin, Paris–Marseilles–Paris, Paris–Vienna, and so forth. Paris was prominent as a starting point or destination because French auto makers were leaders in the early days of the world motor industry, and the Paris newspapers were diligent supporters of racing.

An argument over the relative merits of French cars and those from the younger American industry led a New York newspaper publisher to encourage a different kind of race. He was James Gordon Bennett, proprietor of the *New York Herald*. In October 1899 Gordon Bennett announced that he would put up a trophy, in his name, to be fought for by teams representing the recognized auto clubs of car-building nations. Three cars were to be allowed from each country.

First run in 1900, the race for the Gordon Bennett Trophy attracted little attention. The great town-to-town events were more glamorous, but in 1903, when the Paris–Madrid race was halted after the carnage of its first stage to Bordeaux, the days of such transcontinental races were seen to be numbered. Suddenly, the Gordon Bennett race was the biggest thing in Europe, run on a closed network of roads in a relatively limited area. A German car had won the trophy in 1903, so it was the responsibility of the German Automobile Club to stage the 1904 event. For the course it chose roads in the Taunus Mountains near Bad Homburg, just north of Frankfurt. The task of organizing the race was formidable, with three-car teams from seven countries and intricate scheduling and inspection demands. (Every part of every car had to be made in the entering country.)

The 1904 race was held on 17 June. Three days later, at Bad Homburg, representatives of six of the participating automobile clubs met to discuss their mutual efforts in the field of motor racing. In their meeting, presided over by Count de Sierstorpff, they reflected the view that racing had become too great a burden to be shouldered by only a few clubs. It was time to discuss a united effort. Guided by de Sierstorpff, they decided to found a new body, an association among their clubs, that they would authorize to represent them in both sporting and industrial matters – without relinquishing any of their individual rights and powers – the Association Générale de l'Automobile.

The discussions moved with vigour and optimism. When contacted, seven more clubs agreed to join the founding group. In all, they included the auto clubs of Germany, Austria, Belgium, Denmark, Spain, the United States, France, Great Britain, Italy, the Netherlands, Portugal, Russia and Switzerland. Of these the most powerful and prominent was the Automobile Club de France, which had led in the promotion of club activities and the organization of racing. It was in tacit recognition of this fact that the president of the ACF, Baron de Zuylen, was also named president of the new organization. Paris, and the offices of the ACF, were chosen as its headquarters.

outstanding sportsman. He attended the Ecole Polytechnique in Paris and was as much at home in France as in his native New York. Gordon Bennett came back to the United States to serve as a navy lieutenant in the Civil War but returned to Paris following a scandal in New York that involved a duel. In 1887 he founded the Paris edition of his father's newspaper, the *New York Herald*.

In 1869, as managing editor of the *Herald*, Bennett had been responsible for sending British explorer-journalist Henry Morton Stanley to Africa to find David Livingstone. He helped to finance the 1875 search for the Northwest Passage and in 1877 sponsored the tragic De Long expedition to the Arctic. An erratic but generous man, he gave $100,000 to the *Herald* relief fund for Irish sufferers of the agrarian outrages, yet was known to fire an employee if he did not like his looks. As a sportsman he helped introduce polo to the United States, and he personally skippered his yacht, *Dauntless*, in the transatlantic race of 1870.

Bennett became an early member of the Automobile Club de France and regularly gave financial support to European racing. But he remained an American patriot. The idea of the Gordon Bennett races was the result of his conviction that an American machine could beat the best of Europeans, and his showman's instinct told him that the sponsorship of a series of international automobile races would be a good thing for his newspapers. Gordon Bennett began to realize his idea in 1899 when the pioneer American car maker, Alexander Winton, challenged Fernand Charron to a match race of 1,000 miles. Winner of the 1898 Marseilles–Nice and Paris–Amsterdam races in his Panhard, Charron quickly accepted Winton's challenge, posting 20,000 francs with the *Herald*'s Paris office. Nothing came of Winton's dare, but one month later Bennett announced the Gordon Bennett Cup series and commissioned famed Paris silversmith Auroc to prepare the trophy.

Automobile racing in the United States got under way on 2 November 1895, after H.H. Kohlsaat, who bought the *Chicago Times-Herald* in April 1895, visited Europe in 1894. In July 1895 he persuaded his editor to sponsor a contest. As with the 1894 Paris–Rouen Concours, as its sponsors called it, many more entries, close to a hundred, were received than were ready to race. So few were fully prepared as race day neared that the event was postponed to 28 November, Thanksgiving Day. However, so as not to disappoint the public, an 'Exhibition Run' was scheduled for the original race date, 2 November. For running from Chicago to Waukegan and back, a prize of $500 was to be divided between all finishers within a 13-hour maximum time limit. A Duryea Motor Wagon, driven by Frank Duryea accompanied by his brother Charles, and a Mueller-Benz, driven by the builder's son Oscar, were the sole starters. However, two Kane-Pennington Electric Victorias and a Morris and Salom Electric were exhibited at the start. The Duryea and Benz left the Midway Plaisance in Jackson Park at 8.15 a.m., the 'race' proper starting at Halsted and 55th Street. The Duryea lost 48 minutes repairing a snapped drive chain and, after almost catching the Benz, was ditched by an errant farm wagon. Mueller's Benz completed the 92 miles in 8 hours and 44 minutes actual running time after being on the road for 9 hours and 30 minutes. As the only finisher it won the $500 prize.

Driving on Thanksgiving Day 1895 would have been difficult for today's motorist. The US Weather Bureau's Chicago report for 25–28 November read: 'A severe snowstorm which visited Chicago on November 25th and 26th left 12 inches of snow . . . temperatures ranged from 8 to 13 degrees . . . winds attained a high of 60 miles an hour.' Race-day temperatures did rise to the low 30s Fahrenheit, but 8–10in of snow, slush, and ice remained. Of the eleven competitors that had claimed to be ready the day before, only six made it to the start: Duryea Motor Wagon, De la Vergne Refrigerating Machine Co., Benz, Morris and Salom Electric, R.H. Macy-Benz, Sturges Electric Motocycle, and the Mueller-Benz, which was over an hour late for the start.

At 8.55 a.m. J. Frank Duryea and his umpire, Arthur White, were the first off. The De la Vergne Benz followed but soon withdrew because of trouble getting through the slush between Jackson Park and the official 55th Street starting point. Jerry O'Connor, driving the Macy-Benz, with Lieutenant Samuel Rodman as umpire, started at 8.59 a.m. Within minutes, nearing the Art Institute the Macy-Benz slid into the rear of a horse-drawn streetcar, crossed the Pennsylvania railroad tracks, and collided with an overturned sleigh that had just dumped its occupants, including the *Times-Herald* reporter, in the snow. Later O'Connor made contact with a hack, further bending the Benz's already damaged steering. This last misfortune forced the Macy-Benz to retire. The Sturges Electric left at 9.01 a.m., followed 1 minute later by the Morris and Salom Electric. Sixth and last to leave was the tardy Mueller-Benz, with Oscar Mueller and umpire Charles B. King. They started at 10.06 a.m.

Large, good-natured crowds lined the route. Those attending the Michigan–University of Chicago football game in Lincoln Park paused to cheer the 'motorcycles'; willing hands helped lift stuck machines out of snow-banks, and the Chicago police hustled from point to point clearing a path for the approaching machines. At Evanston the Macy-Benz had less than a 2-minute lead over the Duryea, with the Mueller-Benz 45 minutes behind. Minor delays were caused by the Cottage Grove Horse Cars. Time was lost, and meticulously recorded, for mechanical adjustments: '2 minutes to oil engine; 8.5 minutes to tighten belt; one-half minute right chain off; 6 minutes to bend clutch'. Two relay stations supplied gasoline and pails of broken ice for cooling. Charles Reid, a third rider in Mueller's car, was removed after 35 miles, exhausted and cold. Nearing the finish, Frank Duryea lost 10 minutes when he took a wrong turn, but by then his only competition was the Mueller-Benz, far behind.

As the crowd chilled, its mood changed. At Douglas Park, a group of 200 youngsters first snow-balled the police and then drove them into the street. An attempt to call patrol wagons found that all phone lines had been down since the beginning of the storm. The streets became all but deserted as darkness fell, and fewer than fifty people were in Jackson Park at 7.18 p.m. to see the Duryea win America's first automobile race. At 8.53 the Mueller-Benz crossed the finish line, only 24 minutes running time behind the Duryea, because it had started over an hour later. The Duryea completed the 54.36 mile run in 10 hours and 23 minutes total time – 7 hours and 53 minutes actual running time, at an average speed of 6.66mph. For the final hour, umpire Charles King drove the Benz with one hand on the tiller, the other supporting Oscar Mueller, who had collapsed from exposure.

This is the same Charles Brady King who, on 6 March 1896, drove the first automobile on the streets of Detroit and from 1909 manufactured his own car. King was also one of those responsible for the formation of the world's first automobile club, the American Motor League, established in Chicago on 1 November 1895. Twelve days later, the Automobile Club de France was organized by the Count de Dion at his Quai d'Orsay home in Paris, and 12 December saw Great Britain's Self-Propelled Traffic Association formed.

On 5 December prizes were awarded to the two Chicago–Evanston finishers and seven other entrants: $2,000 to the Duryea for best performance, range of speed, pull and compactness of design; $1,500 to H. Mueller for performance and economy of operation; and $500 to the Macy-Benz for its showing in the race. The farsighted judges also made awards based on tests, as well as race performance, for 'ease of control, absence of noise or vibration, cleanliness and general excellence of design'. However, giving the *Times-Herald* gold medal to the Electrobat, a non-finisher, did cause some dismay. (To this day it is not known why the *Times-Herald* made this decision.) In addition to local newspaper accounts, contemporary reports, calling the event a motorcycle race, appeared in America's first automobile publications, *Horseless Age* and *The Motocycle*. The *Times-Herald*, looking for a term to replace 'horseless carriage', had sponsored a $500 contest to find a new name. 'Motocycle' was the winner, but not for long.

The second automobile race held in America was run on 30 May 1896, and was sponsored by *Cosmopolitan* magazine. Its editor, John Brisbane Walker, arranged for the course to run from New York's City Hall to Irvington-on-Hudson; *Cosmopolitan* was published in Irvington, which also happened to be where Walker had his home. Following a 'parade' of the race cars from City Hall to Kingsbridge, where the race actually began, the field ran up the Hudson to the Ardsley Country Club in Irvington, where the race judges (who included John Jacob Astor, Chauncey Depew, President of the New York Central Railroad, and Frank Thompson, President of the Pennsylvania Railroad) awaited them. The officials were transported from New York City by the New York Central and Hudson River Railroad. They were joined by 400 guests celebrating the country-

club opening. Although the *Cosmopolitan* had thirty entries, only six started. Frank Duryea won the 30-mile run in 7 hours and 13 minutes, pocketing the complete purse of $3,000 in prize money as the only finisher.

Meanwhile, across the Atlantic M. Paul Meyan, one of the founding members of the Automobile Club de France and publisher of the pioneering motoring journal *La France Automobile*, persuaded his editor to sponsor a timed hill-climb at Chanteloup, some 20 miles north of Paris. The route chosen was a 1⅛ mile, 1 in 12 gradient on the morning of 27 November 1898. A total of fifty-four cars turned up for the sponsored event and forty-seven made the climb, a revolutionary electric car built in Paris but driven by a Belgian named Camille Jenatzy making the fastest ascent at a little over 17mph. In second place was a Bollée petrol car, and third a Panhard-Levassor.

Less than a week later *La France Automobile* announced it would be holding an international competition of speed for cars of all kinds, 'at the request of one of our distinguished friends'. The competition would be held on 18 December over a carefully marked 2,000 metre stretch of smooth, level, open road in Achères park, between the towns of St Germain and Constans. On 18 December 1898, a small crowd of people assembled on the normally deserted stretch of road that cuts across the park at Achères. They were about to witness the world's first land speed record.

The inception of the automobile speed record on 18 December 1898 was owed entirely to the introduction of motor-car reliability trials and hill-climbing to the Paris–Rouen area by the debonair Count Gaston de Chasseloup-Laubat. The Count was the younger brother of the Marquis de Chasseloup-Laubat, who with the Count de Dion had founded the now legendary Automobile Club de France.

It was cold and wet on the morning of 18 December, when the dashing Count (the 'friend' of *La France Automobile*) took his chain-driven 40hp Jeantaud electric motor car to the lonely Achères road outside Paris. In the

In 1903 Camille Jenatzy entered the fourth Gordon Bennett Cup race on the Ballyshannon course in Ireland, with the Mercedes '60'. Jenatzy's land speed records of 1899 launched him on to a career path in road racing and the inception of the coveted World Land Speed Record. (Author's collection)

centre of this stretch of road, six timekeepers were fussing about, synchronizing their stop watches and checking once more the marks that had been laid across the road. The 2 kilometre stretch was divided into two, the first kilometre for standing start speeds, with the second for flying start figures. Two timekeepers – one of them Louis Mors of the famous Mors electrical concern – were posted at the start, two at the first kilometre, and two at the second.

Away down the road, some distance from the measured course, a small group of men huddled around the four machines that were to take part in this record run. They included a de Dion tricycle, two Bollées and the Count's electrically powered Jeantaud, an extraordinary affair with a low, boat-shaped body on top of which the driver perched, exposed to the elements, with only his legs actually inside the car. The plan was to time all four vehicles over one standing kilometre followed by one flying.

One by one the vehicular monstrosities bowled down the Achères road, and into the measured 2 kilometre stretch. Anxious consultations followed each timed run, but no announcement was made. Finally it was the turn of Count Gaston de Chasseloup-Laubat. His electric car made a curious, high-pitched ringing hum as the starter, M. Paul Meyan himself, gave the signal and the Jeantaud rushed down the course, swaying dangerously on its narrow pneumatic tyres. The intrepid driver bent low over the steering gear to reduce windage while the Fulmen batteries produced, for a brief burst of a few minutes' duration, about 40hp. He made a single run through a measured kilometre in 57 seconds at an average speed of 39.34mph (63.13kph) and claimed an official world record. Second fastest was Loysel's 3-litre Bollée *Torpille*, a formidable racing machine of its day, at 35.5mph, and third Giraud's Bollée at 33.6mph. The seeds of rivalry had been sown; doubtless someone would soon come along and have a go at beating the new record. . . .

The news that a Frenchman had done such a thing struck like a thunderbolt at the heart of the patriotic Belgian electric car inventor, Camille Jenatzy, known endearingly as the 'Red Devil' because of the colour of his beard. He sat down and penned a challenge to the Frenchman; they would duel with their electric motor cars in what was to be the world's first road race. In a letter to *La France Automobile* Jenatzy expressed his regret at not being at Achères on 18 December; he then issued a 'défi' to Chasseloup-Laubat, declaring his absolute confidence in his ability to beat the Jeantaud electric motor car under the same course conditions, which the Count returned, together with his acceptance of the challenge.

They met on the Achères road on 17 January 1899. Jenatzy, the challenger, was the first to be timed. He passed through the measured kilometre at 41.42mph (66.65kph), the electric batteries of the Chanteloup winner giving out just after he crossed the terminal timing line. For the first time, the land speed record had been broken. Ten minutes later, however, the French Count recorded an elapsed time of 43.69mph (70.31kph) to beat him, burning out the motor of his Jeantaud with the overburdening surge of power he had applied in his quest to regain his record. De Chasseloup-Laubat and Jenatzy agreed to meet again at Achères, and both intrepid drivers went home to build bigger engines for the race. Jenatzy won the next challenge round at 49.92mph (80.33kph) ten days later. By this time the titanic struggle between the two electric car drivers had attracted so much interest that the Automobile Club de France organized rules and appointed official timekeepers and marshals for the now famous runs.

The Frenchman next returned to Achères alone in March to establish yet another new record, 57.60mph (92.69kph). The Jeantaud looked notably different from the previous December; it now had equal-sized wheels and new bodywork made at the Jeantaud carriage works in Paris and sported a 'windcutting' nose, streamlined undertray and a pointed tail. Jenatzy confidently continued working on a new idea that he felt certain would win him back the record. He developed an electric motor with secondary coils that would turn at 900rpm, something not thought possible at that time. Engineered by the Compagnie Internationale des Transports Automobiles Electriques Jenatzy, the new electric car had a semi-elliptically sprung chassis (duplicated at the rear) with perhaps the smallest wood-spoked wheels and certainly the thickest-section Michelin tyres seen at that time. On it was mounted a special cigar-shaped body formed of 'partinium', a new kind of alloy invented by the Frenchman, Henri Partin. This revolutionary aluminium body was designed by Léon Auscher of Carrosserie Rothschild of Paris, the company that fabricated it.

The bullet-shaped La Jamais Contente *shortly after Camille Jenatzy established a new World Land Speed Record of 65.79mph (105.904kph) at Achères on 29 April 1899. The car was powered by two electric motors driven by Fulmen batteries by way of direct drive to the rear wheels. (Author's collection)*

Jenatzy christened his new car *La Jamais Contente (Never Satisfied)*, perhaps to remind himself that he would not submit to his French rival. Once again, he challenged the Count, and the run was set for 1 April 1899. Jenatzy, the challenger, was to go first as was the custom, but he started his run too soon. When he reached the end of the timed kilometre, officials there were still measuring the distance and had not marked the exact spot for the vital timing recognition. Jenatzy was sure he had broken through the 100kph barrier, but due to the lack of urgency shown by the Automobile Club de France officials and timing marshals, the feat could not be recognized, and he could not repeat the run having totally exhausted his batteries on the first run.

Jenatzy returned to the same remote road on 29 April; this time the Count Gaston de Chasseloup-Laubat was present as one of the large crowd of spectators lining the track. The Belgian admonished the timekeepers and received their assurances that there would be no slip-ups on the course this time. They were so intent on accuracy, in fact, that after the run they were still checking their timepieces as Jenatzy dismounted and stormed up to them demanding to know his speed. It was a new record, 65.79mph, or more than 105kph. He had broken the 100kph barrier. Jenatzy held the World Land Speed Record for nearly three years, and the speed record for electric cars for more than half a century, but by then, petrol and steam-powered road cars had caught up and passed the lively electrics with their unavoidable handicaps of heavy batteries and limited range.

TWO

ALTERNATIVE POWER

Jenatzy became the first man in the world to travel at the speed of one mile a minute, and a new and thrilling sport was born. When the record was broken, Léon Serpollet, a Frenchman, did it in a steam-powered car, using for his track the famous Promenade des Anglais in Nice because the Achères road was considered too rough for such high speeds. Léon Serpollet was one of the world's most talented steam car exponents by far and 13 April 1902 was to be his greatest day. Serpollet drove his streamlined steam car, *La Baleine* (*The Whale*), to a speed of 75.06mph (120.79kph), holding his breath nearly all the way through the kilometre in 29.8 seconds, beating four of the latest Mercedes-Simplex '40s', gaining his third Rothschild Cup in a row, and breaking Jenatzy's land speed record by over 9mph. Serpollet allegedly remarked after the run that he literally had to turn his head to inhale.

The World Land Speed Record inched slowly upwards, while sportsmen like American millionaire William K. Vanderbilt Jr, the great Henri Fournier, famed winner of the Paris–Bordeaux and Paris–Berlin runs in 1901, the Hon. Charles S. Rolls, whose name, coupled with that of Frederick Henry Royce, epitomized British motoring at its best, Baron de Forest, and Belgian Arthur Duray held official and unofficial records for short periods of time. Duray first demonstrated his ungainly Gobron-Brillié at a speed trial meeting held outside Ostend in July 1903. It was an unbelievable pass; its radiator and scuttle cowled in, the crippled car flew through the kilometre in only 26.8 seconds, a speed of 83.47mph, while a similar car driven by Louis Rigolly was runner-up. Later that year he raised it to 84.73mph at Dourdan, France. The big 13½-litre Gobron-Brillié with opposed-piston engine went on to score further victories in the Laffrey, Chateau-Thièrry and celebrated Gaillon hill-climbs with Rigolly, emphasizing their versatility and excellence.

The Hon. Charles Rolls took his latest creation, one of the illustrious 70hp 'Dauphin'-type Mors automobiles which outshone all others in the 1903 Paris–Madrid race, to a private course on the Duke of Portland's estate at Clipstone, near Welbeck, in Nottinghamshire, England. It was hoped this would be the first record to be established on British soil. There Rolls was timed by officials of the Automobile Club of Great Britain and Ireland (the ACGBI, forerunner of the RAC) to cover the kilometre in 26.4 seconds – a speed of 84.73mph, equalling Duray's pass at Dourdan, but alas, the ACF declined to recognize Rolls's new figures citing that it had not approved the system of timing employed at Clipstone.

Apart from Arthur Duray's effort at Ostend in July 1903, every successful attempt on the land speed record (LSR) thus far had taken place on French soil. The LSR was still a European possession, even though the famed Ormond Beach, near Daytona, Florida, had already become recognised as the best of the great beach courses. In fact, the Ormond

American millionaire William K. Vanderbilt Jr not only held the land speed record twice, but his books on touring were among the very first and finest of the day. He was also the founder of the celebrated Vanderbilt Cup series. (Author's collection)

LÉON SERPOLLET 1858–1907

Leon Serpollet, a Frenchman, was one of the world's most talented steam car exponents, observed here in his streamlined 4-cylinder, single-acting, steam-powered car at the start line on the Promenade des Anglais in Nice where he broke Camille Jenatzy's land speed record by over 9mph.
(Author's collection)

Léon Serpollet, born in Beauvais, France, in 1858, had a cavalier approach to steam power that immediately appealed. A carpenter's son who spent his evenings working on boiler design, he perfected the flash boiler in 1885. In this, water was pumped into a multi-coiled pipe, which was already heated, to be converted there in a flash into superheated steam. The result was a considerable reduction in the time needed to warm up the car before it was ready to start. As only a limited amount of water was being heated at any one moment, the danger of explosion was also reduced, although it had been greatly exaggerated by the critics anyway.

Serpollet used his boiler, or generator as he preferred to call it, in a tricycle which he built in 1887. Two years later, he had four heavier three-wheeled cars constructed for him by Armand Peugeot. One of these made a journey from Paris to Lyons and back in 1890, taking two weeks to cover the 790 miles (1,270km). A few more of the three-wheelers, which could seat up to five passengers, were produced for Serpollet by the Parisian coachbuilder Jeantaud. By 1892, Serpollet realized that the three-wheeler was too unstable, and turned to making four-wheeled commercial vehicles. They occupied him until 1899, when he obtained financial backing from Frank L. Gardner, an American living in Paris, who had made a fortune in Australian gold mines. A new series of Serpollet cars came into being; they were much more modern, with rear-mounted boilers, horizontally opposed paraffin-fired two- and four-cylinder engines located halfway between front and rear axles, and final drive by single chain to the centre of the rear axle. A hand-operated dual pump fed oil to the burner, and water to the boiler, in constant proportions. From 1904 onwards, this pump was operated by a separate donkey engine.

With Frank Gardner's backing, Léon Serpollet was at last able to make a commercial success of passenger cars. Between 1900 and 1904, the workforce in Gardner's large factory in the Rue Stendhal, Paris, rose from about 60 to 140, and production ran at the rate of 100 or more cars per year. They ranged from light two-seaters to large, ornate touring limousines, one of which was ordered by the Shah of Persia. Serpollet was keen on sport, and in 1902 he drove his streamlined steam car, nicknamed La Baleine (The Whale), to a speed of 75.06mph (120.79kph), setting a new World Land Speed Record. He also fielded teams of racing cars in long-distance events, such as the 1903 Paris–Madrid race and the 1904 Gordon Bennett Trials, but he did not meet with great success.

The steam car dwindled in popularity after about 1904 and when Serpollet died of tuberculosis in 1907, his cars died with him. Fewer than a thousand Serpollet cars were built, but they were by far the most important of the European steam cars.

Beach Garage became the first American 'Gasoline Alley', housing the great racing machines of the day, and to this day is the home of the legendary Birthplace of Speed Association. However, it was to be a Mid-western auto mechanic who would become the first American to drive an American-built car on American soil and set the new record.

Henry Ford had just resigned his position as a general superintendent of the Detroit-based Edison Company to build his own gasoline-powered automobiles. Noting the success of Alexander Winton, Frank Duryea and Ransom Olds, who promoted their cars through racing, Ford built two racing cars, the Ford 999 and the famous *Arrow*. Henry Ford stated his feelings about competition in his autobiography: 'Almost everyone proceeded from the premise that a first class car would automatically develop the highest speed.'

In Ford's first challenge of the fabled Winton, he won a match race. Next, Ford hired as a driver the celebrated bicycle racer, Barney Oldfield, who went out to race Winton and won again – the first time he had ever sat in the driver's seat of an automobile. (Oldfield later recalled that he did not know how to handle the car and so had driven flat-out through the corners due to pure ignorance of the way of the automobile.)

Ford had one more speed stunt to pull off: breaking the World Land Speed Record, which at that time was 84.73mph (136.35kph). Although not a racing driver himself, Ford took his *Arrow* out to Lake St Clair, Michigan, on 12 January 1904. Not far from Detroit, St Clair is a smaller stretch of water in the Great Lakes region and connects Lake Huron with Lake Erie. Upon its frozen surface a mile was measured out, but no kilometre was marked in; the Americans were not bothered with a 'Froggy' thing like that. Ford made a test run, and then proudly

Above: *Henry Ford driving his 1902 racer at Empire City Raceway, New York, while mechanic 'Spider' Huff walks the running-board after beating Alexander Winton. (Author's collection)*

Right: *Henry Ford (left) driving the famous Ford 999 in a wheel-to-wheel duel with Harry Harkness in the Mercedes Simplex at Grosse Point, Michigan in 1903. Ford historians believe this to be a staged photograph (note the track surface of the Simplex's right front tyre). (Author's collection)*

Above: *On 12 January 1904, Ford took his 4-cylinder, 16.7-litre, Arrow out to Lake St Clair, Michigan, and posted the first land speed record set on American soil. Slipping and sliding across the frozen lake, the car flashed through the mile at an average speed of 91.37mph (147.04kph). (Author's collection)*

Left: *Ford calculating his speeds while aide Huff attends to the 16.7-litre engine shortly after the record attempt. Ford said in retirement many years later that he scared himself so badly on that run that, having broken the record, he never again wanted to climb into a racing car. (Author's collection)*

announced to the spectators and timekeepers that man and machine were ready to make an attempt on the record.

With aide 'Spider' Huff at his side, Ford inched on to the frozen, hard-packed ice covering the lake, his spindly pneumatic tyres spinning on the hot cinders that were spread around for adhesion on the melting surface. He hit the first crack, bounded, and almost lost his grip on the frozen steering wheel. Fighting to regain control as the four-cylinder, 70hp engine continued to force more power to the wheels, Ford, with a very meagre metal shield for protection against the icy blast, held on grimly while the *Arrow* hit another crack and bounced higher into the air. Slipping and sliding across the frozen lake, the car flashed through the measured mile at an average speed of 91.37mph (147.04kph). Ford said in retirement many years later that he had scared himself so badly on the run that, having broken the record, he never again wanted to climb into a racing car.

The impetus from Ford's world record, news of which was flashed from coast to coast by the telegraphic service, enabled him to get his fledgling automobile manufacturing business off the ground. He never forgot his lesson – that people equate quality with speed in a motor car. As with many automobile pioneers, Ford did enjoy being around racing cars. For fifteen days he was recognized as the fastest man in the world by the American Automobile Association (known as 'the three As'), but not by the official world body, the Automobile Club de France.

The World Land Speed Record continued creeping upward toward the 100mph barrier. The world's first true drag racing exponent, France's Louis Emile Rigolly, liked to duel wheel-to-wheel from a standing start. He competed in a long series of contests with Arthur Duray, Baron Pierre de Caters and Paul Baras, culminating in a dramatic showdown meeting alongside the canal running from Ostend to Nieuport in Belgium on 21 July 1904.

Having been defeated by Baras in a standing mile race, Rigolly was determined to do something spectacular. He roared through the flying kilometre in the 13,500cc Gobron-Brillié. Rigolly's time was 21.6 seconds, and his speed a resounding 103.55mph (166.64kph). This breaking of the 100mph barrier had a particular impact in non-metric Britain. Four days later Rigolly further demonstrated the versatile performance of the ungainly Gobron by posting a fourth place with it in the Circuit des Ardennes race, whereas Baras had to retire his 100hp Gordon Bennett-type Darracq from the same event.

Rigolly's car was one of the behemothic fuel-devouring devils of the day, typical of the early speed mechanic's approach to achieving more speed – make the engine bigger and more powerful. Vanderbilt's sleek Mercedes, however, had an 8,700cc engine; Duray's Gobron-Brillié had a 13,500cc displacement and Ford's *Arrow*, named after a famous New York Central express train reputed to have travelled at 112mph, was a powerful 16,708cc.

While the European manufacturers were building bigger and bigger engines and even heavier cars to carry them, the Stanley brothers of Newton, Massachusetts, took a very different approach. They wanted to set a record to promote the performance of their ill-fated steam car project, the *Rocket*. Rather than recruit a professional driver like Barney Oldfield or Clifford Earp, the Stanley brothers selected Fred Marriott, head of their factory's maintenance department, to drive their new creation. He would make the record attempt on the vast sands at Ormond Beach.

Since the first speed trials had been made on the 23-mile stretch of Florida coastline in 1902, Ormond Beach had become the traditional home of land speed record attempts. It was there that the great Alexander Winton and Ransom E. Olds raced side by side at 60mph, and the line judges declared them dead-heat finishers. It was to nearby Daytona that the artful Vanderbilt had shipped his Mercedes by charter boat, because there was no dependable route by road. When the skipper eyed the sinister-looking driving machine suspiciously, Vanderbilt offered to drain the highly inflammable petrol from the tank before putting her aboard. Vanderbilt actually emptied the radiator instead of the fuel tanks, because he knew there was no gasoline in Ormond. The boatman didn't know the difference.

Ormond Beach was not a smooth course, but a friable, rippled one that frequently changed its contours as the ebbing tides and continuous sea breeze sculptured the Florida shoreline. The crowd was a partisan one, favouring cars powered by the internal combustion engine as Fred Marriott set off in his steam car across the sands on 26 January 1906. The car hissed quietly to itself. Marriott was timed at 127.66mph (205.44kph) in the mile, and just for good measure he made a return run through the flying kilometre at 121.57mph (195.64kph). Both are records for steam-powered cars that still stand today.

A rare and historic photograph of American Automobile Association Contest Board secretary Samuel Butler, centre, inspecting new timing equipment at Ormond-Daytona in 1906. (Author's collection)

Contemporary newspaper reports reveal the undercurrent of prejudice against the Stanley *Rocket*, a large proportion of the local and indeed national press condemning it as a freak. Even though Fred Marriott became the first man to travel at the rate of two miles per minute, he was robbed of his moment of personal glory, for another driver was crowned speed king of the meet that year.

The steam car played a much greater role in the motoring scene across the Atlantic than it ever did in Europe. This was almost entirely due to the enterprise of the Stanley brothers, Francis E. and Freeland O., who built a reliable steam car at a low price. Owners of a prosperous photographic business, they built their first light steam car in 1897. From autumn 1898 to autumn 1899, they made and sold over 200 of these, far exceeding any other American manufacturer.

The Stanley brothers knew the value of the publicity to be gained from setting a World Land Speed Record, and they knew too well that the sceptics and detractors were still far from impressed by the fact that their car had, in one swoop across the sands at Ormond, raised the all-time record by more than 18mph while running well below full potential power. They returned to Daytona for Speed Week 1907, determined to prove the car's true land speed potential.

The Stanley *Rocket* was rated at only 50hp, but the car, which looked like a torpedo on wheels, weighed a mere 1,600lb. For the 1906 run, Marriott had used only 900psi of steam pressure, but this time he had the boiler up to 1,300psi, and the car had a better gear ratio. The rippled sands, however, were in a terrible condition as Marriott steamed away from the starting line. Taking almost nine miles for his run-up, he entered the measured mile at speeds estimated at between 132mph on the first run and between 196 and 198mph on the second run. Then disaster struck.

Louis Chevrolet, driver of the 22.5-litre, 200bhp, V8 Darracq was the Stanley Brothers' most formidable rival at Daytona in 1906. (Author's collection)

Fred Marriott (top photograph, in duster and goggles) poses with one of the Stanley brothers before setting his record speed of 127.66mph (205.44kph) in the mile, at the wheel of the Stanley Rocket *on 26 January 1906. Trying to better the record the following year, Marriott crashed at Ormond Beach at an estimated 197mph, and was lucky to escape alive. The engine (on the left of the lower photograph) was notably intact. (Author's collection)*

Approaching the 197mph mark, Marriott hit one of the troublesome gullies running across the beach. The nose of the *Rocket* lifted like a kite, the car rose some 10ft in the air, twisting sideways as it careered down the course, smashing onto the beach 100ft down range. The boiler exploded on impact, the car disintegrated, hurtling debris across the Ormond course. Fearing the worst, rescuers were astonished to find the driver unconscious but alive, with four cracked ribs, a fractured breastbone, facial injuries, and his right eye hanging out of its socket. A Mexican doctor who happened to be holidaying close to the crash scene took him to the nearby Coquina Hotel for attention, there slipping the eyeball back into place with a sugar spoon. Marriott quipped, 'Now it's the best eye I have. . . . Thanks Doc!'

The Stanley brothers vowed then and there that they would never build another racing car. In Europe the news of this, the first serious accident in pursuit of the World Land Speed Record, and the subsequent destruction of the *Rocket*, was received with a sigh of relief, though it took no fewer than four years to reinstate the internal combustion engine as the dominant power.

THREE

SETTING UP THE SPORT

The Automobile Club de France did not get around to recognizing any World Land Speed Records not held under its jurisdiction until 1927. In somewhat the same arbitrary manner, from 1906 until 1914, the French Grand Prix was simply known as the Grand Prix. Other nations staged major races – for example, Germany's Kaiserpries and Italy's Targa Florio, using similar regulations – but there was only one Grand Prix.

The Florida beaches, however, began attracting the great European Grand Prix drivers. In 1906 Vincenzo Lancia drove a Fiat and Benz's number one driver, Victor Hémery, ex-Darracq, had the big white *Blitzen (Lightning)* Benz. Engineered and designed by the Benz Company's chief designer George Diehl, the *Blitzen* Benz had already carved out a reputation in Europe, with preliminary wins at Frankfurt, Semmering and Tervueren in Belgium. In 1909 the Benz was sent to Britain and débuted at the new Brooklands track opened at Weybridge in 1907, where Victor Hémery captured Marriott's kilometre record of 121.57mph (195.64kph) on the unweathered banking, posting 125.95mph (202.655kph) for the record.

Four months after Hémery's record at Brooklands, the Benz was sent down to Southampton, loaded on to the liner *Majestic* and transported across the Atlantic to New York, where, after being on temporary display in the Benz Company's showrooms on Park Avenue, it was bought by barnstorming race driver, Barney Oldfield for an alleged $10,000. At Daytona Beach on the morning of 16 March 1910, Barney Oldfield drove the 21½-litre *Blitzen* Benz to a new land speed record of 131.275mph (211.256kph). Initially, the European officials who at that time approved all world records did not recognize the attempt but the lesson was perfectly clear: American drivers were just as fast as the French, English and Germans.

Oldfield's successful land speed record attempt set the stage for the emergence of another American speed pioneer. On 23 April 1911, 'Wild Bob' Burman celebrated his twenty-seventh birthday by driving the same *Blitzen* Benz that Oldfield had raced. Burman clearly proved he was faster on the Daytona sand, covering the flying mile at 141.370mph (227.512kph). The new international rules called for speed runs to be made in two directions to qualify as world records and as a result Burman's great feat was never recognized, but in the United States he was suddenly a national hero. A month later, at the inaugural Indianapolis 500, entrepreneurial tyre manufacturer Harvey Firestone placed a $10,000 crown on Burman's head with the apt inscription 'The World's Speed King'.

Following the First World War, English drivers dominated the land speed record scene. Not until 1922 did Ormond-Daytona, get back in the news when a relatively unknown American 'outlaw' driver, Sigmund 'Sig' Haugdahl, became the first to travel three miles per minute, his 'Wisconsin Special' reaching an estimated 180.27mph – an impressive increase, if

Veteran 'cigar-chewing' Barney Oldfield, who established a remarkable 131.275mph (211.256kph) at Daytona, on 16 March 1910, at the wheel of the famous 21.5-litre Blitzen Benz. (Author's collection)

The spectacular barnstorming American, 'Wild Bob' Burman who, on 23 April 1911, in the 21½-litre Blitzen Benz, *claimed to have broken Barney Oldfield's flying mile record at Daytona Beach, with a one-way run through the mile in 25.4 seconds, equal to 141.37mph (227.512kph). The European ACF naturally rejected the 'one-way' record, the Americans accepted it . . . the inauguration of an era of controversy between the rules and ultimate speed timing. (Author's collection)*

In 1911, minimal safety was the norm at Ormond-Daytona, clearly evident in this rare cockpit photograph of 'Wild Bob' Burman's 21½-litre Blitzen Benz. *(Author's collection)*

The intrepid Ralph De Palma, driver of the exquisite 14.8-litre, 240bhp V12-engined Packard '905'. (Author's collection)

accurate, on the existing record of 156.03mph (251.105kph) set by Tommy Milton in 1920. Haugdahl's one-way run was not recognized, however, as international record rules had been revised. Haugdahl will be remembered as probably the first race driver to balance his tyres by using weights on the wheel rims. Captain George E.T. Eyston, in his book *Motor Racing and Record Breaking*, reports that Haugdahl increased his speed from 160mph to 180mph, solely as a result of eliminating the vibration caused by unbalanced tyres.

Englishman L.G. 'Cupid' Hornsted had become the first man on earth to set a two-way record when he achieved an average speed of 124.1mph (199.72kph), with the aid of a 200hp Blitzen-engined Benz, around the famed Brooklands track in Surrey on 24 June 1914. It was considerably slower than the existing one-way record, but it satisfied the new two-way requirements and was declared 'official' by the newly formed Fédération Internationale de l'Automobile (FIA), a decision that outraged the Americans, for it appeared the FIA itself did not accept Burman's 1911 claim of 141.37mph (227.512kph).

Land speed records were entering a new golden era, but Hornsted's record was fated to last the duration of the First World War. Then in 1924, the Moto Club de France (MCF) announced a records meeting at Arpajon, on the main N20 from Paris to Orléans. Louis Delage decided that René Thomas, the portly French national champion and 1914 Indianapolis 500 winner, should participate in the huge V12, 10.6-litre Grand Prix Delage *La Torpille* (*The Torpedo*). On 6 July, the 12-cylinder Delage established a postwar 'official' record of 143.31mph (230.634kph), but it fell far short of the unrecognized one-way record. The Delage company, first of Levallois, later of Courbevoie, had been famous since 1908, when one of its cars won the celebrated Grand Prix des Voiturettes at Dieppe. Its greatest triumph had been in the 1914 Indy 500, when Thomas, then works driver, took the Delage to first place.

Four months after the Armistice, the great Indianapolis champion, Ralph De Palma, had travelled at 149.875mph (241.199kph) through the measured mile in a 12-cylinder Packard at Daytona on 12 February 1919. His unofficial record was broken on 27 April 1920 by Tommy Milton, who sped across the Daytona course at 156.03mph (251.105kph) in a Duesenberg, powered by two side-by-side 8-cylinder engines. The *Double Duesey*, as it was known, was the brainchild of the Duesenberg

Driven by Arthur Duray, and powered by a lofty 28.35-litre S76 overhead camshaft airship engine, this 300hp Fiat was taken to Ostend on 8 December 1913 in an effort to break the Blitzen Benz hold on the land speed record. In appalling weather Duray clocked 213.01kph (132.37mph) one way through the kilometre, eclipsing Barney Oldfield's 211.256kph (131.275mph) of 1910. Unfortunately, the 4-cylinder Fiat broke down on the return run, robbing him of the title. (Author's collection)

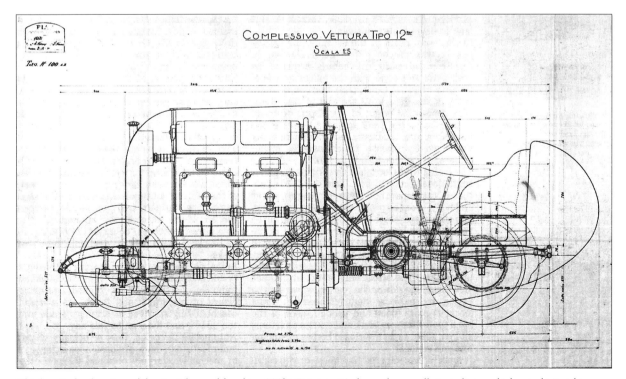

This longitudinal section of the special record-breaking 300hp Fiat type 12 shows the overall streamlining which was designed to achieve high aerodynamic performance. The ballistic shape of the vehicle remained a stylistic feature of Fiat's production throughout the period 1911–21. (Author's collection)

FOUNDING THE ORGANIZATION THAT BEGAN THE FIA

Englishman L.G. 'Cupid' Hornsted became the first man on earth to set a two-way land speed record, when he attained an average speed of 124.1mph (199.72kph) at Brooklands on 24 June 1914 in the 200hp, 2½-litre 'Blitzen'-engined Benz. (Author's collection)

The Fédération Internationale de l'Automobile (FIA) was founded in Paris on 26 June 1904. It had very ambitious goals, which were reflected in the name it initially chose: the Association Générale de l'Automobile. It was the hope of the founders that the association could be involved with all the budding uses of the internal combustion engine, in the air as well as on land, with two wheels as well as four.

It soon became evident that this was too big a task. It also overreached the authority that was given to the group by its member clubs, which after all were chiefly devoted to passenger car owners. (Motorcycles remained a concern of the group until 1922, when a separate club federation was formed for two-wheelers). Very early, a change in name was made to the one the organization used until 1946: the Association Internationale des Automobile Clubs Reconnus, or AIACR.

The Association decided that its general assembly, composed of a representative from each member club, would meet twice a year: at the Paris Salon, in December, and at the Gordon Bennett Trophy race. The latter date was available only in 1905, for that was the last year the Gordon Bennett event was held. The ideal of a contest among nations gave way in 1906 to the Grand Prix, a battle among car manufacturers. Thus, after giving birth to the AIACR, the Gordon Bennett contest passed from the scene.

By 1908 the AIACR had confirmed the regulations by which it was to function. Its expressed aims were to encourage the development of international touring by car, to assure the solidarity of the automobile movement, and to safeguard the material and moral interest of motoring in all nations. Though still a fragile alliance of young clubs in an equally young industry, the AIACR was beginning to define its structure and objectives.

Though motor sports were not mentioned in the first AIACR regulations, this was the area into which the group put its initial efforts. As early as February, 1905, it met to discuss the relative merits of the Gordon Bennett races and the new Grand Prix idea. The following December it first took up the question of a racing calendar for the coming season. This was not then the arduous task it is today. Even as late as 1914 the calendar carried only ten entries; by 1926 it had risen to thirty dates.

Hitherto, the rules according to which cars competed in the Grand Prix (one per year, always in France) were determined by the Automobile Club de France. For the 1908 season, this became the responsibility of the AIACR. It convened in Ostend, Belgium, in July 1907 to set the allowable cylinder bore sizes and minimum weight of the eligible cars for 1908. In all the subsequent years the AIACR/FIA has performed the indispensible and delicate task of setting the regulations for Grand Prix racing and other classes of international competition as well.

The member clubs also conferred on the AIACR the authority to recognize and regulate automotive attempts on land speed records. This too had been the responsibility of the French auto club in earlier years. The first successful attack on the World Land Speed Record to be AIACR-recognized was Victor Hémery's at Brooklands in November 1909. His *Blitzen* Benz was clocked at 125.95mph (202.655kph).

Hémery's record, and those preceding it, were rendered suspect by being made in one direction only. Afterwards, the AIACR decided that future records made over short distances would have to be the average of two runs in opposite directions to cancel the effects of wind and gradient. The decision was reached in 1910 to take effect in 1911. A Benz was again the mark-setting vehicle when the first World Land Speed Record was achieved under this new rule on 24 June 1914 by L.G. 'Cupid' Hornsted at 124.1mph (199.72kph). Thus established the basic principle that has governed all record-breaking since.

Today, the FIA has two divisions. Touring and Automobile is concerned with motoring in general and all matters relating to the motorist, such as road safety, environment, touring, mobility and consumer protection. The Sport division of the FIA is the world governing body for all forms of international motor sport involving land vehicles with four or more wheels; this includes the Formula One World Championship and the World Rally Championship.

Since January 1999, the FIA's headquarters have been in Geneva with those of the Alliance Internationale de Tourisme, an international organization with which the FIA has common interests in all areas concerning motoring, except sport.

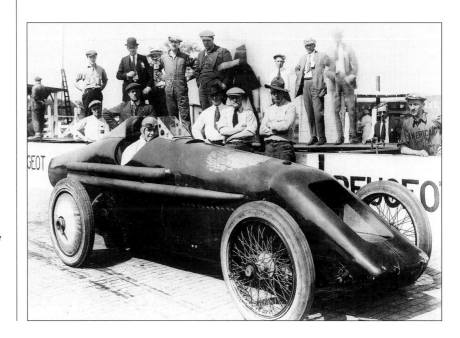

Tommy Milton and the fearsome Double Duesey, *the 10-litre, twin-engined Duesenberg with which he broke Ralph de Palma's record at 156.030mph (251.105kph) on 27 April 1920 at Daytona, attaining a previously unheard of speed of 1 mile in 23.07 seconds. (Author's collection)*

The heart of Ernest Eldridge's 21.7-litre Fiat Mephistopheles was the 6-cylinder, 24-valve, 300bhp A-12 aviation engine of First World War vintage, measuring 160 × 180 mm – giving the formidable capacity of 21,714cc. This power plant drove the rear wheels through a four-speed gearbox and side chains. (Author's collection)

A cutaway section of Ernest Eldridge's massive 21.7-litre aero-engined Fiat Mephistopheles. Before his success at Arpajon, the Fiat Company of Turin had shown little interest in Eldridge's racing activities.

Company, operated by Fred and August Duesenberg, but it was their principal driver Tommy Milton who, while in hospital recovering from injuries sustained in a 1919 race crash, hit upon the concept of using two overhead camshaft straight-eight racing engines, normally used for the Indy 500, in a special car to attack De Palma's record.

Thomas's record was the one that counted, not any of those previously set by the Americans. But on the day the Frenchman set his record, Ernest Eldridge, an Englishman, was at Arpajon to challenge it and the duel they fought recalled the battle between Chasseloup-Laubat and Jenatzy on another French course outside Paris a quarter-century before. Eldridge was driving a highly modified Fiat Mephistopheles, powered by an immense 6-cylinder, 24-valve, 300hp A12 aviation engine of First World War vintage. Eldridge, with mechanic Jim Ames as a passenger, made his two-way run that day at 146.8mph (236.251kph). This annoyed Thomas, who strongly protested against the car on the grounds that it had no reverse gear, as called for by international rules. Officials ruled in favour of Thomas. His record was still the one that counted.

Across the Channel, the British were readying for the challenge with a new car. This was the famous 350hp Sunbeam, which ushered in the era of aero-engined land speed record cars. The car had a modified Sunbeam

Fred and Augie Duesenberg's principal driver, the ingenious Tommy Milton. (Author's collection)

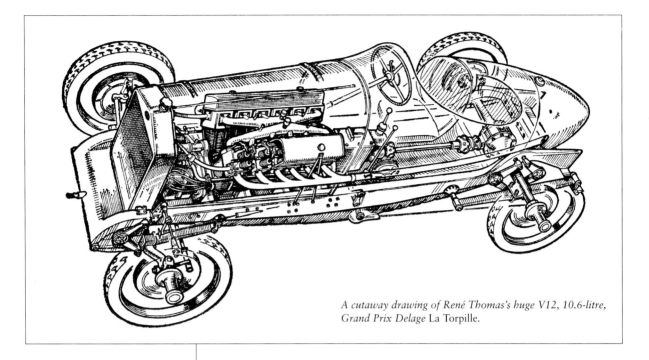

A cutaway drawing of René Thomas's huge V12, 10.6-litre, Grand Prix Delage La Torpille.

René Thomas, the portly French national champion and 1914 Indianapolis 500 winner, broke the land speed record at 143.31mph (230.634kph) during the 1924 Arpajon sprint meeting in the huge V12, 10.6-litre, 280bhp engined Grand Prix Delage La Torpille (The Torpedo). (Author's collection)

Manitou 60°, V12-cylinder aero-engine measuring 18.3 litres. Sunbeam of Wolverhampton had built many of these aircraft engines during the war; they were never outstanding performers, but the RAF's Coastal Command did consider the light alloy Manitou the ideal engine for their coastal defence seaplanes. The Sunbeam first appeared at Brooklands in 1920.

Two years later, Kenelm Lee Guinness (founder of the famous KLG Sparking Plug Company) reached 144mph (232kph) around the Weybridge circuit. On 17 May 1922, Guinness set a new World Land Speed Record of 133.75mph (215.25kph). It was the same car that another Englishman named Sir Malcolm Campbell later purchased to set the first in a series of nine records he was to hold.

MAGNIFICENT MEN, MIGHTY MACHINES

PARRY THOMAS AND 'BABS'

Engines continued to grow as Malcolm Campbell and Major Henry Segrave embarked on their outstanding land speed record careers. Campbell and Segrave were soon joined by another challenger – the Welshman, John Godfrey Parry Thomas.

Thomas had been made chief engineer at Leyland in 1917, when he was just thirty-two, but his pursuit of speed at Brooklands had led him to break with the company in 1923. Unlike Campbell and Segrave, Thomas did not have the resources to build a record car of modern racing specifications and standards. The Higham Special that he purchased for £125 in 1924 was built for the 1920s speed ace Count Louis Zboröwsky who was killed during the 1924 Italian Grand Prix at Monza. The power of the car had not been fully exploited when Zboröwsky was killed, though he had reached 116mph in it. The vehicle had an enormous 400hp, 26.9-litre, 45° V12 American Liberty aero-engine, fitted into a long, sleek chassis made by Rubery Owen of Canterbury, which sported those longitudinal bracing stays designed to impart extra beam strength that were typical of the Brooklands racing cars of the twenties. After Thomas acquired the car, now affectionately known as 'Babs', he streamlined it and fitted the engine with four Zenith carburettors, replaced the Mercedes front axle with one from a Leyland Eight and installed special pistons, which he designed himself.

People liked Thomas. He was a large, friendly man, unmarried, slightly awkward in company, who smoked a lot, had very few topics of conversation apart from automobiles, and whose teeth, it was once said, looked 'as though they had been thrown in from a distance'. On 27 April 1926, Thomas made six runs on Pendine Sands in South Wales, setting a best two-way record of 169.30mph (272.5kph) through the flying mile. He returned the next day and raised the record to 171.02mph (275.22kph), the first man in history to set two World Land Speed Records on two consecutive days. Yet, he was far from satisfied.

Both Campbell and Segrave had set 180mph – three miles a minute – as their goal, and Thomas knew his record wouldn't hold up for long with the aristocratic duo on his tail. It didn't. On 4 February 1927, Campbell averaged 174.88mph (281.44kph) on the flat sands of Pendine and Parry Thomas was once again the challenger.

It was cold and wet when Thomas arrived at Pendine on 1 March 1927. He had been suffering from flu (observers spoke of how ill he looked), but he knew it could be his last attempt on the record, for

It was cold and wet when Parry Thomas arrived at Pendine Sands on 1 March 1927, but on 3 March the weather had improved enough to enable an attempt on the record. Thomas is seen here in the cockpit of 'Babs' shortly before the fatal accident. (Author's collection)

Not unlike a beached whale, this was 'Babs' after the crash at Pendine in which J.G. Parry Thomas lost his life. He was the first driver fatality in twenty-nine years of World Land Speed Record breaking. (Author's collection)

Segrave had taken delivery of a Sunbeam in which he was planning to break 200mph at Daytona. Such a venture was beyond Thomas's pocket. It rained again the following day, but on 3 March the weather had improved enough to enable Thomas to roll 'Babs' out on to the beach. On the first run he trailed black smoke and blamed the trouble on his Zenith carburettors. Smoke was still billowing out of the exhausts when he started his sixth run close to the Beach Hotel. Thomas had just completed the measured mile on his return run when 'Babs' was seen to slew. It suddenly went out of control, rolled, righted itself, then swathed a gigantic arc in the sand, ending up with the engine ablaze. Horrified spectators led by mechanic Jock Pullen rushed to the aid of the driver, but when they reached the wreckage they recoiled at the horrific sight. There sat Parry, upright in the seat of the car, with part of his head lying beside

'Babs' in the sand. The drive chain to the rear wheels had broken at 2,000rpm and slashed through its safety guard like a knife through butter, virtually decapitating Thomas. Death had been instantaneous. And so they buried 'Babs', a Fordson tractor dragging her to a hole that had been dug in the dunes nearby. There were no memorials at the site, but such was the emotion, many photographs were taken of 'Babs' at her burial ground, and these played an important part in what followed forty-two years later.

In 1967, two men called on Owen Wyn Owen, a lecturer in engineering at Bangor Technical College. They had heard of Owen's hobby for restoring old cars, but when they arrived at his house and workshop in Capel Curig, North Wales, nothing prepared them for the sight of the immaculately restored early Bentley, Delage and Argyll cars.

'What's your next project?' they reverently inquired. 'I think I'll dig up Parry Thomas's old car,' Owen replied. Time passed, but one day Owen drove the 140 miles to Pendine and, of course, found there was no memorial, although local villagers who cherished the memory of popular Parry Thomas continued to put flowers on a nearby cairn. (Thomas was buried in the tranquil setting of St Mary's Church, Byfleet, near the site of the Brooklands race track where he made his name.) What Owen did discover at Pendine was a photograph showing 'Babs' maritime burial like the ship at Sutton Hoo and in the image two houses appeared on the headland behind. These two houses survived amid bungalows built since the time of the accident, but it was possible to get a fix from them, and on a map he drew a 20-yard circle to scale. Somewhere inside that circle was 'Babs'. However, to Owen's alarm, 'Babs' was no longer under open dunes. The Ministry of Defence had moved in since 1927, built an experimental rocket range on the beach, and erected a police hut right above 'Babs'. The irony is that this was to prove to his advantage.

'Babs' had been buried on the foreshore. With very few exceptions all rights to the foreshores of this country are vested in the Crown, so any request to dig anything up has to be made to the vast anonymity of Whitehall, and is there quietly forgotten. But Pendine was one of the very few exceptions, where the rights were vested in the Lord of the Manor. In 1967 the British Army was the Lord of the Manor, in particular the General Officer at Brecon, one General Darling. Owen had an old friend who knew General Darling, and each year dined with him at the Royal Welsh Fusiliers' reunion. A few days before that year's reunion Owen wrote to the General, and his friend, suitably primed, sat next to Darling and all through dinner talked about the historical importance of 'Babs' exhumation. Within weeks, Owen got a letter of authority telling him to go ahead, provided he could get the permission of Parry Thomas's next of kin. Several years later, having traced a nephew to Walsall and secured his agreement, Owen made the long journey to Pendine again.

On 27 April 1926, Parry Thomas made his début in the most famous of the behemothic cars, now known as 'Babs'. The Higham Special, which he purchased for £125 in 1924, was built for the 1920s speed ace Count Louis Zboröwsky and had an enormous 400hp, 26.9-litre 45° American Liberty aero-engine. (Author's collection)

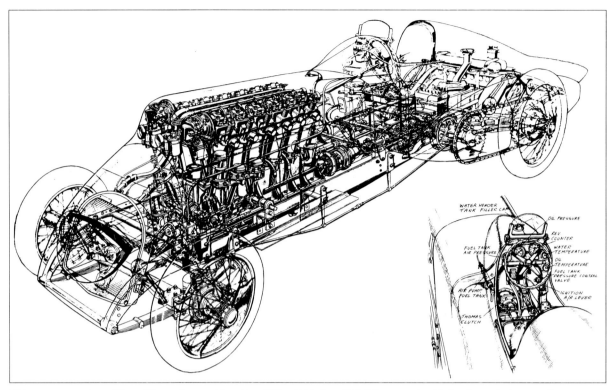

This cutaway section of Parry Thomas's record-breaking 400hp, 26.9-litre, V12 Liberty-engined Babs *shows the improved streamlining and long, sleek chassis made by Rubery Owen. Sporting those longitudinal bracing stays designed to impart extra beam strength, it was typical of the Brooklands racing cars of the twenties. After Thomas acquired the car, he fitted the engine with four Zenith carburettors, replaced the Mercedes front axle with one from a Leyland Eight and installed special pistons he designed himself.*

In remarkable condition after being submerged for forty-two years under Pendine Sands, J.G. Parry Thomas's 'Babs' was exhumed from her watery grave by Owen Wyn Owen. Apart from residual corrosion, the car was almost as she fell on 3 March 1927. (Author's collection)

With the help of some relatives and a JCB, Owen set about digging up 'Babs'. She was in quite remarkable condition considering she had been buried for forty-two years under Pendine Sands. Apart from residual corrosion of the aluminium body panels, and a buckled but not badly rusted chassis, the car was almost as she fell on 3 March 1927 in the terrifying accident that killed her intrepid driver.

After many years of wrangling and searching the globe for parts, Owen Wyn Owen has lovingly restored 'Babs' to her former purposeful form. He has driven her many times at Brooklands, where Count Louis Zboröwsky had raced the Higham Special in its early days. 'Babs' is now being prepared for her final resting place at the National Museum of Wales in Cardiff.

As to the speed in that final, fatal run in 1927, it was never known, for the timing wire had also been broken by the savage contortions of the car. So ended the career of a gallant speed pioneer. Parry Thomas was the first driver to be killed in pursuit of the World Land Speed Record, twenty-nine years after its official beginning.

SIR MALCOLM CAMPBELL – PERSONA GRATA

The First World War cast a shadow of despair over Europe. Motor racing and record breaking paled into insignificance as men's thoughts were eclipsed by the winds of war. The famous Weybridge race track became a dust bowl in a field of desolate pastures in the Surrey countryside. Colonel Lindsay-Lloyd, the ageing Brooklands Clerk of the Course, walked alone along the Outer Circuit recalling the sounds of speed that spawned a succession of champions. The most celebrated champion of them all was the dashing Malcolm Campbell.

Campbell was born to set records. At the age of sixteen he was sent to school in Germany, where he won his first bicycle race. Even as a youngster, speed was his obsession: 'When I drove my first, seven horsepower car, I craved for ten. I wanted to experience the sensation of progressive speed,' Campbell recalled, and he was once fined for riding his father's bicycle at 27mph down Box Hill, Surrey, with his hands in his pockets.

At the age of twenty-four, he built his own aeroplane, but frequent crashes in the Kent orchards were too great a burden on his savings. And in 1910, at the age of twenty-five he entered and won his first automobile race on the Brooklands circuit, in the first car sporting the *Bluebird* livery.

At the outbreak of the First World War, Campbell became a dispatch rider and was commissioned soon after. He then transferred to the Royal Flying Corps. At the end of the First World War he was discharged with the rank of captain. No sooner had peace returned to Europe than Campbell re-entered the racing circuit, taking part in just about every meeting in Europe. Then, fired by the spectacular barnstorming American, 'Wild Bob' Burman, who claimed to have broken Barney Oldfield's flying mile with a one-way run in 25.40 seconds (141.37mph) on the famed Ormond-Daytona Beach, Campbell began his campaign to capture the World Land Speed Record for Britain.

Captain Campbell's first assault on the record was made on the Saltburn sands, Yorkshire, in 1922, a month after Kenelm Lee Guinness set a new record of 133.75mph (215.25kph) at Brooklands in the 350hp Sunbeam. Campbell, already an accomplished racing driver, persuaded Louis Coatalen, chief engineer of the Sunbeam racing team, to let him drive the car. He averaged 135mph (217kph) one way on the sands, but the speed wasn't accepted because the run had been timed by a hand-held Rolex stop watch instead of the electrical timing devices required by the official ruling of the Automobile Club de France.

Less than a year later, Campbell purchased the Sunbeam, which he promptly entered in the international speed trials meeting on the Danish holiday island of Fanöe. On 24 June 1923 he attained a terminal speed of 136.31mph (219.32kph) through the kilometre, and 137.72mph (221.59kph) through the mile. But again, Campbell failed to win recognition. He returned to the sanctuary of his house and workshops at Povey Cross, near Horley, Surrey, where solitude was sublime.

Despite protests from local inhabitants, Campbell hit upon the idea of ploughing two deep furrows some 50 yards apart along the length of the 7-mile Pendine course, to drain the sea water away. This exercise however, made matters considerably worse. It certainly dried up the section close to the ploughed furrows, but appeared to make the course condition midway between the furrows perilous. The idea was later abandoned. (Author's collection)

In between Campbell's two successful runs at Pendine on 25 September 1924, Leo Villa changes tyres on the 350hp Sunbeam. In driving rain, Campbell averaged 146.16mph (235.217kph). The car is resting on boards to prevent it sinking into the wet beach. (Author's collection)

Sir Malcolm Campbell rolls out his new and costly 22.3-litre, 450bhp Napier Lion-engined Napier-Campbell Bluebird *in which he broke Parry Thomas's record at the Pendine Sands in February 1927, averaging 174.883mph (281.447kph) in two extremely wet and bumpy runs, which finally convinced Campbell a new venue for land speed record attempts was needed. (Author's collection)*

Working for the fastidious Campbell kept his mechanic, Leo Villa, occupied at all hours of the day and night. There were customers' cars to be serviced, new cars to be checked over and Campbell's growing stable to be finely tuned and cosseted. Every week saw preparations for a hill climb, speed trial or race on a beach or circuit and, as if that were not enough, Campbell stormed into the workshop late one evening calling for his mechanic: 'Believe me, Villa, that car is bloody fast and I intend to get the record with it.'

Twice he had bettered the existing record, but twice his efforts were rejected. Undaunted, Campbell took the car to Pendine Sands in 1924. By this time he had been joined there by three other contenders, including René Thomas, (winner of the 1914 Indianapolis 500), Parry Thomas and Ernest A.D. Eldridge. On 6 July, René Thomas clocked 143.31mph (230.634kph) at Arpajon in the V12, 10.6-litre Delage, setting a new World Land Speed Record. Four days later, Eldridge upped the mark to 145mph. However, Thomas lodged a protest against the car, claiming that Eldridge's vehicle had no reverse gear fitted.

Eldridge returned to Paris with the car, and, in a hired workshop on the Rue de Longchamp, devised a reverse gear after working round the clock for 48 hours. This time, Thomas could only observe as Eldridge clocked an even faster 146.01mph (234.986kph) on the Arpajon road. There were no protests from the Frenchman . . . the record yet again returned to Britain.

In the Sunbeam car, named *Bluebird* after a successful play running at London's Whitehall Theatre, Campbell finally achieved his goal on 25 September 1924 on Pendine Sands. In driving rain, Campbell hurtled to a record speed of 146.16mph (235.217kph). Malcolm Campbell and the *Bluebird* became household names and, to the World Land Speed Record circuit, a force to be reckoned with.

By this time, however, there were numerous challengers preparing cars to attack the magical 150mph barrier, including Major Henry Segrave. Campbell's trusted mechanic, Leo Villa, and designer C. Amherst Villiers had begun work on a new car, the Napier-Campbell, with which they intended to raise the land speed record to 200mph, but the car was far from ready. The impatient Campbell immediately set Leo and an Italian engineer named Joseph Maina, a friend of Villa's, to work supertuning the old faithful Sunbeam *Bluebird* for one last assault on the 150mph barrier.

After several unsuccessful runs on Carmarthen beach, he returned on 4 February 1927 with his new 450hp Napier Lion-engined Napier-Campbell. Campbell made his first run at the mile, attaining just under 180mph. On the return run, approaching the better 195mph he hit a ripple in the sand left by the retreating tide; he was jolted so violently his goggles slipped over his head, forcing him to drive with one hand and shield his eyes with the other. Despite the incident, Campbell attained a two-way average of 174.883mph (281.447kph); he had the record once again, but the speed was less than his goal.

Meanwhile, Major Henry Segrave was already ship-bound for the New World, where, in the mighty 1,000hp Sunbeam, he was to set a new World Land Speed Record of 203.792mph (327.981kph) on the Florida beach of Ormond-Daytona on 28 March 1927, beating Campbell to both 180mph and 200mph in a single stroke.

Without further ado, Campbell put *Bluebird* into the Vickers windtunnel to evaluate areas of improvement to the aerodynamics of the car. He then consulted Reid A. Railton at Thomson & Taylor of Brooklands and R.J. Mitchell, the designer of the legendary Supermarine Spitfire, who had also helped to design *Bluebird*, and they managed to secure a powerful Schneider Trophy Napier Sprint engine. The redesigned *Bluebird* made her début during the Daytona Speed Week in February 1928. It was 19 February when Campbell rolled her out for her first 200mph dash. On the outward run the car developed a yaw, sending it into a terrifying sideways slide as the indefatigable Campbell momentarily lost control. His return run was as rough as the first, as the speeding car was caught by a gust from an ocean breeze. Nevertheless Campbell regained the record, attaining 206.956mph (333.062kph), but his triumph was short-lived, for Ray Keech increased the speed to 207.552mph (334.022kph) in J.M. White's 81-litre, 36-cylinder three-engined Liberty-powered *White Triplex* – also known as the *Spirit of Elkdom* – regaining the record for the United States.

Campbell, having experienced extreme difficulties in driving on the sands of both Ormond-Daytona and Pendine, decided the time had come to seek a more stable venue for his next attempt at the record. Shortly after his return from the USA, he had a meeting with Leonard T. Scott, who had trekked across the Sahara from Oran to the Niger river. Scott

The retiring Ray Keech, driver of J.M. White's 81-litre, 36-cylinder, 400bhp, Liberty-engined White Triplex – *also known as the* Spirit of Elkdom – *in which he snatched the land speed record from Malcolm Campbell, at a two-way average speed of 207.552mph (334.022kph) at Daytona Beach on 22 April 1928. (Author's collection)*

Lee Bible, team mechanic for J.M. White's famed Liberty-powered White Triplex *driven earlier by Ray Keech, shortly before the accident at Daytona Beach in which he and Pathé newsreel cameraman Charles Traub were to lose their lives (see also page 36). (Author's collection)*

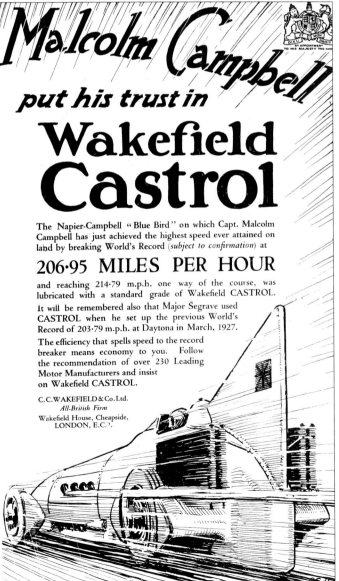

Malcolm Campbell

put his trust in

Wakefield Castrol

The Napier-Campbell " Blue Bird " on which Capt. Malcolm Campbell has just achieved the highest speed ever attained on land by breaking World's Record *(subject to confirmation)* at

206·95 MILES PER HOUR

and reaching 214·79 m.p.h. one way of the course, was lubricated with a standard grade of Wakefield CASTROL.

It will be remembered also that Major Segrave used CASTROL when he set up the previous World's Record of 203·79 m.p.h. at Daytona in March, 1927.

The efficiency that spells speed to the record breaker means economy to you. Follow the recommendation of over 230 Leading Motor Manufacturers and insist on Wakefield CASTROL.

C.C.WAKEFIELD & Co.Ltd.
All-British Firm
Wakefield House, Cheapside,
LONDON, E.C.?.

A poster advertising Wakefield Castrol lubricants used in Captain Malcolm Campbell's Napier-Campbell Bluebird, *with which, on 19 February 1928, he raised the World Land Speed Record to 206.956mph (333.062kph) at Daytona Beach, Florida. (Castrol International)*

told him of an ideal stretch of firm, hard sand ten miles long at least, to the north-west of Timbuctoo in an area patrolled by the Spanish Army. Such a venue sounded too good for a man like Campbell to pass up. Without further ado he purchased a Gypsy Moth aeroplane, which he christened *Bluebird ZS-AAK,* and on 3 November 1928 flew from Croydon airport to the Sahara.

Campbell's search for a new track in the desert nearly ended in disaster. He was homeward bound when the Gypsy Moth suffered engine failure crossing the Atlas Mountains. Campbell's pilot, Squadron Leader Don was forced to make a landing in the sea off the African coast. Fortunately Campbell and Don were not hurt and managed to haul the plane up on to the beach and return home by sea from Gibraltar. Campbell's adventures in the Sahara, however, created worldwide interest and, within a few days of his return to England, a cable arrived at Povey Cross from the motoring correspondent of the *Cape Times* in South Africa. The cable informed him of a dried-up lake bed near Germiston, some 450 miles north-east of Cape Town, but to reach it he would have to make the arduous journey across the Karoo to the Transvaal where there were no roads, and many dry water courses had to be crossed. The nearest railhead was Sak River, about seventy miles away. Campbell had decided against the stretch of sand in the Sahara because it was inaccessible, but the new site, Verneuk Pan, was not a lot better. It hadn't rained at Verneuk Pan for five years. This, from Campbell's point of view was one of its positive attractions; he would at least be assured of a dry run.

In January 1929, Campbell left Southampton aboard the liner *Caernarvon Castle* with *Bluebird,* Leo Villa, Joe Coe, Steve Mac, George Miller and fifty-six packing cases of spares. When they arrived at Cape Town on 10 February, Henry Segrave was already at Daytona with his new car, the three-ton *Golden Arrow.* Campbell lost no time in setting off for Verneuk Pan to make his first survey of the course, while his team attended to the unloading of the *Bluebird* and spares and settled in to Thorneycroft's Garage in Cape Town. The Germiston Town Council loaned Campbell a steam-roller and driver, and further financial contributions were made, both by the South African government and the Corporation of Cape Town and Johannesburg for track preparation.

On 11 March, Campbell, joined in Cape Town by his family, was celebrating his forty-fifth birthday when he received a telephone call. It was Bill Voous at Reuter's Cape Town office with the far from cheering

A cutaway view of the 1931 Campbell-Napier-Railton Bluebird *showing the location of the 26.9-litre, 1,450hp supercharged Napier Lion engine and transmission.*

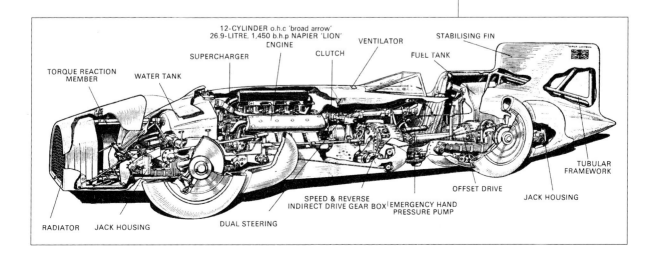

Soon after Malcolm Campbell established a new record of 246.153mph (396.143kph) at Daytona Beach, he returned to England where he was informed that he was to be knighted. Civic receptions followed in both Southampton and London. The Great Southern Railway in recognition of his honour laid on a special train – 'The Bluebird Special' – to take Campbell and his crew back to Waterloo. (Author's collection)

news that Segrave had just established a new World Land Speed Record of 231.446mph (372.34kph) at Daytona in the Irving-Napier *Golden Arrow*, far out of reach of *Bluebird*.

Reid A. Railton, one of a new breed of engineer at Thomson & Taylor of Brooklands, was commissioned to design a new *Bluebird* streamliner around a Napier Lion aircraft engine, capable of producing almost 1,500hp. Meanwhile, Campbell stayed in South Africa long enough to set a number of new British Empire speed records, but the best he could attain against the World Land Speed Record was 218.5mph (351.64kph). While in South Africa Campbell learnt of the death of Segrave on Lake Windermere; he had been attempting the World Water Speed Record in his record-breaking boat *Miss England II*.

At a time when the land speed record was in danger of being captured by the Americans, Campbell returned to Florida with the new *Bluebird* where, on 5 February 1931, he covered the flying mile at 246.153mph (396.143kph). England was in ecstasy. The returning hero on board the *Mauritania* was greeted by a flight of aircraft which dipped their wings in salute of the champion as he approached Southampton water. On disembarking he was greeted by the news that he was to be knighted for his achievements. Civic receptions followed in Southampton and London – there was even a private train dubbed the '*Bluebird* Special', laid on by the Great Southern Railway, to take Campbell and his crew back to Waterloo, where he was welcomed with a government reception at Westminster Hall.

Campbell still wasn't satisfied and the *Bluebird* was altered yet again. Nine months later the car was completed, and the only familiar aspect of the vehicle was its colour. The new *Bluebird* was much heavier than her predecessor, and sporting a V12, ohc, 36.5-litre Rolls-Royce 'R' engine, was much more powerful. Campbell returned to Ormond, where, on 23 February 1933, he set a new World Land Speed Record of 272.46mph (438.123kph).

Sir Malcolm Campbell taking the World Land Speed Record for the eighth time, in the supercharged Rolls-Royce 'R'-engined Bluebird on the famed Ormond-Daytona Beach, Florida, in 1933. His timed speed on the bumpy course was 272.46mph (438.123kph). (Author's collection)

Top: *In 1935, Sir Malcolm Campbell's legendary record car,* Bluebird, *was rebuilt yet again at Campbell's own workshop behind the Brooklands track, under the learned supervision of Leo Villa. This, the final version of the* Bluebird, *incorporated some of the original chassis, front axle and brake drums from the 1927 car. The new design had a completely new body shell with a driver-controlled air-intake slot in the nose, which could be closed for additional streamlining. (Author's collection)*
Middle: *The* Bluebird *support team, with only minutes to spare, make a final inspection of the 36.5-litre, 2,300bhp supercharged Rolls-Royce 'R'-engined car for the vital return run through the mile on the Bonneville course. (Author's collection)*
Bottom: *A cutaway drawing of the 1935 Campbell-Railton Rolls-Royce 'R'-engined* Bluebird.

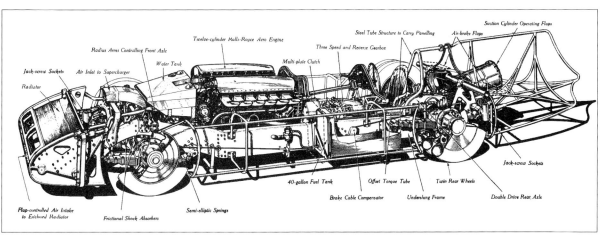

Sir Malcolm Campbell at the wheel of Bluebird, *shortly after raising the World Land Speed Record to 272.46mph (438.123kph), taking the record for the seventh time, on the famed Daytona Beach. (Author's collection)*

For Sir Malcolm, however, the beach had far outlived its usefulness as a venue for attempts at the record and he set out to find a far longer and harder course. His journey ended on the vast Bonneville Salt Flats in Western Utah. This was to be the setting of his new assault on the record, where, on 3 September 1935, he fulfilled his ambition with a 301.12mph (484.51kph) average. His first assault through the flying mile lasted exactly 11.63 seconds; the return run lasted 12.08 seconds, establishing a two-way average speed of 301.129mph (484.818kph).

For Sir Malcolm Campbell, this was surely the pinnacle of his outstanding career. Having established just about every record he had set out to attain on land, he turned his attention to water, where he achieved no fewer than four World Water Speed Records in three years. The ambassador of speed had well and truly established Great Britain and, indeed, the *Bluebird* name in almost every chapter of land and water speed record history.

Shortly before his death on New Year's Eve 1948, Sir Malcolm Campbell had already made plans to raise the World Water Speed Record to 200mph in the jet-powered *Bluebird* three-pointer. He was finally at rest in his birth-place town of Chislehurst, Kent, in the same grave as his mother and father.

In the years ahead Sir Malcolm's son Donald was to pick up the gauntlet left by his father in pursuit of ultimate speed on land and water.

MAJOR HENRY SEGRAVE – THE ENGLISH GENTLEMAN

Major Henry Segrave, the debonair test driver for the Wolverhampton-based Sunbeam Motor Company, was the obvious choice to drive the first in a new series of potential land speed record Sunbeams. He was a staunchly patriotic Englishman, winner for Sunbeam of the 1923 French Grand Prix and fourteen other road and track races.

Powered by a V12, twin ohc, 4-litre, 306bhp, supercharged engine, the Sunbeam was the latest racing machine to emerge from the stable of Louis Coatalen, chief engineer and racing team manager for the famous Sunbeam-Talbot-Darracq group. Segrave wasted no time in taking the new Sunbeam to Brooklands for trials in September 1925. Lacking the now familiar red racing team colours, the car was clocked at 145mph (233kph) through the half-mile. A number of predictable teething problems were overcome and the car, finally painted red, was ready for an attempt on the record.

The power behind the punch of Segrave's 4-litre Sunbeam – the 12-cylinder, twin overhead camshaft, 'Grand Prix' type block and heads of the 306bhp supercharged engine. (Author's collection)

On 16 March 1926, Segrave and his team of eight mechanics arrive, on the windswept Lancashire coastline. With very little pomp and even less publicity, the Sunbeam was rolled out on to the Southport beach. After walking the length of the course, which was still glistening from the retreat of the ebbing tide, Segrave was ready to go. Trailing a plume of spray, the Sunbeam hurtled down the beach to a new record of 152.33mph (245.149kph).

The following month J.G. Parry Thomas raised the record to

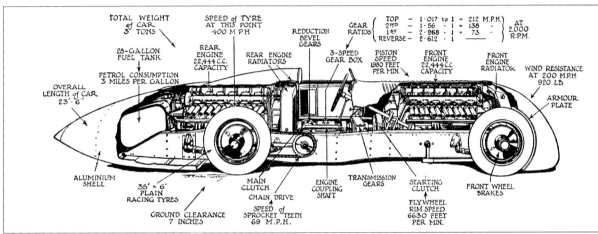

169.30mph (215.25kph) on Pendine Sands. Not content with the speed, Thomas went on the sands again the following day, raising the record to 171.02mph (275,22kph). That very record however, nearly cost the respected Welshman his life, nevertheless, he still became the first man in history to set two World Land Speed Records in two consecutive days. The following year Thomas lost his life at Pendine trying to raise Campbell's 174.883mph (281.447kph) mark set on 4 February 1927. Experts are divided as to the cause of the tragedy at Pendine, some claiming the man was at fault, but without doubt, the conditions on the beach that day were a major contributing factor. Campbell's mechanic, Leo Villa, held a personal theory as to the cause of the tragedy. His feeling was that the new guard which Thomas had fitted over the top of the drive chain just before the record attempt may have been responsible for his death. In the ordinary way a chain breaks on load, and if the guard had not been there, he thought the chain might just have opened out and stretched its length harmlessly along the sand. This was pure conjecture on Villa's part, but he believed it was the guard that prevented the chain from detaching itself from the sprockets, and of course if a broken chain got tangled up in anything there was bound to be trouble.

Another factor which Villa thought contributed to Parry Thomas's death was his habit of driving with his head to one side of the screen. This was something he had picked up at Brooklands, where he always drove fast cars up near the top of the bank. And of course it meant that when the drive chain snapped, he didn't stand a chance.

Top: *The tapered form of Segrave's 1,000hp Sunbeam shortly before she was driven to a new World Land Speed Record of 203.792mph (327.981kph) at Ormond-Daytona on 29 March 1927, bettering Campbell's seven-week-old figure by over 28mph. Bottom: This schematic view of the remarkable Sunbeam shows the disposition of the two 22½-litre, 12-cylinder Matabele aero-engines, engine radiators and 28 gallon fuel tank. (Author's collection)*

In 1927, Henry Segrave set sail for the United States onboard the SS Berengaria *with a new car, the remarkable 1,000hp Sunbeam, powered by two 22½-litre, 12-cylinder Matabele aero-engines, with the objective of eclipsing Campbell's record. This was indeed achieved soon after Segrave arrived at Daytona. The car is seen here at Southampton Docks on her triumphant return to England, now sporting the livery 'The First Car in the World to attain a Speed of over 200mph'.(Author's collection)*

The following year, Segrave set sail for the United States on board the SS *Berengaria* with a new car, the remarkable 1,000hp Sunbeam, with the objective of raising the record of 174.88mph (281.44kph) set by Malcolm Campbell driving the Napier-Campbell *Bluebird*, the first to fully adopt the *Bluebird* livery, and also the first car to be specifically built as a record breaker.

Driven by two V12, twin ohc, 22.5-litre, 435bhp, 48-valve Matabele aero-engines, and weighing in at 3 tons 16 cwt, the Sunbeam required a course 9 miles long to attain its anticipated speed, and this factor alone ruled out most of the European beaches. Pendine, Saltburn, Southport, Perranporth and Fanöe were far too short and most were certainly unpredictable. Segrave decided – and with his noted charm and diplomacy, convinced his sponsors – that the famous Ormond-Daytona beach was the only suitable venue for the attempt.

Apart from its phenomenal speed capabilities the design and layout of the car were of unusual engineering interest. The stresses and strains, enormous wind resistance and forces encountered at the anticipated 200mph regime, represented an entirely new field for the designer, Louis Coatalen, simply because the highest speeds hitherto attained on land had been far short of this figure. Sunbeam's experience in the design and production of racing cars at their Moorfield Works and in building high-powered aircraft was unique; and this experience had been brought thoroughly to bear in connection with the design of Segrave's car, together with the fullest use of wind tunnel experiments and knowledge of aerodynamics. By such means Sunbeam was confident it had produced a car capable of safely accomplishing its objectives.

Segrave's visit to Daytona was widely publicised, and for good reason: he was the first European of the postwar era to attempt an official World

Land Speed Record on the Florida beach, and he was claiming that he intended to surpass the 200mph mark.

On his inaugural run, a party of school children carelessly walked through the timing traps, making it impossible for the United States Automobile Club (USAC) officials to certify any speed higher than 163mph, though with regret Segrave knew he had well surpassed that speed. There was a crowd of spectators estimated at between 30,000 and 35,000 on hand when, on 29 March 1927, Segrave made what was considered to be his 'last chance' at the record. Buckled into his seat, he fired the mighty V12 aircraft engines and within seconds he was gone; manipulating the two three-speed gearboxes, he entered the speed traps at just short of 200mph as a gust of wind caught the car, sliding it sideways. Segrave fought for control and was struggling hard to maintain his course as he left the measured mile. He thumped the brakes and literally incinerated them. With a stream crossing the beach dead ahead, he had no alternative other than to steer the car out into the shallow water to slow her down. The car finally came to a halt, the brakes were quickly replaced during the turnaround, and with 11 minutes remaining within the regulation hour, Segrave launched the 1,000hp Sunbeam back down the beach to establish a new World Land Speed Record of 203.792mph (327.981kph). Segrave had beaten Campbell to both 180 and 200 miles an hour in a multiple stroke of speed, skill and determination. Moreover, in doing so he made obsolete the expensive Napier-Campbell *Bluebird*.

Sir Henry O'Neale de Hane Segrave, the Baltimore-born son of an Anglo-Irish father and an American mother, was undoubtedly Britain's greatest Grand Prix star of the Golden Age of the 1920s. (Author's collection)

This view of the incomplete chassis of the Irving-Napier Golden Arrow *shows the massive frame construction and location of the 925hp Napier Lion engine which drove the rear wheels from a position set low between the twin propeller shafts, located on each side of the driver's seat. (Author's collection)*

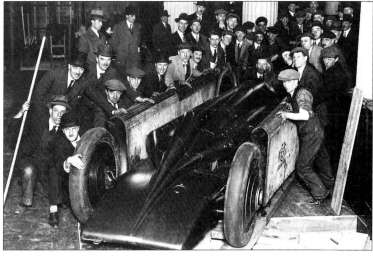

The Golden Arrow *being wheeled into Olympia for the 1928 London Motor Show. (Author's collection)*

Campbell set off on an aerial expedition to seek a more suitable venue
for his attempt to regain the record. While Campbell was away, Segrave
announced he was to have another crack at the record with an all-new
vehicle designed by the renowned Captain J.S. 'Jack' Irving. Both
Campbell and Segrave had turned their back on Sunbeam by then, but
Segrave had found corporate sponsorship and his new car was already
well on the way to completion at the Robin Hood Works of the KLG
Sparking Plug Company at Putney Vale.

Segrave and Irving went to Napier to hire a powerful engine, a
Schneider Trophy unsupercharged racing unit, producing 925hp. Irving
designed a remarkable multi-plate clutch with servo assistance – the first
in a concept that was subsequently adopted by both private and
commercial vehicle manufacturers. The car was to become a household
name, the Irving-Napier, or popularly the *Golden Arrow*. Major Henry
Segrave drove the 3-ton *Golden Arrow* to a new World Land Speed
Record of 231.446mph (372.34kph) at Daytona Beach on 11 March
1929; a record that once again proved to be far out of the reach of the
Napier-Campbell *Bluebird*.

Segrave was convinced the *Golden Arrow* was capable of a greater
speed, but soon after he set the new record he witnessed a horrifying
tragedy that was to turn him away from further attempts at the World
Land Speed Record. American Lee Bible, team mechanic for the famed
White Triplex driven earlier by Ray Keech, wanted to shoot for the
Englishman's record. In fact, and as some onlookers explained, he was
driving too fast in preliminary trials, and seemed oblivious of the danger

of the sands. He worked the car rapidly up to 200mph on practice runs. On a third (unofficial) run at the mile, the car veered out of control, skidding sideways at some 128mph. It then appeared to lunge into the sands, throwing debris over 300ft of the course, hitting a Pathé newsreel cameraman who couldn't get out of the way of the rolling car. Both Bible and the cameraman, Charles Traub, were killed instantly.

Major Henry Segrave returned to England and was knighted shortly after his record success. Eager to return to some sort of record breaking, he turned to Lord Wakefield, founder of the Castrol Oil Company in Cheapside in the City of London, or as the company was then known, C.C. Wakefield & Co. Ltd. Such was Lord Wakefield's enthusiasm for the fast-growing sport of power-boating that in September 1930 he financed the building of a potential record-breaking boat *Miss England II*, and Sir Henry Segrave was chosen to pilot her.

Disenchanted that Hubert Scott-Paine, the chief of the British Powerboat Company at Hythe, was trying to claim all the kudos for designing and piloting *Miss England I*, Fred Cooper and Sir Henry Segrave, with the full support of Lord Wakefield and Castrol, decided to change their boatbuilder to Saunders-Roe Ltd of Cowes. The Cooper-designed *Miss England II* soon took shape at Sam Saunders' Isle of Wight yard. Powered by two 1,800hp supercharged Rolls-Royce 'R' Type aero-engines, the single-stepper was taken to Lake Windermere to make an official attempt at the record on Friday 13 June 1930. England's largest lake suddenly became populated with every conceivable type of spectator craft, not to mention a small flotilla of newsreel boats and the press corps from Fleet Street; not exactly fair for such an untried craft.

In common with tradition, Sir Henry went out on the second of what were to be three trial runs prior to an attempt at the World Water Speed Record, when at a staggering 98.76mph (158.93kph) he hit a submerged

The Irving-Napier Golden Arrow *returns to England after Major Henry Segrave set a new World Land Speed Record of 231.446mph (372.34kph) in March 1929. The road from Southampton to the KLG's Robin Hood Works at Putney Vale was lined with jubilant onlookers. The car is seen here pausing briefly at Wandsworth Town Hall. (Author's collection)*

After setting a new speed record the Golden Arrow *is lifted aboard the SS Oramo at Tilbury Docks, London, on the first leg of a world tour, backed by the British section of the Society of Motor Manufacturers and Traders, and Lord Wakefield, founder of the Castrol Oil Company, as part of a campaign to attract overseas trade orders. Such was the prestige of record-breaking in the 1920s that the result of the initiative attracted £11.5 million in advance orders for product related components and lubricants. (Author's collection)*

Sir Henry Segrave's boat Miss England II *travelling at full throttle on Lake Windermere shortly before she capsized, killing her helmsman Sir Henry and his mechanic Victor Halliwell. (Author's collection)*

The upturned hull of Miss England II *appeared remarkably intact after the fatal accident on the Westmorland lake. There was no evidence pointing towards the cause of the tragedy, although at the inquest, Ulverston coroner Mr F.W. Poole reported that twenty minutes after the disaster, a water-logged branch was seen 250 yards to the stern of the boat. The sole survivor was chief engineer Michael Willcocks. (Author's collection)*

LORD WAKEFIELD 1859–1941

In March 1899, Charles Cheers Wakefield founded the firm of C.C. Wakefield & Co., Limited, later to become Castrol, corporate sponsor of many British land speed record cars. (Castrol International)

Charles Cheers Wakefield, the founder of the Castrol company that has made such an extraordinary contribution to record breaking attempts, was born on 12 December 1859 in Wavertree Vale, Liverpool. The youngest son of a Liverpool Customs Official and lay preacher, his school days were spent at the Liverpool Institute.

In 1891 he came to London and was associated with the American-owned Vacuum Oil Company. In 1899 he founded the firm of C.C. Wakefield & Co., Limited, which, as a manufacturer of high-class lubricants, achieved great prosperity. Elected to the Court of Common Council in 1904, he served as Sheriff of the City of London in 1907 and 1908. At the close of his term of office he received a Knighthood from King Edward VII.

In the world of motoring and power-boating, Lord Wakefield financed L.G. 'Cupid' Hornsted's 200hp Blitzen-engined Benz, Kenelm Lee Guiness's celebrated 350hp Sunbeam, Ernest Eldridge's 21.7-litre Fiat Mephistopheles, and Malcolm Campbell's record-breaking *Bluebird* cars and boats. He sponsored Major Henry Segrave's *Golden Arrow* LSR car and *Miss England II* record boat, and Captain George E.T. Eyston's *Speed of the Wind* and *Thunderbolt* cars. Whether for racing or for individual achievement in the air, or on land and water, invariably his now renowned Wakefield 'Castrol' Motor Oil was the lubricant chosen by those who reaped success.

At the outbreak of the Second World War, Lord Wakefield's first thought was for the safety of his staff and he immediately put into effect plans already made for the evacuation of his offices from London to the country. During 1940 he controlled the many adjustments that were needed to place his company's production on a war footing. His work, which was without respite, imposed a heavy strain on his health and quite suddenly, early in December 1940, the day following his eighty-first birthday, he was taken seriously ill. Five weeks later on the 15 January 1941, he passed away peacefully at his home in Beaconsfield, Buckinghamshire.

log from a fallen rowan tree at the far end of the lake. The log catapulted Sir Henry and the boat across the glass-like surface of Lake Windermere, submerging him and his crew under the upturned hull of *Miss England II*. The support team rushed to the scene in a flotilla of craft, searching for Sir Henry. He had captured the World Water Speed Record from the American, Garfield Wood in *Miss America VII*, but the attempt had cost him his life.

Segrave, aged only thirty-four, died of a punctured lung after three hours of conscious pain. One mechanic, Victor Halliwell, was drowned, while the other, Michael Willcocks, survived with severe bruising. The English Gentleman had lost his life in the pursuit of speed.

NORMAN 'WIZARD' SMITH – THE ANZAC CHALLENGE

Less than two years after the Windermere tragedy came news of a new, unexpected challenger from the other side of the world. An Australian endurance driver, Norman 'Wizard' Smith, who had none of Segrave's connections or works facilities, was going blithely ahead to build a machine of almost identical specifications to Segrave's Irving-Napier *Golden Arrow*. Fred H. Stewart, a Sydney businessman, was to sponsor the attempt and Don Harkness, a brilliant engineer and partner in the prominent Sydney engineering firm of Harkness & Hillier, would design the car.

Norman Smith had already enjoyed a distinguished career on the Australian endurance and point-to-point circuit with the Purr-Pull sponsored Model B-4 Ford and the Essex 4 racers, when, in 1928, Lord Wakefield, of Castrol fame, first introduced his Wakefield Trophy for presentation to each driver able to set a new World Land Speed Record. By then racing and point-to-point record breaking had already become of secondary interest to Smith. Like Henry Segrave, Ray Keech, Kaye Don, Parry Thomas and Malcolm Campbell across on the other side of the world, his sights were already set at much higher elevation. Like Segrave and company, he desired now to explore speeds in an area where few men had ever been before. Like them, he now desired nothing less than to become the fastest man on earth!

Smith had learned that far away in Western Australia there was a place called Lake Perkolilli – a dry and flat salt-pan, only occasionally covered with water – which possessed a near-perfect speed track around its outside perimeter. Smith went there and, in a Studebaker, got down in grim earnest to the task of setting endurance records that would earn him credibility as a serious contender for the World Land Speed Record. His 6-hour (75.8mph) and 12-hour (71.4mph) records, and the 24-hour marathon during which his car covered 2,416km against the clock, were still standing as Australian and Australasian records thirty years later, even though all three were established in 1928!

In fact 1928 was a vintage year for the 'Wizard'. Having decided to drive his Studebaker back east from Western Australia, and with his old rival John 'Iron Man' Burton firmly in mind, Smith in characteristic fashion quietly gathered together some food and water, a cheap pocket compass, and a satchelful of survey maps; then stepping into his big Studebaker at Fremantle, where the western edge of the Australian continent meets the Indian Ocean, he disappeared in a cloud of dust out of human ken. Five days later, with his car battered and filthy but still idling silkily, he drew up outside the Central Post Office – not of Sydney, but of

Norman Smith [signature]

Brisbane! There he was welcomed by his wife, and the two drove quietly away for Smith to take a shower and have a hot meal, after which he attended a party given in his honour.

Gradually the incredible tale came out. In fractionally more than five days Smith had completely crossed the almost-roadless continent, travelling over 500 miles (805km) farther than had Burton and slicing a whole day off the latter's time. He had jolted along through blazing days and pounded through swamps and across boulders during the precarious nights. With only small-scale maps and a pocket compass to guide him he had passed along from outback station to outback station, refuelling wherever he could; had repaired his own blown-out tyres and attended to his car's maintenance as he went. When he finally arrived at Brisbane at the end of the trail he had had only one two-hour spell of sleep during the entire marathon drive. What, Australia was asking, would 'Wizard' Smith try next? The answer was not too long in coming.

In Sydney, in the expert hands of Don Harkness, the car upon whch Norman Smith's land speed record hopes were pinned was gradually taking shape. Harkness designed the vehicle – appropriately dubbed the *Anzac* – around an enormous Rolls-Royce Eagle aero-engine donated by the Royal Australian Air Force and capable of developing 360hp – this at a time when 1,000hp would seem to have been the minimum required. Power or not, the car itself was rapidly nearing completion.

The chassis of the *Anzac* was basically that of a standard Cadillac sedan, strengthened, lengthened and underslung at the rear to accommodate the mighty 1922 aero-engine whose measurements Harkness had been given by the RAAF. The chassis itself incorporated stock Cadillac brakes, road wheels, and three-speed gearbox, while the racing-shell body, which had been designed but not yet fabricated, looked exactly like that of an elongated and ultra-heavy conventional racing car. It carried an ordinary small flat racing windscreen plus a small seat for the riding mechanic – Don Harkness, it was agreed, would ride alongside Smith during any record attempts – and an aircraft-type pilot tube on the front of the car to measure speed.

The *Anzac*, although thoroughly outclassed for land speed record potential, was nonetheless a racing machine to be reckoned with. In shape it bore little resemblance to the lowslung, semi-envelope record-breaking cars that, in Wakefield Trophy competition, it had no chance whatsoever of catching; nevertheless by standards of only two or three years earlier it was both a handsome car and contemporary. In profile the *Anzac* was necessarily high, as not only had its massive V12 engine somehow to be accommodated underneath the bonnet, but a driver and riding machine had both to fit 'on', rather than in – there being simply no way by which their position could be lowered because of the height of the bulky Cadillac chassis plus the transfer case.

All four wire wheels were fully exposed and carried Firestone racing tyres on detachable well-base rims. Interchangeable crown wheels and pinions provided by Harkness for the Cadillac differential gave Smith a choice of two final-drive ratios, the higher of which provided for a theoretical maximum road speed close to 200mph. That was to be the gearing selected by Smith for his forthcoming runs at Ninety Mile Beach at the far end of New Zealand's North Island, since approach distance at the venue was almost unlimited.

Oblivious to the possibilities of Lake Eyre, some 400 miles north of Adelaide, in South Australia, Smith set off to tour both Australia and New Zealand, giving exhibitions and driving at high speeds between cities, while searching for a venue for his record attempt. In New Zealand, just as in Australia, wherever he went Smith now made judicious enquiries about a possible site at which he might attempt land speed records. In turn he inspected, and rejected, long beaches at Muriwai near Auckland, at Ohope in the Bay of Plenty and at Bluecliffs, down in the uttermost south of the South Island. Nothing seemed suitable. But as he continued to barnstorm the country one New Zealander after another kept telling him of a stretch of beach right up north that was said to be 90 miles (145km) long, and was known to the Maoris as Oneroa-a-Tohe and to Europeans as Ninety Mile Beach. Ninety Mile Beach – the wide, flat and curving strand of sand that begins at Ahipara, a short distance south-west of Kaitaia, and runs away off in a north-westerly sweep until it comes to an abrupt end at Scott's Point, beyond Te Paki Stream – is about as far north as the land will let you go in New Zealand and is really an impostor, as it measures not 90 miles (145km) but only 56 (90km).

When Smith arrived at Kaitaia accompanied by his wife, the *Anzac* was already at the Star Garage, ready, polished and waiting. The big car had in fact already been photographed several times by Kaitaia's two weekly newspapers in the street outside the garage, usually with proudly beaming locals seated at the wheel or leaning in studied stances against its side. To reach Kaitaia from Sydney the *Anzac* had already been through something of an ordeal. First it had to be shipped across the treacherous Tasman Sea aboard the steamship *Rarotonga* and was then customs-cleared at Auckland by the Auckland Automobile Association, representing the British Royal Automobile Club (RAC) and the International Committee on Motor Racing. To make matters even more difficult, having left Auckland in pouring rain Smith found as he progressed north that the weather, instead of easing, was growing steadily worse. When, at length, he arrived at Kaitaia the whole of New Zealand's Northland was in the grip of a tropical cyclone, a storm which was to wage unabated for four whole days, with water sweeping in flood through Kaitaia township itself and creating havoc across the length and breadth of the countryside.

Smith was no stranger to rain or to wind, but when he was able to visit Hukatere, his chosen site about midway along the sands at Ninety Mile Beach, he drove cautiously and his mouth dropped open. He was aghast at what he saw. The broad flat strand which he had so admired during an earlier reconnaissance was a shambles! Piles of upcast seaweed and debris festooned the shoreline above the low-water mark for as far as the eye could see, while the once-level beach, now a wilderness of humps, ripples and water-filled hollows, was so corrugated that it was punishing to drive along it even at low speed.

But if Oneroa-a-Tohe had chosen upon that occasion to show her visitor the worst of her many moods, she was determined with equal coquettishness soon to show him her very best as well. For with the storm over, only two tides had come and gone before the beach presented a diametrically opposite picture – all kelp washed up high, the hard low-tide sand stretching along for mile upon mile unruffled, glass-smooth and as hard as concrete. It was a great opportunity and Smith insisted it should be seized upon without delay.

The year 1930 was approaching, and Norman Smith knew two new land speed record contenders were now entering the lists. They were celebrated British racing drivers Kaye Don and Giulio Foresti, the latter in charge of an Italian-designed car which had been financed by Egyptian royalty. They called the car the *Djelmo*, and Foresti, who raced Schmid and Bugatti cars at that time, could be counted upon to make it produce its utmost. Don, on the other hand, had produced a behemoth of a car named the Sunbeam *Silver Bullet* and designed by former Sunbeam designer Louis Coatalen, one of the most brilliant auto-designers Britain had ever known. Smith knew he could not possibly compete with the likes of Don and Foresti with his 360hp *Anzac*. World marks were simply not possible over short distances; there was still, however, the 10-mile record within his reach, as well as records for both New Zealand and Australasia.

Low tide came that 1929 day at late afternoon and Smith, with Harkness's help, tow-started the big car and warmed it up with a few practice runs along the sand. Then the mechanics swiftly ripped out all of the twenty-four 'soft' spark-plugs and replaced them with the 'hard' plugs needed for high speeds. That done, the still-warm engine started almost instantly when shoved by a dozen willing helpers. Smith and Harkness pulled down their goggles, bright flame belched from the *Anzac*'s exhausts, and the big car disappeared northward down the beach in the direction of Ahipara. Upon reaching the end of the marked course, Smith launched the *Anzac* almost immediately into the return run.

The southward 10-mile run, made at an average speed of nearly 156mph (251kph), had included bursts when Smith's airspeed indicator told him he was exceeding 170mph (276kph), whereas on his return trip he was never able to top 150mph (242kph) at any time. When the crackling-hot car trundled slowly back down the beach and came to rest in the midst of a swarming, cheering crowd, official calculations showed that Smith had averaged 148.63mph (239.75kph) for the two-way 10-mile run. It was a new Australasian (and New Zealand) record and a very respectable one too. In addition he had covered the measured two-way mile in 24.65 seconds – an unofficial land speed record of 146.34mph (235.93kph).

Later, after his return to Australia, Smith was to find that his world record over the 10-mile distance had been disallowed on the grounds that the timing apparatus used had been 'inadequate'. However, even as things stood, he returned to Australia thoroughly satisfied and authorized Don Harkness almost immediately to design and build a bigger, faster car – one that would have true Wakefield Trophy and world record potential.

Smith found a beneficiary in Sydney businessman and ex-politician Fred H. Stewart, but Stewart insisted upon a condition: when completed, Smith's new enterprise was to be christened the *Fred H. Stewart Enterprise* and this was in fact the unwieldy title by which the new record-breaker became known. The car itself was built by Harkness & Hillier (the firm that later produced the Harkness & Hillier racing aircraft) around one of the latest Napier Lion racing engines loaned by the British Air Ministry via the RAAF. Supercharged by a centrifugal blower, its power output had

been boosted from 900hp in normal aspiration up to 1,450hp. The mighty engine was carefully installed in a massive girder-rail chassis with multiple cross-bracing to form a car that measured a full 32ft (10m) overall. Instead of the full-length inter-wheel sponsons that housed the surface radiators on Segraves's almost identical Irving-Napier *Golden Arrow*, Smith and Harkness used ice cooling and fitted rear-wheel fairings, which extended to form twin stabilizing fins. So low was the car, even without Smith seated therein, that the *New Zealand Herald* quipped, 'It will be able to run on its wheels even if turned upside down.'

As with Campbell's various *Bluebird*s, Smith's car incorporated a built-in jacking point at each corner of the chassis wherein a quick-acting screw jack could be inserted and cranked down to facilitate rapid wheel changes. The car's panel work, by Gough Brothers, was superbly executed as was the bright golden duco which, relieved only by bright red lettering and a blue Australian ensign outlined on each tall tail fin, glistened from end to end of the 3-ton car.

Even as the huge golden *Fred H. Stewart Enterprise* lay dolefully at Harkness & Hillier's premises while shipping arrangements were being made for her long journey across the Tasman Sea to New Zealand, Prime Minister George William Forbes wrote to the Auckland Automobile Association (AAA) suggesting the possibility of inviting Malcolm Campbell and Kaye Don to Ninety Mile Beach for a 'Speed Pageant'. However, the facilities provided at the Bonneville Salt Flats, in the United States, no doubt made it a better proposition to go there than to haul a large racing car and entourage all the way to New Zealand.

If Smith's whole notion of trying to snatch the flying mile Wakefield Trophy from Campbell in a car that was barely capable of reaching the speed required was open to question, the Australian's manager, J.H. Mostyn, showed no recognition of any such limitations. To those pressmen who lingered around the Hukatere base camp soon after the team arrived at Ninety Mile Beach and who would listen to Mostyn, he was all optimism.

'The 10 and 15 mile records are in our pockets,' he proclaimed. 'And we ought to have no difficulty at all with the flying mile.'

If talking sets new land speed records, Mostyn already had them in the bag. Thus the *Enterprise* was taken in late December 1931 to Ninety Mile

The Fred H. Stewart Enterprise *is unveiled to the press at the Hukatere base camp shortly after Norman 'Wizard' Smith arrived at Ninety Mile Beach. This photograph gave Don Harkness, back in Sydney, Australia, his first sight of the huge, unsightly radiator fitted in New Zealand after earlier cooling troubles. (Author's collection)*

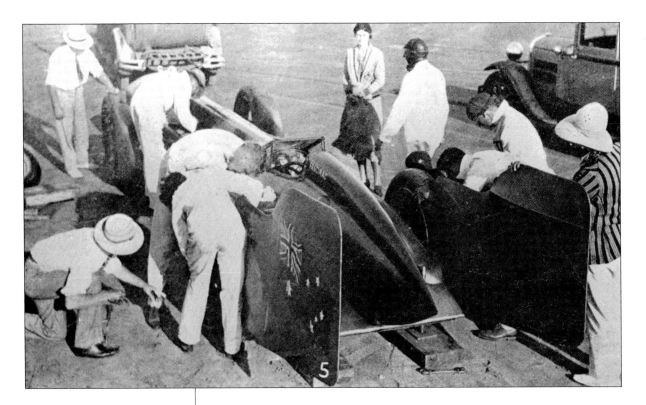

The Fred H. Stewart Enterprise *was taken to Ninety Mile Beach, North Island, New Zealand, in December 1931 and prepared for her inaugural assault on the land speed record. Instead of the full-length inter-wheel sponsons, which on Segrave's almost identical Irving-Napier* Golden Arrow *housed the surface radiators, Smith and Harkness used ice cooling and fitted rear-wheel fairings, which extended to form twin stabilizing fins. (Author's collection)*

Beach but Smith was geared-up to attack only one record – that of 10 miles.

The New Zealand course was troublesome from the start. The practice run on 11 January was a disappointment for Smith. The conditions were poor; the sands had been pitted with unexpected holes and rippled with short sharp undulations and jagged toheroa shells which threatened Smith's stock of tyres. However, it seemed to be improving with every tide.

Low spring tide came and went and it was not until 26 January 1932 that beach conditions appeared favourable enough for Smith to attempt the 10 mile record. The flags were already in position. The timing team raced down to the water's edge and rapidly erected tripods and delicate instruments. Once down upon the sand the big car started easily, then tore off northward, wheels spinning fiercely under acceleration as Smith gave the throttle an exploratory nudge. Immediately the first run was completed the electric timing figures came in – 150mph almost exactly. The crowd buzzed with excitement, for a whole convoy of cars had scorched off southward along the beach in the wake of the decelerating Smith and it seemed an age before any of them returned bearing news.

It must have been a full half-hour – the actual time-lag was never recorded – before a bellowing roar in the distance heralded the approaching *Enterprise* on the return run. This time its bodywork seemed to sparkle like a jewel as its driver pressed onward at high speed into a setting Pacific sun. Throughout the return pass Smith drove without the protection of his goggles and kept the car going at a more or less steady speed well below its maximum. Then 3 minutes 59.945 seconds after he had passed the AAA's northern 10 mile sign there was a huge jubilation at the timing-box, for the time represented a speed of just over 178mph (287kph). His average over the two runs – 164.084mph (265.45kph), a new world record! Norman 'Wizard' Smith had beaten his own previous

world 10 mile record, unofficial though it was, by a margin of 27mph, but it was well below the 300mph target they had hoped to reach.

Smith's great aim from the outset was the mile – the 'absolute' record – but conditions at Ninety Mile Beach never improved sufficiently and he had to abandon his assault. In 1936 he drove 10,000 miles (16,000km) right around Australia in a Pontiac sponsored by General Motors Australia, taking only forty-five days for the journey despite primitive and, in places, non-existent roads.

Incredible though it may seem, he faded gracefully into obscurity. This courageous and very modest sportsman, who waited impatiently for nothing more than a fighting chance to risk his life, was later dubbed not 'Wizard' but 'Windy' Smith by the Maoris of New Zealand's Northland – an epithet that was to dog him until his death on 1 December 1958.

Wheels spinning fiercely under acceleration, the Enterprise *hurtles down Ninety Mile Beach on 26 January 1932. Shortly after this photograph was taken Norman 'Wizard' Smith hit a rough patch, couldn't see the course and became airborne. He was forced to reduce his speed to 90mph to clean his goggles and windshield. Despite this he averaged 164.084mph (265.45kph). (Author's collection)*

FORESTI AND VILLA – ITALIAN INTERLUDE

In 1927 Smith knew that there were at least three people going after the 180mph record. One was an Italian designer Edmond Moglia, who was building a 355hp car in France for Prince Djelalledin, an Egyptian living in Paris, who was the brother of King Hussein Kiamil Fuad of Egypt; this mysterious car, aptly called the *Djelmo*, (a combination of their two surnames) was to be driven by Giulio Foresti.

Foresti not only ran a sales and service depot in Bryanston Square, London, for the legendary Itala empire of Turin, Italy, but also had his own workshop at Brooklands, where he tested and raced for the Itala team and the Ballot brothers, Maurice and Albert, before driving for Schmid and Bugatti at Brooklands and Italy's Targa Florio.

Among Foresti's engineering protégés at Bryanston Square was the fifteen-year-old former page boy Leopoldo Alphonso Villa, whom he had taken on as an apprentice after he was sacked from Romano's Restaurant in the Strand. Leo Villa, as he became known, went on to serve both Sir Malcolm and Donald Campbell as their unfailing and unequalled chief engineer and racing mechanic.

During the First World War Foresti had been responsible for the organization of all transport for the Italian Flying Corps in Britain, but he had also managed to keep the garage and workshop in Bryanston Square. Shortly after Villa joined Foresti in Bryanston Square, they took delivery

In November 1927, Giulio Foresti made an abortive attempt on the British national record at Pendine in the French 10-litre, straight-eight Djelmo. Projected in 1924, the mysterious car was financed by Prince Djelalledin, an Egyptian living in Paris, and designed by the Paris-based Italian engineer Edmond Moglia, of Sunbeam-Talbot-Darracq fame. Foresti's hopeless attempt on the record ended when the car slewed at speed and overturned, flinging the driver out on to Pendine's treacherous sands, dislocating his shoulder. (Author's collection)

of a 90hp Austro-Daimler, which they intended to race at Brooklands against the mighty Sunbeams. Foresti's Austro-Daimler had a cylinder bore of 130 mm and a stroke of 170 mm, giving a cubic capacity of 9,026cc. The new 6-cylinder Sunbeams against which they were racing had a bore of 81.5mm, and a stroke of 157mm giving a cubic capacity of only 4,914cc or 5 litres, yet they were a good deal faster.

Foresti and Villa took the Austro-Daimler to Brooklands towards the end of 1919, fitted it with new Palmer Cord tyres – three plain ribs, no tread – and within half an hour of their arrival they were out on the track racing against Malcolm Campbell, Major Henry Segrave, Victor Hémery and Kaye Don. Foresti and Villa touched 80mph on the track, but remained low down on the banking hoping to avoid the 'niff' from the sewage farm situated on the inner circle of the track alongside the section known as Railway Straight. Indeed, to this day many veterans of the old Brooklands track still recall the pungent smell of sewage as their cars passed under the Members' Bridge. Foresti took first place with Campbell third. It was an outstanding season for Foresti and Villa with the Austro-Daimler. Having entered all of the renowned races at the track, including the 100mph Short and Long Handicaps and the Two Mile Sprint Race, they beat Campbell in a Peugeot to first place by a handsome margin.

In August 1920, Foresti took over the agency for the Isotta Fraschini car in Britain. Built in Milan, this was one of the first straight-eights, a 40hp luxury motor car with eight cylinders in line. It was undoubtedly Foresti's success at Brooklands that prompted the Italian company to award him the Isotta Fraschini concession.

Foresti left England for Monte Carlo early in 1921, revoking his concessions for the Itala, Dialto and Isotta Fraschini car agencies for the more lucrative challenge of racing cars for some of the European organizations, leaving Villa, now aged twenty, in charge of an empty showroom and service depot. Villa soon followed and on 29 March 1921 they entered their first Targa Florio race in Sicily in a 3-litre Itala. But owing to the political situation and the unrest caused by Benito Mussolini and his Black Shirts, work at the Itala factory in Turin had come to a standstill. Despite the riots and pickets at the Itala Works, Foresti and Villa climbed over the wall under cloak of darkness and got on with the job of preparing their car for the Targa Florio. Within a month the car was ready. They gave her a cursory test around the back streets of Turin, then drove straight down to Genoa where they were shipped to Palermo aboard the old tramp steamer *Anna Catania*.

The 3-litre Itala was a production car, sporting 4 cylinders with side valves. Transmission was through a four-speed 'crash' gearbox via a Hele Shaw wetplate clutch and a live axle with open propeller shaft. The transmission brake was foot operated, the brake drum being situated at the rear of the gearbox. The hand brake operated on two drums with internal expanding shoes on the rear wheels. Suspension was by semi-elliptic leaf springs all round. A single Solex carburettor was fitted and a standard wet sump with spur gear pump was the source of lubrication.

Motor racing in the early twenties was a gripping sport – especially the Targa Florio, or Circuito delle Madonie, as it was otherwise known, where a crash or breakdown in the mountains of Sicily might leave you at the mercy of bandits! Foresti and Villa avoided this fate and had many successful runs on the circuit in the Itala.

Following their victory in the 1921 Targa Florio, Foresti and Villa were invited by the Ballot brothers to Paris, where two 2-litre sports models were being prepared for the 1922 Targa Florio. Maurice Ballot hired them to drive one of his cars. Their team mate was to be the famous French racing driver Jules Goux, with Pierre du Cros as his racing mechanic. The 2-litre Ballot, was designed by the former Peugeot designer, Ernest Henry, who had produced a 4.5-litre, 4-cylinder engine in 1912 for the company's Grand Prix racing cars. After the war, Henry joined the Ballot firm, which had made rather ordinary proprietary engines and was about to launch a programme of Grand Prix and sports cars.

The Ballot was a very advanced car with an engine of 2 litres capacity, 4 cylinders, with twin overhead camshafts, a bore of 69.5mm and a 130mm stroke. Carburation was via a single Claudel Hobson carburettor and the single engine developed 72hp at 4,000rpm. Of standard production, it was a hand-

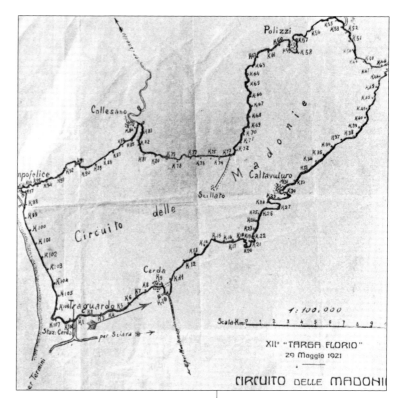

An early map of the gruelling Targa Florio, or Circuito delle Madonie, as it was otherwise known. (Author's collection)

Giulio Foresti at the wheel of the 2-litre Ballot shortly before the start of the 1922 Targa Florio. Jules Goux and Pierre du Cros came in second overall, and first in the 2-litre class. Foresti and Villa finished second in the 2-litre class, and fifth overall. The outright winner had been Count Masetti, driving a Mercedes, but it was a victory for the reputation of the Ballot car. (Author's collection)

fabricated car, sporting a four-speed gearbox, a live axle and a dry leather cone clutch. Suspension fore and aft was by semi-elliptic springs mounting Hartford shock absorbers. The crankcase, gearbox and rear axle casing were all aluminium castings, hand-turned and polished. As a final touch of luxury, each Ballot car was fitted with a solid silver radiator cap, which took the form of a statuette of a nude nymph, carrying a laurel wreath and blowing a hunting horn. The Ballot was a far more advanced car than the 3-litre Itala.

Conditions at Targa Florio had not changed significantly since the previous year. After a lively practice run, Villa removed the cylinder block, ground down all the valves and prepared the car for the race itself. The 1922 Targa Florio proved to be a disappointment for Foresti and Villa, but at least they made the finishing line. Jules Goux and Pierre du Cros came in second overall and first in the 2-litre class. Foresti and Villa finished second in the 2-litre class and fifth overall. The outright winner had been Count Masetti, driving a Mercedes, but it was a victory for the reputation of the Ballot car.

In order to gain maximum publicity for their new 2-litre sports car, the Ballot brothers, insisted that Goux and Foresti should drive their cars back from Genoa to the Ballot showrooms on the Champs Elysées in Paris.

In 1922 Malcolm Campbell took on the British agency for both the Itala and Ballot marques, as well as employing Leo Villa, leaving Foresti to pursue his lifelong ambition of driving a land speed record contender, but first he had to find a sponsor.

In October 1924, Foresti was approached by the Paris-based Italian engineer Edmond Moglia, the former chief engineer for Talbot, the French part of the vast Sunbeam-Talbot-Darracq empire, who told him of a highly sophisticated and costly car he was building to attack Campbell's World Land Speed Record of 146.16mph (235.217kph), set on 25 September 1924 in the Sunbeam *Bluebird*. Moglia's car was based on a design concept pioneered by Louis Coatalen and Vincenzo Bertarione of Sunbeam

Giulio Foresti and Leo Villa in the Ballot during the 1922 Targa Florio, or Circuito delle Madonie, as it was otherwise known, where a crash or breakdown in the mountains might leave you at the mercy of bandits! (Author's collection)

in reply to the V12, 10.6-litre Delage driven by René Thomas at Arpajon. Due to lack of funding Coatalen and Bertarione never built the car and sold the design to Prince Djelalledin for £6,500.

The pale-blue vehicle had the appearance of a conventional Grand Prix racing car, much smaller than the existing record-breakers. The massive 10-litre engine had twin overhead camshafts, straight-eight with cylinders in two blocks of four, and four valves per cylinder. Its bore was 107mm and its stroke 140mm. Carburation was via four Claudel Hobson carburettors that were estimated to develop 355hp at 3,000rpm.

Giulio Foresti's hopeless attempt on the British record ended in November 1927, when Pendine's treacherous sands overturned the Djelmo, flinging the unhelmeted driver out on to his head. Miraculously, he escaped unhurt. The car was a complete write-off and Foresti and Edmond Moglia went back to the Continent never to be seen on the record-breaking scene again. (Author's collection)

The engine-bearers were bolted direct to the chassis, affording it valuable bracing, and a two-speed-plus reverse gearbox in unison with the 10-litre engine was used. The eight exhausts discharged directly into a large chamber extending beyond the undershield midway between the front and rear wheels. The aluminium chassis encased the front dumb-irons, coil springs and radiator base. The front springs passed through the solid forged front axle, commonplace on Fiat and Bugatti racing cars. The rear wheels were 37½in crab-tracked with 56in at the front of the car and void of differential. The rear semi-elliptic springs were underslung adjacent to an enclosed rear axle. The clean and purposeful bodywork was most impressive, particularly from the front.

The initial plans were to take the *Djelmo* for an attempt on the record in 1925, either on the vast alkali playa of Muroc Dry Lake, high in the Mojave Desert, California, or on the beaches of Ormond-Daytona. But during road tests at Arpajon and Miramas it was discovered the car would not be ready for an attempt on the record until 1927.

Foresti and Moglia brought the *Djelmo* to Pendine Sands in South Wales in August of that year, as Prince Djelalledin was reluctant to underwrite the cost of shipment to the USA. Soon after their arrival on the Carmarthen beach they encountered persistent engine trouble. Foresti did manage some very respectable speeds, but the 146.16mph (235.217kph) record which stood when the *Djelmo* was first laid down had been raised by Major Henry Segrave earlier that year to 203.792mph (327.981kph) in the 1,000hp Sunbeam. By the time Foresti was ready, he could only make an attempt on Campbell's British record of 174.883mph (281.447kph) set at Pendine on 4 February 1927.

Foresti's hopeless attempt on the British record ended in November 1927, when Pendine's treacherous sands caught the car at a speed said to be well in excess of 150mph. Suddenly, the *Djelmo*, with one wheel hitting a patch of water, went into a broadside skid, swung around and overturned, flinging the driver out on to the sands, dislocating his shoulder. The *Djelmo* was a complete write-off and Foresti and Moglia went back to Europe never to be seen on the record-breaking scene again.

Only Kaye Don and Norman Smith were still in the field.

Top: *The unfortunate Sunbeam*
Silver Bullet *was a truly astonishing*
machine, weighing over 4½ tons.
The car theoretically should have
reached 125mph in first gear, and
yet in the record attempt at
Daytona on 31 March 1930, Don
couldn't get her going any faster
than an averaged timed speed of
186.046mph (297.6kph), well
below the current record. Bottom:
A partly cutaway view of the
Sunbeam Silver Bullet, *showing the*
location of the two enormous
Sunbeam-Coatalen 12-cylinder
engines mounted in line, with
centrifugal supercharger coupled in
tandem behind them, and twin
propeller shafts copied from the
Irving-Napier Golden Arrow.
(Author's collection)

KAYE DON AND THE SUNBEAM SILVER BULLET

By the spring of 1930, when Campbell's thoughts again turned to record-breaking, Kaye Don had already been out to Daytona with his much publicized Sunbeam *Silver Bullet*, and had got nowhere.

Less than ten months after Segrave set his 231.446mph (372.34kph) record at Daytona, Louis Coatalen, creator of the 4-litre and 1,000hp Sunbeams, came forth with his incisive reply to Captain J.S. 'Jack' Irving's 3-ton *Golden Arrow* – the *Silver Bullet*. Coatalen was confident the car would surpass the record set by Segrave in the Irving-Napier *Golden Arrow*, and hired the celebrated Brooklands racing driver Kaye Don to drive the all-new behemoth.

The *Silver Bullet* was meticulously constructed and was propelled by two enormous 12-cylinder Sunbeam-Coatalen engines mounted in line, with centrifugal supercharger coupled in tandem and twin propeller shafts copied from Irving's 1929 *Golden Arrow*. The two V12, twin overhead camshaft engines specially designed for the car were cast in aluminium with Nitralloy steel cylinder liners measuring 140×130mm, giving a cubic capacity of 24 litres. The cylinder blocks were angled at 50°. The car had a proclaimed output of 4,000hp from its two special engines that were coupled, not by direct shafting but by drop gears and a secondary shaft. A

The aesthetic beauty of Frank Lockhart's 16-cylinder, four ohc, 3-litre, Stutz Black Hawk *belied the instability and tendency to yaw that eventually cost him his life on the sands of Daytona on 25 April 1928. The car was entering the measured mile at over 220mph when the right rear tyre collapsed, smashing the car and killing Lockhart. (Author's collection)*

The enterprising Californian, Frank Lockhart, was only twenty-five when he lost his life on the sands of Daytona at the wheel of the sleek Stutz Black Hawk. *(Author's collection)*

three-speed gearbox gave estimated speeds of 125, 166 and 248mph at 2,400rpm.

The crankshaft and big ends ran in roller bearings, and supercharging was by a huge blower turning at 17,000rpm, charging from two huge Amal carburettors. There was no radiator; instead, engine cooling was by 75lb of ice and water in two tanks through which the coolant flowed. This was good for five miles at full throttle before the temperature exceeded 185°F. The cooling concept was pioneered by the American car designer/driver Frank Lockhart in 1928. Lockhart's car, the experimental 3-litre, 16-cylinder Stutz *Black Hawk*, proved hard to control at high speed and at Daytona on 25 April 1928 the car was entering the measured mile at over 220mph, when the right rear tyre collapsed, smashing the car and killing Lockhart.

The *Silver Bullet* was a truly astonishing machine weighing over 4½ tons. Its total length was 31ft, and it stood only 40in high. Its silver bodywork was long and slender, interrupted only by the form-fitting cockpit. The wheels had aerodynamic after-fairings, similar to the *Golden Arrow*, with twin rectangular stabilizing fins and a horizontal hinged air brake in between on the tail of the car. Suspension was semi-elliptical all round.

Kaye Don and the Sunbeam entourage left England for Daytona on 5 March 1930, but contrary to the expectations outlined in the press releases, it soon became clear the thoroughbred was not up to the task. The engine proved capable on the test bed at Wolverhampton, but the supercharging arrangements were such that soon after the *Silver Bullet* arrived at Daytona it was discovered that under power the close proximity of the exhaust manifolds to the inlet chambers caused the incoming gas to explode before reaching the cylinders, resulting in fires. The unfortunate Sunbeam *Silver Bullet* was doomed from the start.

The car should theoretically have reached 125mph in first gear alone and yet in the record attempt on 31 March Don couldn't get her going any faster than an averaged timed speed of 186.046mph (297.6kph), well below the current record. Morale in the Sunbeam camp was low. There was even friction between Coatalen and Don, whom one American

Kaye Don had little chance of success at Daytona Beach in March 1930. The bumpy course played havoc with the long chassis'd
Silver Bullet, *seen here entering the timing traps on the first run through the mile. (Author's collection)*

The supercharging arrangements on the Sunbeam Silver Bullet *were such that under power the car proved very prone to catching*
fire. Morale in the Sunbeam camp was low; there was even friction between Louis Coatalen and Kaye Don. Another attempt was
planned, but Sunbeam abandoned its efforts. The car was eventually sold to Lancashire drivers Jack Field and Freddy Dixon, who
both tried unsuccessfully to reach acceptable speeds on Southport beach in 1934, only to discover the car was still prone to catching
fire. (Author's collection)

newspaper accused of being scared of the car. The truth, however, was the car simply could not run as expected. It was unlike Coatalen and Don to leave matters standing and the team returned to England with the intention of modifying the *Silver Bullet* for another attempt, but Sunbeam abandoned its efforts with the car, and it was eventually sold to Lancashire drivers Jack Field and Freddy Dixon, who both tried unsuccessfully to reach acceptable speeds with the car on Southport beach in 1934, only to discover the *Silver Bullet* was still prone to catching fire. They abandoned their attempt.

Kaye Don, like Segrave, turned his attention to the World Water Speed Record and in 1931 he piloted Segrave's *Miss England II* to a new record in the Argentine. *Miss England II* had been salvaged from Windermere after Segrave's death and thoroughly overhauled, repaired and modified. Her hull was now sheathed in ¹⁄₁₆in stainless steel. Just over two weeks after the American, Garfield Wood, regained the record from Segrave in *Miss America VII*, the patriotic Don, piloting the modified *Miss England II*

on the Paranà River, Argentina, set a new World Water Speed Record of 103.49mph (167kph). Three months later, on Lake Garda, Italy, Don and *Miss England II* improved their record to 110.28mph (194.02kph).

In 1932 news came through that a third *Miss England* was being built at the Hampton-on-Thames yard of John I. Thornycroft Ltd, and that the Rolls-Royce 'R' Type aero-engines had now been rebuilt to give her over 4,000hp. Kaye Don and *Miss England III* succeeded in lifting the record to 119.81mph (192.04kph) on Loch Lomond in Scotland. Among the spectators cheering with delight was Segrave's former mechanic, Michael Willcocks. Such runs gave Don hope to believe that his experiences with the Sunbeam *Silver Bullet* at Daytona were long since past.

Prior to driving the Sunbeam Silver Bullet *Kaye Don enjoyed much success at Brooklands driving for Sunbeam, breaking no fewer than four International Class C records in the legendary Sunbeam cars, depicted here in an early Castrol advertisement. (Castrol International)*

Kaye Don, the celebrated Brooklands racing driver hired to drive Louis Coatalen's unfortunate Sunbeam Silver Bullet. *(Author's collection)*

AB JENKINS - MORMON CONQUEST

In 1933, David Abbott (Ab) Jenkins, a devout Mormon of Welsh parentage from Salt Lake City, set a remarkable 24-hour endurance record of 117.77mph (189.09kph). Driving a 12-cylinder Pierce-Arrow, equipped with a 200hp engine with 488 cubic inch displacement, he raced the car on his Bonneville Salt Flats backyard, covering some 3,000 miles in 25 hours 30 minutes 36.32 seconds.

Although in his late sixties, Ab Jenkins embarked on a career with the sole objective of snatching the World Land Speed Record from under the very noses of the 'ruddy' Englishmen, who turned up on the Bonneville Salt Flats with their exotic streamliners to capture and retain the record over a span of twenty-three years. This was raised from a mere 146.16mph (235.217kph) by Malcolm Campbell in 1924, to 394.20mph (634.267kph) set by John Cobb in September 1947. The record was broken only once for the United States – by Ray Keech who established a record of 207.552mph (334.022kph) in J.M. White's Liberty-powered *White Triplex* in 1928. Although the Bonneville course became famous as a result of the record-breaking exploits of Campbell and Cobb, it took the personal campaigning of Ab Jenkins to attract the top European competitors to Utah for their record attempts.

In 1934 Jenkins raised the 24-hour record to 127.229mph (204.754kph) driving a car with a similar chassis to J.M. White's vehicle and equipped with a now familiar streamline racing bodyshell. The 12-cylinder Pierce-Arrow engine was equipped with six carburettors, special manifolds and high compression heads. The car was christened the 'Ab Jenkins Special'.

In his 4,800lb, 700hp racing car David Abbot 'Ab' Jenkins, a devout Morman of Welsh parentage from Salt Lake City, set speed and endurance records at every distance from from 50 to 10,000 miles and from 1 hour to 48 hours on the famed Bonneville Salt Falts. (Author's collection)

In 1935, the first Duesenberg Special to appear on the salt was engineered and designed for Ab Jenkins by Augie Duesenberg. The engine was a variation on a theme of an earlier design completed by the famous Duesenberg brothers, Fred and Augie, shortly before Fred's untimely death. Built by Lycoming, the engine was a supercharged straight-eight, developing 350hp, with a 420 cubic inch displacement. A number of these chassis were built and sold 'off the shelf' at a cost of $11,000 each. The bodyshell was the first to be designed with the aid of a wind tunnel test facility. The work was carried out at the Ohio State University, which would conduct the transonic and supersonic tests of the rocket-powered land speed record car *The Blue Flame*. With his new car, and with Tony Gulotta as relief driver, Jenkins established a new 24-hour record of 135.58mph (218.19kph) at Bonneville during the 1935 season.

The first of Jenkins' *Mormon Meteor* cars made its appearance in 1936. It was clearly designed from the ground up for speed. The chassis was a special Duesenberg with wire wheels. The bodyshell was built at Indianapolis by Augie Duesenberg, Ab Jenkins and a select team of expert mechanics.

Successful British challenges to Jenkins' endurance records in 1935 had convinced the most famous man in Utah that aero-engines would be needed to power future vehicles. He found what he wanted in New Jersey, in the possession of the famous aviator Clyde Pangborne. Ab returned to Indianapolis with a complement of two Curtiss Wright Conquerors-V-type, 12-cylinder, water-cooled powerplants that developed 700hp. One of these aero-engines was used by Pangborne and Hugh Herndon Jr in their famous round-the-world flight of 1931 and for the first non-stop crossing of the Pacific Ocean.

Salt Lake City's afternoon newspaper, the *Deseret News*, had held a contest to name the new car, which was how it came to be dubbed the

1936 was a hard year for Ab Jenkins, with Captain George Eyston and John Cobb on hand to make the contest a three-cornered event for the endurance records. Eyston was first in the slot with his Rolls-Royce Kestrel-engined car Speed of the Wind. *With backing from Lord Wakefield and the Castrol Oil Company, this mighty vehicle was specially designed by Eyston for the long-distance Class A figures, achieving success at Montlhéry and Bonneville, where he set a new 24-hour record of 149.096mph (240.012kph), followed soon after by the 48-hour record of 136.34mph (219.41kph). (Author's collection)*

Laying down the line: this rare photograph shows the sighting strip being marked into the salt at Bonneville in the 1950s. (Author's collection)

Mormon Meteor. Jenkins himself carried that tag for the rest of his life, and so did each of his racing cars. The *Mormon Meteor* was completed in time to race in 1936 and, using Babe Stapp, the famed Indianapolis champion, as relief driver, Jenkins once again rewrote the record books for endurance driving.

To relieve the boredom of the long drive, Jenkins steered with one hand and wrote notes with another. He pitched the notes over the side while passing his pits, roaring along at more than 120mph. His remarkable record speed of 151mph (243.02kph) was never accepted however, as the American Automobile Association had not timed it. The fact remained that Jenkins and Stapp had covered 2,710 miles in 24 hours. However, Jenkins' performance did catch the AAA's attention and the American record-sanctioning body agreed to provide official timing for their next run.

It was a hard year, with Captain George Eyston and John Cobb on hand to make the contest a three-cornered event for the endurance records. Eyston was first in the slot with his *Speed of the Wind*. He set a new 24-hour record of 149.096mph (240.012kph), then went on to establish a 48-hour record of 136.34mph (219.41kph).

Jenkins and Stapp, with the *Mormon Meteor*, made the next bid but were interrupted after the 500-kilometre (310 mile) and 500-mile (805km) records had fallen. A front universal joint burned out, and the *Meteor*'s run was aborted for vital repairs. New records, set before the race was ended by misfortune, included: 500 kilometres – 164.47mph (264.68kph); 500 miles – 152.34mph (245.16kph); 12 hours – 152.84mph (245.97kph).

Cobb then took to the circular track and replaced Eyston's 24-hour record with a speed of 150.163mph (241.663kph), but Jenkins and Stapp were far from finished. Returning to Bonneville in late September 1936, they captured for America every record from 50 miles to 48 hours

Castrol has been involved with excellence in the field of record breaking since Charles Cheers Wakefield first introduced his new Wakefield Castrol Motor Oil in 1906. Indeed, not only was Wakefield Castrol Motor Oil used in many of the legendary land speed record cars, but Castrol has sponsored no fewer than twenty successful attempts. Shown here and overleaf are early Castrol advertisements celebrating Malcolm Campbell's 1928 and 1931 Bluebirds, Henry Segrave's 1,000hp Sunbeam and Irving-Napier Golden Arrow. (Castrol International)

A rare cockpit photograph of Henry Segrave's 1,000hp Sunbeam. The driver sat directly above the engine coupling shaft for the front and rear 22½-litre, 12 cylinder Matabele aero-engines. (Castrol International)

Malcolm Campbell's remodelled Bluebird *in its sleek 1931 form, redesigned by Reid A. Railton at Thomson & Taylor of Brooklands, nearing completion in the Chelsea coachbuilders of Gurney, Nutting & Co., where the bodyshell was constructed and fitted. (Castrol International)*

Conceived in a dream, the body shell of Athol Graham's City of Salt Lake *was built around a drop tank taken from the belly of a Second World War Boeing B-29 Superfortress bomber, cut into three sections, forming the nose, centre and sandwiched tail section, and was powered by a 3,000hp V12 Allison aero-engine mounted at the rear and driving the rear wheels. Sitting in the cockpit, taken from a surplus P51 Mustang fighter, Graham, with USAC timekeeper Joe Petrali presiding, discusses a run in which he attained a two-way average speed of 344.761mph (554.829kph), nearly equalling Mickey Thompson's flying mile record. (Author's collection)*

Right: *On 1 August 1960, Graham fired up his $2,500, V12 Allison-powered vehicle, sponsored by STP and Firestone. Some 2 miles down range, the car veered slightly off course, began to slide, pitching violently, turned, became airborne and crashed. Graham hadn't worn a seat belt or safety harness.*
On impact, the firewall shattered the cockpit breaking his spine. Graham died three hours later in Tooele Hospital. Above: Athol Graham's 1960 City of Salt Lake with his wife Zeldine in the cockpit. After Graham's death, the car was rebuilt twice, first by Otto Anzjon and later by Harry Muhlbach, both of whom drove the car to near fatal crashes. (Author's collection)

Above: *The beautiful lines of Donald Campbell's* Bluebird *at Lake Eyre, some 400 miles north of Adelaide in South Australia. After several unsuccessful attempts on the dead lake, Campbell eventually cemented a new World Land Speed Record of 403.1mph (648.728kph) on 17 July 1964.* Left: *Corrosion from the salt had badly affected* Bluebird's *exterior and also the internal electrical connections, and the Bristol-Siddeley Proteus engine proved very difficult to start. Leo Villa and his team worked around the clock to prepare the 'Skipper's' car for the final assault at Lake Eyre. (Author's collection)*

Above: *Mickey Thompson built* Challenger I *around four V8, ohv, 6.7-litre 700hp Pontiac engines – one pair driving the front wheels, the other the rear. In 1960 the enterprising Thompson supercharged the engines and on 9 September covered the measured mile at a one-way average speed of 406.60mph (654.329kph) beating John Cobb's record by over 12mph. (Author's collection)*

Below: *By the time Mickey Thompson reached Bonneville on 30 October 1968 with his new Ford Autolite Special the salt was already wet from sporadic rains. Despite the threat of further rain approaching from Stansbury Mountains to the east, Thompson hurtled his streamliner across the salt to 425.03mph (683.01kph). The rains came, robbing Thompson of a chance of a return run at the record.*

Mickey Thompson at Bonneville with Challenger I. *The car was comparatively small by land speed record standards, being some 8ft shorter and 3ft narrower than John Cobb's behemothic* Railton-Mobil-Special. *It was powered by four V8, ohv, 6.7-litre, 700bhp Pontiac engines with two General Motors, Rootes-type superchargers and fuel injection, mounted in pairs, side by side, driving the front and rear wheels through two prewar La Salle three-speed gearboxes. (Author's collection)*

Best Wishes
Bob Summers

Above: *In simplest terms, Bob Summers' remarkable* Goldenrod *is the fastest automobile of all time. With an official World Land Speed Record of 409.277mph (658.636kph) set on 12 November 1965 at Bonneville. (Author's collection)*
Below: *Dr Nathan Ostich prepares the* Flying Caduceus *for its inaugural run at Bonneville. For three years, the Los Angeles physician waged a battle with the elusive record in his sleek 28ft jet car. (Author's collection)*

Above: *Designed by Ray Brook, the* Flying Caduceus *was the first jet-powered car to attack the World Land Speed Record. Powered by a General Electric J47 turbojet unit from a Boeing B36 bomber, the car made its début at the Bonneville Salt Flats on 6 August 1960. (Author's collection)*
Below: *Approaching a speed of 331mph (533.02kph) 7 miles down range, the* Flying Caduceus *suddenly veered to the left in a terrifying slide. The left-hand front wheel buckled, and snapped from its bearing. Fighting to regain control Dr Nathan Ostich fired his safety chute and and the car remained stable until finally coming to a shuddering halt at the end of the salt. (Author's collection)*

Above: *The* Green Monster *is towed onto the course at Bonneville in preparation for the greatest speed duel in automobile history. Art Arfons' lifelong friend and project associate Ed Snyder (standing) confers with the intrepid driver sitting in the cockpit. (Author's collection)*
Below: *Art Arfons'* Green Monster *after cementing his third World Land Speed Record at Bonneville on the morning of 7 November 1965, with an average speed of 576.553mph (927.829kph) in two consecutive runs. (Author's collection)*

inclusive. The times: 24 hours – 153.823mph (247.55kph); and for the 48 hours – 148.641mph (239.213kph).

At the close of the most colourful season so far on the salt, all parties withdrew to their respective workshops to build or rebuild their cars. The *Mormon Meteor II* included only minor changes, for example the installation of a revolutionary new design concept of a vertical tail fin at the rear of the car. A potential World Land Speed Record car was beginning to emerge from the chrysalis of time and experience.

Ab Jenkins, the carpenter from Salt Lake City, first saw the salt in 1910 when he drove his motorcycle to a speed of 60mph. The first record-breaking attempted ever essayed at Bonneville was in 1914, when American Indianapolis racing star 'Terrible' Teddy Tetzlaff came to the salt flats to drive Ernie Moross's famed *Blitzen* Benz, the car that had gained its reputation in the hands of Barney Oldfield and 'Wild Bob' Burman. His aim was to break Burman's controversial flying mile American record of 141.370mph (227.512kph) set up at Daytona on 23 April 1911. There was no official timing, only Moross's men with stop-watches. The chief timing official announced a time of 25.4 seconds for the distance, averaging 141.73mph (228.030kph), ⅕ second faster than Burman. Moross, meanwhile, had suggested to spectators that they hold their own watches on the run because 'this run is not phony. Everything is square, honest, and above-board.' Individual timers caught Tetzlaff in everything from 19.2 seconds to recognize the claim of 141.73mph, which compared with the official two-way world mark of 124.100mph (199.720kph), set by L.G. 'Cupid' Hornsted, and Bob Burman's one-way American record of 141.370mph.

The most spectacular event to promote the Bonneville Salt Flats as a potential land speed record speedway, took place in 1925, shortly after the completion of the Lincoln Highway, linking Salt Lake City with Wendover. W.D. 'Bill' Rishel, lifelong friend of Ab Jenkins and, in 1900, the first man to drive a car across the saline highway, asked his old friend if he would race the Denver & Rio Grande excursion train from Salt Lake City to Wendover, a distance of 125 miles. Ab Jenkins said he would – provided

On 20 July 1951, Ab Jenkins set twenty-four new International Class A and American records in the Mormon Meteor III, *the most notable being a 196.36mph (361.01kph) average for 100 miles. The car was designed by Augie Duesenberg around Ab's specifications, and seven mechanics helped construct the most famous Jenkins racer. (Author's collection)*

there was a purse of $250 riding on the outcome. The money was quickly raised and the race was on – the dawn of sponsorship had broken!

Riding with Ab were a Miss Paula McCafferty, secretary to the Studebaker dealer who provided the car, and Tommy Dee, a Salt Lake City policeman who sat in the back seat and took most of the rough jolts. Streaking across the Salt Flats, Ab beat the train by no less than 4 minutes 29 seconds, but it took more than his $250 prize money to pay for repairs to the badly shaken car. That very run cemented the confidence of all associated with speed and record-breaking: Bonneville became a household name in the workshops and garages from coast to coast.

Jenkins went on to establish even more records on Bonneville's circular course. He set more than 500 during his racing career, and he was so popular in his hometown that he was elected mayor of Salt Lake City. At the age of sixty-eight, Ab returned to Bonneville for what many people thought would be his last appearance. On 20 July 1951, just short of a year before the birth of this author, Ab Jenkins set twenty-four new International Class A and American records, the most notable being a 196.36mph (361.01kph) average for 100 miles.

In July 1952, Ab, tired of his desk in the Utah State Capitol Building, was signed by the Firestone Tire and Rubber Company to appear on a strenuous tour of the United States. In addition to personal 'cameo' appearances, Ab's publicity routine consisted of driving at 80mph and purposely blowing out a front tyre to demonstrate the safety factors incorporated in his sponsor's supreme product, the first in the historical development of what has become known as 'the safety tyre'.

In August 1952, the *Mormon Meteor III* was turned out to pasture for the last time and presented by Ab Jenkins to the children of Utah, where it now stands sentinel, amid the stately surroundings of the Utah State

Capitol Building in Salt Lake City. This car was recently restored to its former clean and purposeful form by Ab's son, Marvin.

At sixty-nine, Ab Jenkins embarked on a career to capture the most coveted prize of all – the World Land Speed Record. At an age when most of us would be well into retirement and limiting our activities to tending the vegetable plot in rural Essex, the devout Mormon set about designing and building a jet-powered car capable of attaining a terminal velocity in excess of 500mph. To power the LSR car – tentatively named the *American Meteor* – a J30 or the larger J34 turbo-jet, manufactured by Westinghouse, would be used. These powerful engines develop between 3,000 and 4,000hp a piece, at speeds of 375mph and up. A vertical tail fin would again be incorporated in the design. Jenkins observed the power-to-weight ratio of many of the early jet-powered research aircraft at such speeds. He noted that without a substantial tail fin, aircraft were left with the thrust of an engine mounted at the rear of the craft exceeding the weight of the fuselage forward of the propulsion system; this produced the very simple, although often tragic, result of the rear overtaking the front of the aircraft.

On 1 August 1960, Salt Lake City garage owner Athol Graham fired up his $2,500, V12, Allison-powered *City of Salt Lake*, sponsored by STP and Firestone. Some two miles down range, the car veered slightly off course and began to slide, pitching violently, turned, became airborne and crashed. Graham hadn't worn a seat belt or safety harness. On impact, the firewall shattered the cockpit breaking his spine. Graham, thirty-six, died three hours later in Tooele Hospital near Salt Lake City.

Two years after the tragic death of Athol Graham, on the morning of 10 September 1962, Glenn Leasher had already completed what was to be the first in a series of runs on the salt in Romeo Palamides's J47 jet-powered car, *Infinity*. On his second run into the mile the car (without a

Below and opposite: *Romeo Palamides' jet-powered* Infinity *is rolled out on to the salt for what LSR history has recorded to be a reckless foray in the quest for the record. Glenn Leasher from San Mateo, California, lost his life in pursuit of the coveted title 'Fastest Man on Earth', when the vehicle exploded in a series of rolls that scattered its remains over two miles of the hallowed Bonneville Salt Flats. (Author's collection)*

A few pieces of steel framework, the seat, safety harness, and a solitary boot were among the recognizable bits of wreckage that remained after Glenn Leasher, twenty-six, was killed in an attempt on the record at the Bonneville Salt Flats on 10 September 1962, driving Romeo Palamides' General Electric J47 5,200lb, thrust jet-powered Infinity. *To this day the wreckage remains in the Utah Highway Maintenance Yard in Wendover. (Author's collection)*

vertical tail fin) began to yaw and slide approaching 250mph; the car rolled and exploded killing Leasher instantly. Some say this was due to the absence of a tail fin, others claim Leasher ignored the advice of timekeeper Joe Petrali, to gradually 'build up' his speeds. Less learned LSR sceptics were quick to put the tragedy down to the inexperience of Leasher; a somewhat common practice when the victim is unable to reply to the scepticism of the 'armchair' experts of speed.

As far back as 1952, Ab Jenkins had predicted the mandatory inclusion of a vertical tail fin in the design of any land bound vehicle or projectile, for both guidance and greater stability at speeds in excess of 200mph.

While his 12-cylinder, 700hp *Mormon Meteor* had a speed potential of 275mph, Jenkins' proposed assault on the World Land Speed Record never came of age. Ab Jenkins was born in 1883 and died in his sleep in 1956 at the age of seventy-three. On the day of his death the plans for the *American Meteor* jet car were almost complete; only four days previously he accepted from Firestone the delivery of four transonic tyres, tested at speeds in excess of 450mph (725kph). The Grand Old Man of speed had gone . . . but his legacy lingers on!

EYSTON AND COBB AND THEIR SILVER LEVIATHANS

Between 1937 and 1939, the Bonneville speedway saw two gallant Englishmen, Captain George E.T. Eyston and the statuesque John R. Cobb, pick up the gauntlet left by Sir Malcolm Campbell in their celebrated pursuit of the World Land Speed Record.

Captain Eyston began his quest for the record as early as 1923 on the European road and track circuit, establishing numerous long-distance and class records, and was a regular at the Montlhéry track, outside Paris, driving Bugattis, Rileys, MGs, a lively Hotchkiss and a Panhard-Lavassor. In 1935, Eyston, with co-drivers Bert Denly and Chris Staniland, cemented many long-distance Class A records in his Rolls-Royce Kestrel-engined car *Speed of the Wind*. With backing from Lord Wakefield and the Castrol Oil Company, this mighty vehicle was specially designed by Eyston for the long-distance Class A figures, achieving success at Montlhéry and Bonneville, where, in 1936, he set a new 24-hour record of 136.34mph (219.41kph).

In the spring of 1937, Eyston commissioned the renowned French coach-builder and aerodynamicist Jean Andreau to design the body of a new leviathan with which he intended to shatter Campbell's 301.13mph (484.51kph) record set at Bonneville on 3 September 1935. Construction of the car, dubbed *Thunderbolt*, soon followed at the Bean works at Tipton, Staffordshire. Again, Castrol stepped in with backing and the car was assembled in less than six weeks. Eyston's *Thunderbolt* was the largest petrol-engined record car ever built and when the all-British team arrived at Wendover, Utah, on 3 October 1937, the world's press was already in attendance along with a growing crowd of followers.

The car was powered by two supercharged Rolls-Royce Schneider Trophy engines having a combined displacement of 73 litres and an output of 4,700hp. Of the eight wheels, four were closely paired at the front, with steering similar to a conventional 'twin-steer' lorry, and four were placed in pairs at the rear on a driven axle, all steering. There was independent

Portrait of a legend . . . Captain George E.T. Eyston, undoubtedly the most prolific Land Speed Record breaker of them all, was also the inventor of the Powerplus supercharger which was used on many of his racing and record-breaking cars, including the 7-ton, twin-Rolls-Royce aero-engined Thunderbolt. He was made an OBE in 1948. (Author's collection)

A welcome break from Bonneville for Eyston and Cobb – the British Empire Trophy Race at Brooklands reveals Captain George Eyston in his Panhard-Levassor taking the banking with rear wheels off the track, closely followed by John Cobb. The 1935 race was won by Eyston after Cobb was disqualified from first place – the French team dubbed Eyston 'Le Recordman'. (Author's collection)

In the spring of 1937, George Eyston commissioned the renowned French coach-builder and aerodynamicist Jean Andreau to design the body of a new leviathan, Thunderbolt, with which he intended to shatter Sir Malcolm Campbell's record of 301.129mph (484.818kph), set two years earlier. It had four wheels at the front (like the bogie of an express steam train), all of which were connected to the steering wheel. The rear wheels were twinned, not unlike those on a large lorry. (Author's collection)

This was the first picture of Captain George E.T. Eyston's Thunderbolt nearing completion at the Bean works at Tipton, Staffordshire. The 'mile-eater' was twice the power of Sir Malcolm Campbell's Bluebird and was designed to reach a colossal, unheard of speed of 400mph (640kph). In reality the car in this form attained a two-way average speed of 345.5mph (555.93kph) on the Bonneville Salt Flats. (Author's collection)

suspension all round, inboard front 'clutch' type disc brakes, and a rear transmission disc brake jointly developed by Borg & Beck and Lockheed Martin.

The spectacle of the whale-like aluminium 'Thunderbolt' must have been an awe-inspiring experience for both the press and followers as it was uncrated for the record attempt on the hallowed salt flats. Shortly after dawn on 19 November 1937, the retiring Captain Eyston was ready to go. Push-started by a modified Ford Prefect with a reinforced front bumper to save transmission, he made his first run cautiously, saving his speed for the timing traps. The flying kilometre was timed at 491.03kph (305.59mph). After all the wheels were changed and the mighty *Thunderbolt* refuelled, within sixteen minutes Eyston made the return run, recording a much faster 514.01kph (319.11mph). The eight-wheeled,

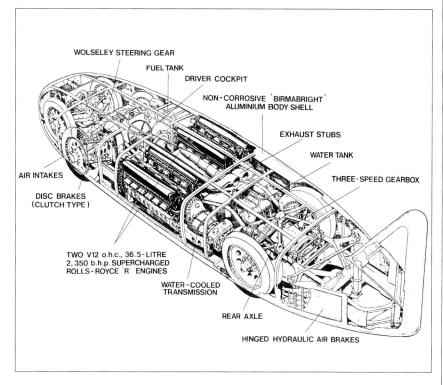

WOLSELEY STEERING GEAR
FUEL TANK
DRIVER COCKPIT
NON-CORROSIVE 'BIRMABRIGHT'
ALUMINIUM BODY SHELL
EXHAUST STUBS
WATER TANK
THREE-SPEED GEARBOX
AIR INTAKES
DISC BRAKES
(CLUTCH TYPE)
TWO V12 o.h.c., 36.5-LITRE
2,350 b.h.p. SUPERCHARGED
ROLLS-ROYCE 'R' ENGINES
WATER-COOLED
TRANSMISSION
REAR AXLE
HINGED HYDRAULIC AIR BRAKES

Top: *Eyston's* Thunderbolt *was push-started at Bonneville by a modified Ford Prefect with a reinforced front bumper to save transmission. The course on the southward run was far from satisfactory on the morning of 19 November 1937; this did not deter Eyston from breaking the indefatigable Sir Malcolm Campbell's record. Left: A schematic view of the 7-ton* Thunderbolt, *showing the location of the two V12, 36.5-litre, 2,350bhp supercharged Rolls-Royce 'R' engines, three-speed gearbox and water-cooled transmission within the whale-like 'Birmabright' aluminium bodyshell. (Author's collection)*

7-ton *Thunderbolt* averaged 501.374kph (312.00mph) for the kilometre and 311.42mph (501.01kph) for the mile, setting a new World Land Speed Record for man and machine in perfect harmony.

'When I first topped 300 miles an hour,' Eyston told reporters, 'I had a number of mingled sensations. One moment I felt the salt was curving down in front of me. The next, I felt as if we were speeding through a body of water in a high-powered speedboat instead of riding on wheels. Another time it was quite a casual ride. The last time it was a hell of a ride, and I don't mean that profanely.'

Within half an hour, the unpredictable Utah weather broke, and Bonneville's first winter rains began to approach the salt flats from the north. Without further ado, Captain Eyston ordered his team to pack up and return to Britain, vowing to return.

Less than a year later, Captain Eyston returned to Bonneville with a modified *Thunderbolt*, sporting a new front cowling with a significantly smaller intake, a fully enclosed cockpit, a longer tail and larger air scoops for the mighty centrifugal superchargers of the two Rolls-Royce 'R' engines. On a trial run he nearly asphyxiated when the enclosed cockpit filled with fumes at 270mph, causing him to career off the marked course due to the lack of visibility. That problem remedied, he was ready for his record try on 24 August 1938. He roared through the timing traps at a staggering 347.155mph (559.05kph), way over his existing record set the previous year. American Automobile Association chief timekeeper Art Pillsbury counselled him: 'Just put your foot down in that damned thing and let it go. You're ready to set a new record. Get it done and make it good.' Eyston replied with an impressive pass. There could be no doubt, this was a new record, but as the silver leviathan came to a halt, Pillsbury, high up in the AAA timing tower, realized with horror no mark had been registered on the timing tape. Pillsbury said not a word and began the 30-ft descent from the tower in tears. Eyston simply consoled Pillsbury and informed the expectant press: 'Well, my good fellows, this was just a practice run. My car was running very well, and I am encouraged that I can break the record. I shall make a formal attempt in the very near future.'

There was no animosity or recrimination between the driver and timekeeper, and three days later Eyston was back on the salt. Eyston and Pillsbury did confer and the consensus of opinion was that the combination of the blazing sun, the silver fuselage of the aluminium car, and the blinding whiteness of the crystalline salt were to blame for the timing failure. Eyston painted the car matt black with a yellow disc and arrow on each side, confident that it would overcome the problem of visual registration by the timing 'eye'. This time there were no problems and at exactly 9.35 a.m. on 27 August 1938 Captain George E.T. Eyston upped his record by a sensational 33mph, to 345.5mph (555.93kph), attaining 347.49mph (559.05kph) on the outward sortie and 343.41mph (553.022kph) on the return.

Two weeks later, John Rhodes Cobb turned up on the salt with the remarkable turtle-shaped Railton. Cobb clocked several runs under the watchful eye of its creator, Reid A. Railton, BSc, A.M.I.A.E., before attempting an assault on Eyston's record. Railton had previously worked with Parry Thomas and skilfully designed Campbell's *Bluebird*s between 1931 and 1935. Both Railton and Cobb ironed out a number of teething problems and within days both the car and its driver were ready for the assault.

For his second attempt on the record, George Eyston had Thunderbolt *modified. Seen here being rolled out of the Bean works, the car is now sporting a new front cowling with a significantly smaller intake, a fully enclosed cockpit, a longer tail and larger air scoops for the mighty centrifugal superchargers of the two Rolls-Royce 'R' engines. (Author's collection)*

On the morning of 15 September Cobb shattered Eyston's record with a timed speed of 353.3mph (568.57kph) one way and a slower 347.2mph (558.76kph) on the return run through the mile, establishing an average speed of 350.2mph (563.471kph). 'An outstanding performance; John's got it,' shouted Eyston watching the run with Railton. But, no sooner had Cobb begun to celebrate the fruits of victory, than Eyston rolled out the *Thunderbolt* to establish a higher record of 357.5mph (575.217kph). The World Land Speed Record had been broken twice by the duo in less than 24 hours.

Captain Eyston held the record for a year, but on 23 August 1939 John Cobb returned to Bonneville to reclaim it. Conditions on the salt could not have been better for Cobb; it was firm and there was no sign of wind. Without further hesitation Cobb roared from the starting line and the Railton streaked across the salt attaining a new record through the mile of 369.74mph (593.56kph). This was to be the last record established

Sir Malcolm Campbell and Captain George E.T. Eyston listening to each other's recorded accounts of the Land and Water Speed Records on the Castrol stand at the 1938 Earl's Court Motor Show.
Sir Malcolm (left) described his World Water Speed Record on Lake Halwill, Switzerland, where he attained a two-way average speed of 130.93mph (210.71kph) in the 2,500hp Rolls-Royce 'R' type Bluebird single-step hydroplane, and Captain Eyston described his World Land Speed Record on the Bonneville Salt Flats, where, at the wheel of Thunderbolt, he set a new record of 357.5mph (575.217kph). (Author's collection)

before the outbreak of the Second World War. (During the war Cobb was in service as a pilot with the British Air Transport Auxiliary, the civilian operation responsible for aircraft ferrying.)

No sooner had peace in Europe been achieved, than Cobb and Railton went to work on a number of modifications to the Railton at Thomson & Taylor of Brooklands. Initially the car was not totally changed, but for a new auxiliary drive to prevent the possibility of the engine stalling during gear changing sequences on freewheel. Prior to the outbreak of war the Railton was without clutches and flywheels on the two 12-cylinder, ohc, 'broad arrow', 26.9-litre, 1,250bhp supercharged Napier Lion engines. The gear ratios were also changed, raising them slightly for easier management at high speeds. In addition, the vehicle was fitted with new Dunlop tyres that were tested for speeds in excess of the low 400mph regime. In recognition of the prestige that World Land Speed Record breaking developed, the Mobil Oil Company offered financial backing for the project in return for the publicity that a new record would offer. This was clearly the inauguration of realistic corporate sponsorship by way of product endorsement and logistic support association. The car, in recognition of Mobil backing, was renamed the *Railton-Mobil-Special*.

On 16 September 1947, John Cobb began his shakedown runs with the new *Special*. 'She handled like a dream,' Cobb reported to Railton and confirmed both man and machine were ready to go. Cobb fired both engines, working up slowly through the gears of the two 1,250hp engines, and the car, wheels spinning, accelerated toward the horizon. Cobb's

Main picture: *John Cobb in the*
Railton-Mobil-Special *approaches*
the timing corridor at Bonneville.
Within seconds, he was within the
flying mile, attaining a two-way
average speed of 394.2mph
(634.267kph). Inset above: *In 1936*
John Cobb commissioned Reid A.
Railton – designer of Campbell's
Bluebirds *from 1931 to 1935 – to*
design a new land speed record car.
The result, the beautiful Railton,
was later renamed the Railton-Mobil-
Special, *in recognition of Mobil's*
backing. Inset below: *John Cobb.*
(Author's collection)

outward run through the mile was clocked at 385.645mph (620.5kph). It was very fast, but still below the 400mph mark Cobb had established as the goal.

Within the hour, the car was refuelled and John Cobb began his return, south-to-north run. Within a span of less than nine seconds, he was already within the flying mile, attaining a mean speed of 415mph, with an official timed recording of 403.135mph (648.781kph). Cobb had established a two-way average speed of 394.2mph (634.267kph). It had taken the intrepid fur-broker from London seven weeks to better his pre-war record. Within days the Bonneville speedway became waterlogged and the season came to a rapid halt, with a Briton yet again holding the World Land Speed Record.

Like Segrave, Don and Campbell before him John Cobb was not content with holding the World Land Speed Record alone and turned his career path to water. On 29 September 1952, he set out to regain for Britain the World Water Speed Record and the coveted Harmsworth Trophy, held by the Americans since the 1920s. His boat, the behemothic *Crusader*, was the tool for the job.

The 31-ft vessel became the first powerboat to be specifically designed and built for turbojet power. As for Sir Malcolm Campbell, the powerplant was a de Havilland unit, the Ghost as developed by Major Frank Halford from the Goblin; the tricycle – or reverse three-pointer hull concept – was worked out jointly by Reid Railton together with Commander Peter du Cane. The latter's Portsmouth-based Vosper yard fabricated the futuristic looking hull out of plywood and high-tensile alloy.

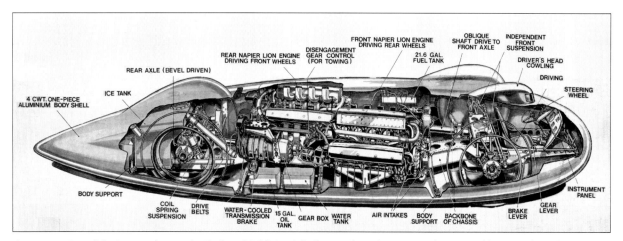

A cutaway view of the immensely complex Railton-Mobil-Special, *showing how the two 26.9-litre, 1,250bhp supercharged Napier 'Lion' engines, two gearboxes and four-wheel drive were accommodated in the 4 cwt one-piece aluminum bodyshell.*

The two 12-cylinder ohc, 'broad arrow', 26.9-litre, 1,250bhp supercharged Napier Lion engines of the Railton were located at an angle, one each side of the cranked backbone chassis. The rear wheel track was narrower than the front for both stability at high speed and housing within the turtle-shaped, one-piece, removable bodyshell. (Author's collection)

For easier assembly and maintenance, the turtle-shaped bodyshell of the Railton *was built in one piece. It is seen here at Thomson & Taylor of Brooklands. Following John Cobb's record breaking pass at Bonneville on 16 September 1947, the Motor & Cycle Trades Benevolent Fund, of Great Portland Street, London, published a limited edition booklet entitled* The Story of John Cobb's Racing Railton. *The booklet was sold for the benefit of workers in the motor car, cycle and allied trades. (Author's collection)*

The very last photograph of John Rhodes Cobb, seen here at the helm of Crusader, *shortly before the return run through the mile on Loch Ness, Scotland. On the south to north return run, the nose of* Crusader *appeared to lift, when, at a staggering 240mph (387kph) the front planing shoe hit the wake of a spectator boat, bounced, and then distintegrated. On impact, Cobb was thrown 150ft ahead of the burning wreckage. (Author's collection)*

John Cobb's three-pointer hydroplane Crusader *was powered by a mighty de Havilland Ghost 48 MkI 5,000lb thrust, straight-jet engine, loaned by the Ministry of Supply, Woolwich, seen here bouncing badly and almost clear of the water seconds before the ill-fated crash at Loch Ness in 1952. (Author's collection)*

With Captain George Eyston as his manager, Cobb and the *Crusader* team went up to Loch Ness. Working this revolutionary craft up through speeds of 50, 100, and then 150mph, Cobb, who had never driven a speedboat before, described the sensation as 'like driving a London omnibus without tyres on!' *Crusader* met with her fair share of teething troubles on the loch. At speeds approaching 200mph, *Crusader's* front planing shoe showed signs of weakness. Commander du Cane offered to take the boat back to Portsmouth for strengthening, but Cobb declined, assuring him that he would only do 190mph in the boat.

On the outward run against the record two days later, Cobb attained a particularly buffeting 206.89mph (332.88kph), some 30mph greater than the existing record. On the return run, the nose of *Crusader* appeared to lift, when, at a staggering 240mph (387kph) the front planing shoe hit three large swells as he entered the wake of a spectator launch, bouncing the *Crusader* even higher out of the water. She porpoised violently, water rushing into her jet intakes, flooding the hull, and Cobb was thrown fifty yards ahead of *Crusader*, which disintegrated in a blinding explosion.

Cobb, watched by his horrified wife Vera, was terribly injured and died of heart failure soon after. At the age of fifty-two, the pioneer of speed on land and water was killed in pursuit of a new frontier in the name of King and Country.

FIVE

LAST OF THE PURISTS

DONALD CAMPBELL – IN HIS FATHER'S SHADOW

Donald Campbell grew up slight of stature, a victim of rheumatic fever as a child, and he seemed content to enjoy the country life at his home in Horley, Surrey, and a passive career as partner in a machine-tool business in Redhill. He was only fifteen when his father, Sir Malcolm Campbell, broke the World Land Speed Record at Bonneville. He had always lived in the shadow of his father, who by now was a national hero and remained so until he died of a heart attack on 1 January 1949. As a boy, Donald was reputed to have once said he regarded his father as a god.

Inspired by his father, Donald soon embarked on his own career of speed and after five years of setting and holding World Water Speed Records on Ullswater and Coniston Water, in Westmorland, and on Lake Mead, Nevada, in the *Bluebird K4* prop-rider, he entered the land speed record sphere with a new gas turbine-powered car bearing the famous *Bluebird* name.

It was following his second successful waterborne attempt in November 1955 on Lake Mead that Donald Campbell conceived his ambition to try for the land speed record as well. From that moment, he was a man with a single, dedicated purpose: to develop a turbine car faster and more stable than any other vehicle that had gone before and at the same time to show to the world what could be achieved by pooling British industrial resources to design and build such a machine. As it transpired, the project could not have been more timely, for there were no fewer than five other contenders in the chase for the title 'Fastest Man on Earth'; moreover, all five were financed by corporate America. These included Craig Breedlove, Art Arfons, Walt Arfons and Mickey Thompson. As this chapter will later reveal, Thompson had very little time for the Englishman and was one of the loudest critics of the British initiative – unlike Craig Breedlove, who not only respected Campbell but became a great personal friend.

Five painstaking years went into the design and construction of the new *Bluebird*, and the result was all-British. Sixty-nine leading British companies, manufacturing everything from ball-bearings to the turbine engine itself, had to grapple with and overcome problems never before met in the field of engineering – for the car they were to build was venturing into the realms of the unknown. First came the design, then research into hundreds of intricate details, then testing and more testing, until by the time the vehicle was completed over 5,000 drawings had been made and nearly one million man-hours expended on the project. But the final test remained, and rested on the shoulders of the man whose vision had become a reality – Donald Campbell.

In 1960 Donald Campbell, son of the illustrious speed king Sir Malcolm Campbell, entered the World Land Speed Record area with a new turbine-powered car bearing the famous Bluebird *name. (Author's collection)*

Work on the design of the new car began in January 1956, and was entrusted to Kenneth and Lewis Norris at Norris Brothers Consulting Engineers, the designers of the *Bluebird* boat. The basic requirement was for a peak speed of 500mph (800kph). The immediate objective, however, was a new World Land Speed Record of 400mph-plus and Campbell had already decided that the engine he required was a Bristol-Siddeley Proteus free turbine. Four-wheel drive was considered essential and to accommodate this the engine would require substantial modification.

From the earliest planning stage, the designers were governed by the regulations laid down by the Fédération Internationale de l'Automobile, which state that to qualify for a land speed record a car must be 'a land vehicle, propelled by its own means, running on at least four wheels, not aligned, which must always be in contact with the ground; the steering must be assured by at least two of the wheels'. The last stipulation was most important. It meant that there had to be direct drive from the engine to at least two wheels. At the time this ruled out the use of a pure jet or rocket engine. And manufacturing transmission and reduction gear units to take the power from the engine to the wheels was one of the most difficult problems that had to be resolved.

The finished car weighed 8,000lb, giving it an unprecedented power to weight ratio of approximately 2lb for 1bhp. The engine developed more than 4,000bhp. The overall body dimensions were: length, 30ft; width, 8ft; height, 4ft 9in; wheelbase, 13ft 6in; and track, 5ft 6in. Suspension was fully independent, with wishbone and Girling oleo-pneumatic spring and damper units allowing plus or minus 2in vertical wheel movement. The steering was of conventional pattern to give a wheel deflection of 5° each side of the centre line. Brakes consisted of two systems: air brakes to slow the car from peak speed to 400mph and disc brakes – acting inboard on each side of the front and rear reduction gears – to be used to bring the car to a halt.

An essential consideration in the design concept was to achieve maximum strength with minimum weight and, with this in mind, the frame was constructed in a unique way. This involved the use of light alloy foil formed into a 'honeycomb' sandwich, ¾in thick, and faced on each side with alloy sheeting, the whole being sealed under pressure with Araldite. Four longitudinal members of the honeycomb material formed the basic frame, joined together by four cross-members forming separate compartments for the cockpit, engine, transmission gear units and wheels. Air from the intake at the front of the car was ducted on each side of the cockpit to the engine. Two fuel tanks, with a total capacity of 25 gallons, were mounted one each side of the car, slightly forward of the rear wheels.

In view of the vital importance of the project to British prestige, Donald Campbell felt that a trustee council should be formed of leading public figures who would take over the project in the event of his illness or death. This council was formed in 1957 under the chairmanship of the Duke of Richmond and Gordon, the members being the Duke of Argyll, Mr Charles Forte, Mr Eric Knight, Mr A.G.B. Owen, the Hon. Greville Howard, Mr Cyril Lord, Mr R.W. Coley, Mr Victor Mischon and Mr P.J.P. Barker. In the event of Campbell's indisposition or death two reserve drivers were nominated – Squadron Leader Peter Carr, AFC, RAF, Rtd, who was also managing the project, and Squadron Leader Neville Duke, the celebrated Second World War fighter pilot and former holder of the World Air Speed Record. The fact that both of these men were distinguished pilots was no accident. It was felt that driving a record-breaking car involving huge power and turbine technique at speeds never before achieved by man was

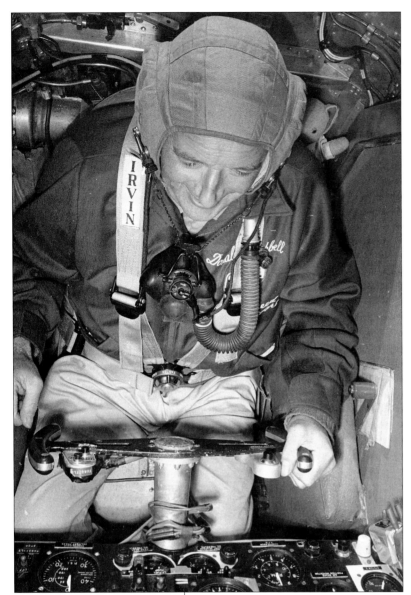

Donald Campbell sitting at the controls in the tiny cockpit of the Bluebird-Proteus, prior to making his return run through the mile at Lake Eyre. The instrumentation was by Smiths Instruments Limited, steering wheel by Bluemel Brothers Limited and the safety harness was the 'flying' type from Irvin Brothers. Donald Campbell was the first LSR driver to adopt the yoke-type steering wheel. (Author's collection)

Donald Campbell's view of Bluebird's open cockpit and instrument panel . . . Beyond – the vast expanse of the course at Lake Eyre. (Author's collection)

more closely related to test flying than to driving a Grand Prix racing car, which called for very different skills and experience – a theory that would later be adopted by Richard Noble in recruiting Squadron Leader Andy Green to drive his triumphant *Thrust SSC*.

Squadron Leader Carr retired from the Royal Air Force in 1959 to coordinate the land speed record project and also to act as first reserve driver. His release from the RAF was given special approval by the Air Council. He was no newcomer to high speeds. Before his release he commanded a Hunter squadron and earlier was responsible for much secret ultra-high-speed research flying. Prior to this, he had been seconded to the United States Air Force, where, at Las Vegas, Nevada, he was directly concerned in the service development of the F100. It was, in fact, at Las Vegas that he first met Donald Campbell, during the water speed record attempt on Lake Mead in 1955. Coincidentally, both men were decorated by Queen Elizabeth II at the same investiture in March 1957.

A steering committee was formed in the early stages of the project to advise on policy and planning. It comprised a senior executive member of each group concerned in a major role. It was made up of the following organisations: the Owen Organisation (Mr Alfred Owen, CBE); The British Petroleum Company Limited (Dr K.E.W. Ridler); Dunlop Rubber Company Limited (Mr Evan Price); Joseph Lucas Limited (Mr Nigel Breeze); Smiths Industrial Instruments Limited (Mr F.J. Hurn); Bristol-Siddeley Engines Limited (Sir Arnold Hall, FRSMA, ACGI, FRAeS.); Ferodo Limited (Mr G. Sutcliffe, OBE, TD); Norris Brothers (Mr Kenneth W. Norris); Tube Investments Limited, including The British Aluminium Company and Accles & Pollock Limited (Mr Leslie Hackett); and Squadron Leader Carr. The committee guided an advisory council made up of a representative from each company concerned or associated with the endeavour.

The chassis and body of the vehicle were built by Motor Panels Limited of Coventry – a member of the Rubery Owen Organisation, where engineering coordination was conducted under the direction of Mr J.M. Phillips, the Managing Director. Installation was effected in the same factory under the supervision of Leo Villa with facilities provided by the Rubery Owen Organisation.

There was no clutch or conventional gearbox in the *Bluebird*. Power was transmitted by the gas stream between the primary and power turbines – there being no direct mechanical link between the two. In operation, air was inducted at the intake and passed to a multi-stage compressor. Here it was compressed and fed into a series of combustion chambers. Fuel was injected into the air stream in each chamber and burned, imparting additional energy to the incoming air. Some of this energy drove the first turbine, which in turn drove the compressor. The excess power, governed by throttle opening, was automatically absorbed by the second, or power, turbine, which was directly connected through the reduction gears to the drive shafts connected to the four wheels of the car.

No tail fin was fitted initially, but the symmetry was somewhat spoiled by the large wheels and specially developed Dunlop 700×41 tyres (with ⅟₆₀in treads) giving an overall diameter of 4ft 4in and designed for 475mph – a total of eighty were provided by Dunlop for the project.

Torque was smoothly transmitted to the wheels throughout the entire speed range without the necessity of clutch or gear change. In operation the engine was started and run up to a predetermined compressor speed with the car locked on the brakes. When this point was reached the brakes would be released allowing the car to accelerate at a rapid but progressive and controlled rate to the maximum speed. Full torque could not be

Leo Villa, the engineering entrepreneur, companion, and devoted friend to both Sir Malcolm and Donald Campbell, who always referred to his famed employer as 'The Skipper' (Author's collection)

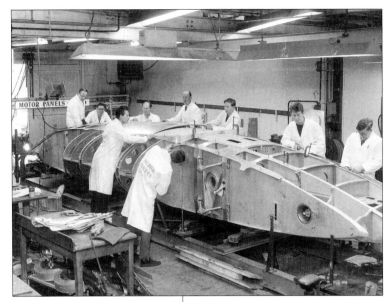

Behind closed doors at the Coventry works of Motor Panels Limited, the birth of a legend in the form of Donald Campbell's Bluebird CN7, is seen here for the first time during the early stages of construction. Designed by Kenneth and Lewis Norris at Norris Brothers Limited – consulting engineers and designers of the 3,750lb thrust-jet Bluebird K7 three-pointer boat – the remarkable vehicle is still considered by many to be the most aerodynamic car ever built for the purpose of attacking the World Land Speed Record. Clearly visible are the four longitudinal members which form the basic structure of a light alloy foil shaped into a 'honeycomb' sandwich, ¾in thick, and faced on either side with alloy sheeting. (Author's collection)

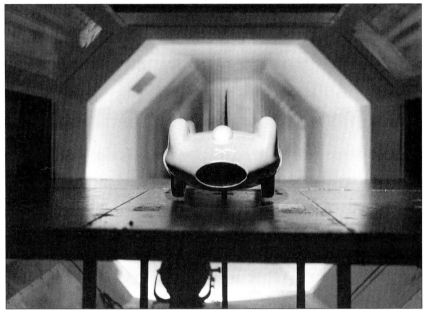

The modified Bluebird-Proteus model in the wind tunnel at the Imperial College, London. Note the build-up of shock waves forward of the tail fin. (Author's collection)

applied until the car had reached 200mph (320kph); if applied at a lower speed it would result in drastic wheel spin.

Achieving sufficient power to break the land speed record was one problem for Campbell and his team. Stopping the car in the distance available was just as great a difficulty. The maximum length of the Bonneville Salt Flats straightway was 15 miles and since, under the international regulations governing such attempts, two runs have to be made, the final time being the average of these two runs, the measured mile is naturally in the centre. There is, therefore, a distance of 7 miles in which the car has to stop after reaching anything up to the estimated speed potential of 500mph (800kph). The disc brakes had a considerable task – to bring the car from 400mph to a halt in 60 seconds. Because of the limitations of weight and space, the design, by Girling Limited, departed from normal practice. To economise on weight, the calipers that carried the linings were made of magnesium alloys. There were two calipers, each consisting of three pairs of brake linings, acting on each side of each of the rotating discs, making twenty-four pairs of linings in all. The discs were keyed into the driving hubs so that they could slide along towards the fixed linings as wear took place. The brakes were power operated with compressed air from 3,000psi storage cylinders, the circuit being duplicated for safety. The total amount of energy to be dissipated during the 60 seconds of braking was an estimated 75 millionftlb.

The Bluebird Project was not only a tremendous effort to further human knowledge and capability, but at the time was a major endeavour to keep Britain ahead. This was the first time such a project had been based on a turbine engine, and the knowledge and experience gained with new materials, structures, breaking systems, tyres, bearings and suspension, and indeed the vital lubricants, all helped to enhance Britain's ability to engineer and design a vehicle with the capability of regaining the World Land Speed Record from the American invaders with their jet-powered missiles.

The construction of the *Bluebird* car – known officially as *CN7* (the CN stood for Campbell-Norris) – was completed by May 1960 and the vehicle was taken to Goodwood for a press preview and a trial run.

During the inaugural trials at Goodwood, Campbell took the car around the course at about 80mph, driving with the brakes on to keep the speed down. This test enabled him to get the feel of the cockpit and instrumentation, but he had never driven under full power until he arrived at Bonneville in August 1960. The only major defect that was noticed was minor distortion of the rear panelling around the exhaust, caused by the extreme heat. After all, the Bristol-Siddeley Proteus free turbine engine was normally used in the Bristol Britannia airliner. The problem was soon rectified by Motor Panels Limited and the *Bluebird* was shipped to the United States for her sternest test.

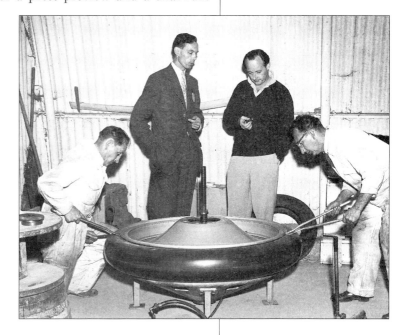

Donald Campbell with Don Badger of Dunlop discussing one of the eighty tyres he was to take with him to Bonneville. (Author's collection)

Campbell's first glimpse of the blinding salt flats came on 4 September, when he watched Mickey Thompson turn 372mph (598kph) in his powerful *Challenger 1*. He later spoke with the American hot-rodder who went out of his way to play on Campbell's superstitions. Thompson, shrugging his shoulders, told him, 'I've seen the salt an awful lot better than it is right now.' The more he teased, the paler Campbell grew, and Thompson gleefully poured it on. Campbell had always been a superstitious man and made sure his lucky mascot Mr Woppit was with him during all his record attempts on land and water.

On 5 September, *Bluebird* was uncrated and prepared for her first sortie across the salt flats. Donald depressed the accelerator and she moved off smoothly, attaining a mere 120mph (194kph). This was Donald's first run in the car and he reported the acceleration to be 'fantastic'. After a 20-minute delay, Ken Norris and Leo Villa gave Campbell the thumbs up sign for the return foray. It was better – 170mph (274kph). Two further trial runs were made on 15 September, attaining 175mph (282kph) and 240mph (387kph) respectively, but it was a rough ride for Campbell.

A very rare photograph of Donald Campbell's first attempt at the record on the Bonneville Salt Flats in 1960. Campbell made several passive runs in the Bluebird, increasing his speed stage by stage. (Author's collection)

The shattered hulk of Donald Campbell's Bluebird after the 1960 crash at Bonneville during the fifth trial run. It was never known exactly what caused the crash. The car was travelling at some 360mph (580kph), when it was seen to stray across the marking line, veering off in a wide arc to the left of the course, becoming airborne shortly before the 2-mile mark, tumbling and bouncing on the crystalline salt before landing and skidding to a halt nearly 100 yards down range. (Author's collection)

One of the shod wheels of Bluebird torn off at over 350mph in Campbell's near-fatal crash at Bonneville on the 16 September 1960. (Author's collection)

On the morning of 16 September, the impatient driver was ready for the fifth trial run in which he intended to go for broke. Don Badger of Dunlop warned Campbell of the 475mph limit of the tyres, but Villa noticed Donald grin as he closed the cockpit canopy. As the *Bluebird* disappeared over the horizon, there was an almighty crash – the car was seen to tumble over and over in a cloud of salt. Villa cried, 'My God, Ken, the Skipper's in trouble.' They rushed to the scene – wreckage was strewn across the course, two of the wheels had sheared off. When they reached the shattered remains of *Bluebird*, the engine was still screaming with a menacing whine. Norris and Villa raised the canopy and cut off the engine. Campbell was sitting in the cockpit, bleeding from a deep cut on his cheek, but still conscious. He was rushed to the nearby Tooele Hospital, where, only one month earlier, Athol Graham had lost his life after pursuit of the record on the same course, driving the V12 Allison-powered *City of Salt Lake*.

Donald Campbell, alone in the cockpit of Bluebird, *is pushed unceremoniously on to the course at Lake Eyre to prepare the car for her first trial on the dead lake. (Author's collection)*

*At Lake Eyre, official timekeeper
Bill Bates prepares to clock Donald
Campbell's attempt at the World
Land Speed Record – the first and
only attempt at the record on
Australian soil at the time.
(Author's collection)*

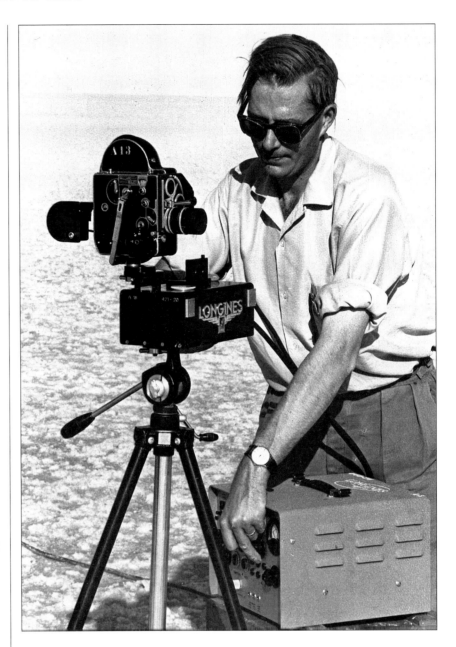

*Below: A schematic view of Donald
Campbell's Bluebird-Proteus CN7,
showing the disposition of the
Bristol-Siddeley Proteus 4,100hp
gas turbine power unit, two single-
speed gearboxes and four-wheel
drive. (Author's collection)*

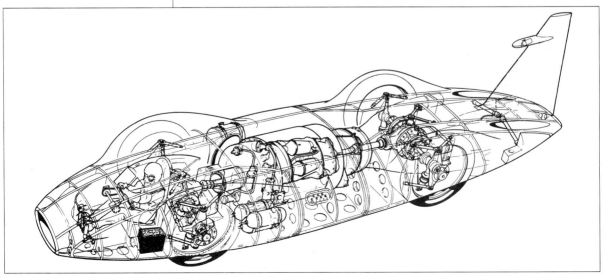

It was never known exactly what caused the *Bluebird* crash. The car was travelling at some 360mph (580kph) when it was seen to stray across the marking line, veering off in a wide arc to the left of the course, becoming airborne shortly before the 2-mile mark, tumbling and bouncing on the crystalline salt before landing and skidding to a halt nearly 100 yards down range. The near-fatal accident totally wrote off the costly *Bluebird* and left Campbell with a fractured skull, a pierced eardrum and diverse cuts and bruises, but he was well enough to walk into hospital accompanied by his wife Tonia and Squadron Leader Peter Carr.

Thus the *Bluebird-Proteus CN7* saga at Bonneville ended. Campbell immediately inaugurated a search of the globe for a better, longer track than Bonneville and eventually accepted the learned recommendation of his long-standing sponsors BP, who told him of a vast dry lake in South Australia known as Lake Eyre, some 400 miles north of Adelaide. Squadron Leader Carr flew out to Australia to reconnoitre and reported that Lake Eyre 'looked just the job'. The *Bluebird* team was back in business.

The nearest inhabited point to the selected course was Muloorina, a sheep station less than 30 miles away. The Southern Australian government agreed to grade 65 miles of road from the railhead at Marree to Muloorina and from there to the lake, and to construct a 400 yard causeway on to the vast expanse of Lake Eyre itself. BP Australia appointed John Gilbert to coordinate the initiative. Donald Campbell's second attempt to capture the World Land Speed Record was under way.

Cutting the salt islands on the track for the Bluebird-Proteus's *first trial run on Lake Eyre. Here one of the two salt cutters, which were specially equipped for this purpose, is shown in grinding action. In the background are (left) the BP film unit vehicle, and the* Bluebird *chase car. (Author's collection)*

The enormous Bristol-Siddeley Proteus 4,100bhp gas-turbine power unit undergoing extensive test runs at Bristol Siddeley's Patchway works prior to placement in Donald Campbell's 1964 Bluebird-Proteus car. Similar versions of the same power plant were used in the Britannia airliner. (Author's collection)

After several unsuccessful attempts, thwarted by severe weather conditions on the dead lake, Campbell eventually cemented a new land speed record of 403.10mph (648.728kph) on 17 July 1964, breaking John Cobb's record of 394.20mph (634.267kph) set at the Bonneville Salt Flats in 1947.

Campbell was jubilant about his eventual success and was eager to reflect that he had actually forgotten to take Mr Woppit along for the ride. Campbell never did rid himself of the tormenting superstitions that haunted his life. On the evening of 3 January 1967, he was playing solitaire in his room at the Sun Hotel overlooking Coniston Water, when he turned up two consecutive cards, the Ace and the Queen of Spades. 'Mary, Queen of Scots, turned up the same combination of cards,' he later remarked to Connie Robinson, the proprietor of the hotel, 'and from this she knew she was going to be beheaded. I know one of my family is going to get the chop. I pray it will not be me'.

The following day he was aboard his Bristol-Siddeley Orpheus jet-powered boat *Bluebird K7*, making the return run to Coniston in an attempt to raise the World Water Speed Recrod to over the 300mph mark when disaster struck.

With Norman Buckley in charge of timekeeping, Campbell made a near perfect down run of 297mph (478kph). But then, instead of refuelling and waiting for the wash created by his waterbrake to die down, Campbell made an immediate return run in a boat whose lack of fuel made it dangerously light and lively.

Donald Campbell and his faithful mascot Mr Woppit absorb the peace and tranquillity of the English Lakes. Within three days he was to lose his life in pursuit of his own World Water Speed Record, a tragic end to a family tradition of speed with excellence. (Author's collection)

Below: Donald Campbell seen here in the cockpit of the Bluebird K7 jet-boat in which he broke the World Water Speed Record on six occasions in five years. In 1965, Campbell replaced the old Beryl engine with a Bristol-Siddeley Orpheus developing 5,000lb thrust. He intended to put the record over the 300mph mark. (Author's collection)

Donald Campbell in the Bluebird
K7 *jet-boat, about to make the fatal
return run on Coniston Water.
Campbell was barely four minutes
into the run when, at an estimated
320mph, the boat soared into the
air, somersaulted and crashed to the
glass-like surface of the lake.
(Author's collection)*

Right: *Tonia Bern-Campbell lays a
bouquet of roses on the memorial
plaque to her late husband in the
centre of Coniston village. Donald
Campbell lost his life in pursuit of
the World Water Speed Record on
the 4 January 1967, when the
Bristol-Siddeley Orpheus jet-
powered boat Bluebird K7
somersaulted at over 300mph on
Coniston Water. Despite the tireless
efforts of Royal Navy divers, under
the command of Lieutenant-
Commander Futcher, Campbell's
body was never found – a tragic
reminder of those men who lost
their lives in the transition from
land to water. (Author's collection)*

IN MEMORY OF
DONALD CAMPBELL, C.B.E
QUEEN'S COMMENDATION FOR BRAVE CONDUCT
WHO DIED ON
JANUARY 4th 1967
WHILE ATTEMPTING TO RAISE
HIS OWN WORLD WATER SPEED RECORD
ON CONISTON WATER

The *Bluebird K7* took off, flipped into a backward loop at an estimated 320mph (515kph) and with Campbell still calmly making his running commentary over the radio: 'She's doing 260 . . . 280 . . . 300 . . . she's tramping! I can't see much . . . She's going. She's going . . . Oh . . .' When the boat hit the shimmering surface of the Westmorland lake, there was a blinding flash amidst a plume of spray, and Donald was gone. Had *Bluebird K7* completed her loop, it is possible that Campbell might have survived, albeit with terrible injuries.

The next day, Royal Navy frogmen searched the lake for Campbell's body but he was never found. At a depth of 140ft, they found the main hull of *Bluebird K7*, Campbell's steering wheel, seat belt and even his lucky mascot Mr Woppit. Thus the legend of the racing Campbells was complete. Together, father and son established twenty-one land and water speed records over a period that covered more than four decades.

Donald Campbell suffered that particular comparison which any son of a famous father has to endure: the 'old boy' had broken the record nine times, and this was no doubt the driving force behind the obsession that took Donald Campbell to a watery grave in the English Lake District. Before his death, he was already working on plans for a rocket-powered car to break the sound barrier. Engineered and designed by Ken Norris, the 22ft long delta-shaped projectile, appropriately dubbed *Bluebird Mach 1.1 (CMN-8)*, was to be powered by a complement of two 4,200lb thrust Bristol-Siddeley BS 605 rocket-assisted take-off (RATO) engines. Indeed, such was the initial interest in the project, the Jamaican government offered to construct a 14-mile track between Falmouth and St Ann's Bay on which Campbell could run the vehicle.

Despite several attempts to revive the project it would seem the rocket car died with him on that winter's morning in 1967.

MICKEY THOMPSON – A CHAPTER FOR THE CHALLENGER

The men who have reached into the unknown thresholds of speed are clearly not ordinary mortals. For John Cobb, the motivation was an obsession with excellence; for the indefatigable Sir Malcolm Campbell, it was undoubtedly a way of life. But in common with most warm-blooded Englishmen, dedication led them all to eventual success. It sometimes takes a British success to awaken the Americans, and when Donald Campbell scorched a path back into the land speed record books in 1964, he woke a sleeping giant in the form of an old adversary – Mickey Thompson.

Mickey Thompson's obsession with speed dated back to 1937 when he first visited the Bonneville Salt Flats with his father, who told him of the speed feats of men like Campbell, Jenkins, Eyston and Cobb, but it was Frank Lockhart, killed during a land speed record attempt at Daytona Beach in 1928, who was his boyhood hero.

He was born Marion Lee Thompson Jr, on 7 December 1928 in San Fernando, California. At the age of fourteen he assembled his first hot-rod, a chopped and channelled, five-window '27 Chevy coupé, and later sold the same car for $125, enabling him to buy a modified Model A roadster that he raced against Merle Finkenbinder of the famed Revs Hot Rod Club on El Mirage dry lake. Thompson hurtled the roadster to 79mph (128kph) – a particularly impressive pass considering he was riding on farm machinery tyres, guaranteed to only 5mph.

In 1949 when the first Bonneville National Speed Trials took place and the cult of 'hot-rodding' was born, Mickey Thompson was only twenty-one.

Mickey Thompson's outstanding record of accomplishments included 485 national and international speed and endurance records, and his ability to turn a passion for speed into a multi-million dollar industry made him a highly respected and wealthy entrepreneur. Sadly, Mickey, and his wife Trudy, met a tragic death in 1988 when they were murdered in front of their home in Bradbury, California. (Trudy Thompson/Author's collection)

To support his expectant wife Judy and his 'addiction' to speed he joined the *Los Angeles Times*, qualifying as a pressman seven months later. On the side, the Californian hot-rodder held two and sometimes three extra jobs until he had saved enough to go to the 1950 Bonneville Speed Week as a spectator. The following year he returned as a competitor, gunning a tandem-engined roadster to 141.065mph (227.03kph), vowing to return the following year. In 1952 he hurtled his unorthodox hot-rod to a national speed record of 194.34mph (313.02kph) in the streamliner class, eclipsed only by Bill Kenz and Roy Leslie in a twin-engined roadster. Never satisfied, Thompson then became a celebrated competitor in the 1954 Pan American and 1955 Mexican Road Races, running against the likes of Carroll Shelby and Umberto Maglioli.

Thompson was getting closer to his goal. Since 1927, the World Land Speed Record had been broken fifteen times, all on American soil – first at Ormond-Daytona and then Bonneville. During that span only one American had wrested the title from the British – Ray Keech, who established a record of 207.552mph (334.022kph) in J.M. White's Liberty-powered *White Triplex* in 1928, but Keech's record only stood for one year. Thompson was gunning for John Cobb's record of 394.2mph (634.267kph) set at Bonneville on 16 September 1947, and decided to build a new car for the attempt. By 1957 the streamliner was completed, just in time for a press preview at the Beverly Hilton Hotel, Los Angeles, arranged by Goodyear, which was sponsoring the car. Thompson called his new machine *Challenger I* and first ran the car in tests in 1959 on the vast Rosamond Dry Lake at the legendary Edwards Air Force Base, California, close to Rogers Dry Lake, formerly famous as Muroc Dry Lake.

In 1949, Muroc Army Airfield had been renamed Edwards Air Force Base in memory of Captain Glen W. Edwards, an Air Force test pilot who had been killed in the crash of the Northrop YB-49 experimental Flying Wing jet bomber during a performance test on 5 June 1948, but the dry lakes were also known to a number of racing aficionados living out in the high desert, many of whom worked at the NASA Flight Research Centre at Edwards, who found in the hard, smooth surface the perfect speedway to race their hot-rods.

Challenger I was comparatively small by land speed record standards, being some 8ft shorter and 3ft narrower than John Cobb's *Railton-Mobil-Special*, and was powered by four V8, ohv, 6.7-litre, 700bhp Pontiac engines with two General Motors, Rootes-type superchargers and fuel injection, mounted in pairs, side by side, driving the front and rear wheels through two pre-war La Salle three-speed gearboxes.

The magnesium alloy wheels, made by Halibrand, were shod with Goodyear tubeless tyres, supplied by his sponsor and to Thompson's exacting specifications. The Pontiac engines had been stripped and modified by Fritz Voight, and were equipped with dynamic Hilborn-Travers fuel injection. In addition to conventional wheel-braking Thompson is attributed as having introduced the first parachute braking system used on a land speed record vehicle; it was pioneered by Jim Deist.

Two years earlier Thompson had proved his worth as a potential contender for the World Land Speed Record at the 1957 Bonneville Speed Week. He was scheduled to run at the National Hot Rod Association (NHRA) National Speed Trials in Oklahoma City, but en route to Oklahoma he stopped at Bonneville with his tandem-engined roadster, sporting his entry number for the Oklahoma meet, '555'. Bill Kenz was the first to inspect the modified roadster, but little did he know that Thompson was not there by mistake. He intended to better

7842-60C

Mickey Thompson's Challenger I takes shape in his Long Beach, California, engineering shop. The four-engined car burned fuel at the rate of 1 gallon per mile when Thompson approached the 400mph barrier at Bonneville. The Pontiac engines had been stripped and modified by Fritz Voight, and equipped with dynamic Hilborn-Travers fuel injection. (Author's collection)

the Kenz and Leslie American record of 266.2mph (428kph) set in 1952. Two days later he turned a two-way average of 266.866mph (428.05kph), wiping the Kenz and Leslie mark off the record books for good. Bill Kenz congratulated Thompson on beating a record he and Leslie had devoted a lifetime to achieve. Going that fast with such little effort gave Thompson the confidence he needed to go after John Cobb's record.

Thompson attained an impressive 203.792mph (327.981kph) during trials at Edwards, but during one pass across the Mojave Desert the selector rods broke, leaving the car in second gear. *Challenger I* then hit a clay polygon on the dry lake, which launched the speeding vehicle into an uncontrollable spin. Out of this apparent chaos Thompson emerged shaken but not deterred. By 23 August 1959, Thompson and his crew had arrived at Bonneville to shake the car down prior to the record attempt. Two days later he posted a 300mph (483kph) run through the timing traps when his braking parachute deployed coming out of the mile. He said:

I was still doing over 300 when I felt a tug to the right. I barely breathed on the steering, got it straightened out, and then there was a stronger whip to the left. Then came a harder whip, and a harder one. I grabbed the wheel tight to anchor my arms to protect them when the inevitable flip and crash came. Then the damn chute got caught in a different area of their air stream and yanked me far to one side. That sent me into a sideways skid for over 700 feet across the salt. By a miracle the car did not flip, and it slowed to a point where I could steer it again.

Regardless of the chute problems he still managed to clock 332.8mph (535.3kph), becoming the first American to surpass the 300mph barrier. After much delay through rain and high winds, Thompson returned to Bonneville on 1 October, but the course was waterlogged. Four days later he readied the car for the all-out assault on the record. Thompson ran *Challenger I* close to the 300mph regime, when, at a staggering 295mph (475kph) the underpan broke loose. He fired his braking chute and guided the car to a stop well before the end of the course. The following day he booked the course for 8.00 a.m., but had to shut down for repairs due to gearshift failure. Then, before rain prevented any more record attempts, Thompson powered *Challenger I* to a new flying mile record of 367.83mph (592.01) and broke four world records for 5 kilometres, 5 miles, 10 kilometres and 10 miles in the process.

First to congratulate him was Rodger Flores, a young Mexican-American boy who helped him build the car and worked at the Thompson residence in Alhambra, California. There was still time that day for another all-out assault on the record. Using a more potent fuel mix of 40 per cent nitromethane he tried again.

The introduction of the first parachute braking system used on a land speed record vehicle is attributed to Mickey Thompson. Challenger I *is seen here in a rare photograph during trials at Rosamond Dry Lake at Edwards Air Force Base, California in 1959. (Mickey Thompson)*

Thompson was coming out of the mile when his left arm disconnected the oxygen supply to his face mask, leaving him choking in an enclosed cockpit filled with toxic fumes. The ever-courageous Thompson held his breath and started to black out, but he managed to cut the power and bring the car to a halt at the end of the course before falling into a coma. An ambulance arrived to take him to hospital but ran out of fuel before it left the vast Bonneville Salt Flats. Thompson regained consciousness, climbed out of the ambulance and walked back to the *Challenger I* camp two miles away. The silver-suited hot-rodder was greeted with applause by his crew and followers. Minutes later rain closed the salt flats for the 1959 season.

While Mickey Thompson was stealing the headlines, a group of challengers were preparing for a 1960 showdown on the salt. They were Athol Graham and his V12 Allison-powered *City of Salt Lake*, Dr Nathan Ostich in a General Electric J47 turbojet car, the *Flying Caduceus*, the ingenious Art Arfons with the mighty General Electric J79 turbojet-engined *Green Monster*, and Britain's Donald Campbell, with a Bristol-Siddeley Proteus free turbine-powered *Bluebird*. Thompson knew the most likely contender to succeed was Donald Campbell. Thompson returned to Bonneville in 1960 with a modified car. The Pontiac engines were now supercharged with four General Motors, Rootes-type diesel blowers, raising the output by 1,000 to a menacing 3,000hp. *Challenger I* was also more streamlined, improving aerodynamics at high speed.

Graham's bid ended in his fatal crash. Dr Nathan Ostich's *Flying Caduceus* suffered engine ducting problems, and Campbell ended his effort in a crash that nearly cost him his life, leaving the salt flats free for Thompson, before and after the Southern California Timing Association (SCTA) Bonneville Speed Week trials.

THE INTERNAL COMBUSTION ENGINE

Mickey Thompson and his great rivals the Summers brothers were the last in an illustrious line of land speed record chasers who harnessed the power of the internal combustion engine. Since Thompson and the Summers, all record cars have been rocket or jet-propelled – and purists would argue that, therefore, since the Summers brothers there has been no new World Land Speed Record. But the story of using the power of combustion to move a vehicle started more than a century before Thompson rolled *Challenger I* out on to the Bonneville Salt Flats.

The development of the internal combustion engine was made possible by the earlier development of the steam engine. Both types of engines burn fuel, releasing energy from it in the form of heat, which is then used to do useful work. The steam engine, however, is an external combustion engine, because the fuel is burned in a separate part of the engine from the cylinder containing the piston. Anything combustible can be used as a fuel in the steam engine, such as wood, coal or petroleum products, and the liberated energy is used to heat a fluid, usually water. The hot water vapour expands in a confined place (the cylinder) to push the piston. In the internal combustion engine, the burning of the fuel takes place in the combustion chamber (the top of the cylinder). The combustion is very sudden, amounting to an explosion that pushes the piston.

During the eighteenth and nineteenth centuries, as the steam engine was made more efficient, advances were made in engineering and metallurgy which made possible the first successful internal combustion engines. The operation of steam engines was not fully understood at first; in 1824 the French physicist Sadi Carnot published his theories, which led to the science of heat exchange (thermodynamics). Fifty years before that, James Watt had already begun to develop packings and piston rings to prevent the escape of energy past the piston on his steam engines. By 1800, the British engineer Henry Maudslay was making improvements to the lathe which led to machinery capable of producing precision-made parts for engines, and in the 1850s more volatile fuels were being refined from petroleum.

In 1860 J.J.E. Lenoir, a French engineer, built a successful engine that was essentially a modified steam engine using illuminating gas as the fuel. In 1867 the firm of Otto and Langen began producing an engine that transmitted the power of a freely moving piston to a shaft and a heavy flywheel by means of a rack-and-gear device, using a freewheeling clutch in the gear, so that it turned freely in one direction and transmitted power in the other.

Meanwhile, in 1862, Alphonse Beau de Rochas had published in Paris his theory of a four-stroke engine of the type used in the modern car. While de Rochas never built any engines, his theory included compression of the fuel mixture in order to raise its temperature, and he also realized that a four-stroke design would be more efficient at scavenging (intake of fuel mixture and exhaust of burned gases) than the two-stroke.

A two-stroke engine provides for intake of fuel, combustion and exhaust of burned gases with each back-and-forth motion of the piston (that is, with each revolution of the crankshaft). A four-stroke engine requires four strokes, that is, two complete back-and-forth movements of the piston (two revolutions of the crankshaft). The two-stroke engine delivers twice as many power impulses as the four-stroke engine to the crankshaft, but the four-stroke is much more efficient at scavenging, if all other things are equal. The two-stroke design is also wasteful because unburned fuel is exhausted with the burned gases.

In 1876, Otto and Langen began building the Otto 'silent' engine (it was a good deal quieter than their earlier model). It was the first modern internal combustion engine – a four-stroke design that compressed the fuel mixture before combustion. After 1878, it was also manufactured in the United States, where it was an inspiration to Henry Ford in his early research.

On his first run that year Thompson found the salt to be in poor condition. The first pass pounded him so hard as he roared across the salt that he was sick inside his face mask during deceleration. When this author interviewed Thompson in 1976, he remarked: 'I thought I was gonna drown in my own vomit on that run, it was hell.' (Mickey Thompson was covering the Hal Needham/Bill Fredrick speed of sound bid with the *SMI Motivator* on the Alvord Desert, Oregon, for CBS Television on that occasion.) Nevertheless, during that nauseous run he still managed to clock 372.67mph (599.01kph). That pass was so wild he decided to return at the end of the week in a slot left by Donald Campbell.

On the morning of 9 September 1960, Thompson tried again and *Challenger I* roared across the Bonneville Salt Flats into a 5mph head wind, attaining a terminal velocity of 406.6mph (654.329kph), over 12mph faster than Cobb's 1947 record of 394.2mph (634.267kph) in the *Railton-Mobil-Special*. Thompson's speed was the fastest ever attained in an automobile. During the return run it soon became obvious the car was in trouble as it approached the timing traps; he was about to cement a new record, when, at speed approaching 210mph (338kph) a three-dollar driveshaft snapped when he shifted into third gear. Replacing the broken shaft would have taken longer than the permitted hour, so Thompson pulled out, content with topping the elusive 400mph one-way mark. He was so near yet so far when he dejectedly vowed, 'We'll be back in a week.' He did try again two years later but poor salt conditions denied him success.

Thompson had planned to return to Bonneville, but that was before he fractured his back piloting a twin-engined powerboat across Lake Mead, Nevada, during the winter of 1962.

Above: *The working crew of* The Blue Flame *manages a smile shortly before commencing a series of low-speed trials at Bonneville on the morning of 17 September 1970. Gary Gabelich clocked a leisurely 185.086mph (297.866kph) on his inaugural run, but during this sortie an engine backfire caused a minor explosion in the combustion chamber, melting the exhaust nozzle. (Author's collection)*

Below: *Shoehorned into a marvel of motion engineering Gary Gabelich, alone in* The Blue Flame, *prepares to ignite the awesome 35,000hp rocket motor that will launch him into history. (Author's collection)*

Gary Gabelich emerges from the cockpit of The Blue Flame shortly after setting the new World Land Speed Record at Bonneville. (Author's collection)

Main picture: In a split ear-shattering second, the 35,000hp, rocket-powered The Blue Flame disappeared in a stream of white smoke as it streaked toward the deep-blue horizon and the target, almost 2 miles down range. (Author's collection)

Gary Gabelich is besieged by the press and media shortly after his record-breaking run at Bonneville in 1970. (Author's collection)

The Wynn's sponsored 12,000hp Courage of Australia *was the first in a series of outstandingly successful thoroughbred rocket cars to be engineered and designed by Bill Fredrick. Powered by a 6,100lb thrust Fredrickinetics monopropellant hypergolic rocket system, the 27ft dragster broke the timing beam at 311.41mph (501.01kph) in 5.107 seconds on 11 November 1971, at the Orange County International Raceway in Irvine, California, setting a new World Land Speed Record for the quarter mile. Driven by Vic Wilson and 'Courageous' John Paxson, the* Courage of Australia *was designed as the prototype for a land speed record car that was to be backed by an Australian consortium for an attempt on the record at Lake Eyre in 1972; due to the worldwide economic recession, however, the project never evolved. (Author's collection)*

Left: *Bill Fredrick, engineer and designer of the Budweiser Rocket, had always dreamed of breaking the sound barrier on land. This was his third rocket car. His land speed career began with the introduction of his first car, the 23ft jet-powered* Valkyrie I *which he débuted at Bonneville in 1962. (Author's collection)*

Right: *The curious frontal aspect of the SMI Motivator, at rest on the Alvord Desert. While supersonic aerodynamic theories had to be used, the vehicle was based on a simple design concept using computational fluid dynamics (CFD) – a simulation technique culminating in the launch of an instrumented model of the car along the 35,000ft high-speed test track facility at the White Sands Missile Range, Holloman Air Force Base, New Mexico. (Author's collection)*

Below: *A study in attention . . . The Success Motivation Institute-sponsored SMI Motivator was testament to Bill Frederick's ability to create a car with supersonic capabilities. Both Kitty o'Neal and Hal Needham drove the 48,000hp rocket car to speeds in excess of 600mph in 1976. It is seen here after completing a day of trials on the immense Alvord Desert in Pregon. (Author's collection)*

Above: *At exactly 7.26 a.m. on 17 December 1979, Stan Barrett turned a page in automotive history. The $1.2 million three-wheeler blasted off in a cloud of dust and, like a bright red needle with a huge ball of flame flying from its tail, scorched a path across the bed of Rogers Dry Lake, high in the Mojave Desert. During the speed of sound run Barrett was subjected to 4 gs of force, pulling a further g at over 600mph when he hit the Sidewinder. (Author's collection)* Right: *A delicate needle trailing a swirling vortex of fire and dust in testament to the violence of its passage, the* Budweiser Rocket *blasts through the sound barrier at a staggering 739.666mph (1,190.377kph) or Mach 1.0106. This remarkable photograph was taken from a US Air Force Northrop T-38 chase plane flying 100ft above Barrett. (USAF/Author's collection)*

Stan Barrett was a leading Hollywood stuntman before driving the controversial Budweiser Rocket.

Above: Stan Barrett was 12 seconds into the run when, at a staggering 612mph (984kph), he hit a button on the small butterfly steering wheel igniting 12,900 additional horsepower from the Sidewinder missile booster system. (Author's collection)

Right: The Budweiser Rocket, with the rear wheels literally off the ground, roars through the timing corridor beyond the speed of sound. Some claim that there was a supersonic boom. Other observers, including this author, heard only a small rumble like distant thunder. (Author's collection)

A Project Speed of Sound team engineer checks the power plant housing on the Budweiser Rocket at the Edwards Air Force Base. (Author's collection)

In 1963 NASA was working on the M2-F1 Lifting Body programme at Edwards Air Force Base and needed a tow vehicle with great power and speed. The solution to its problem did not take long to find. Fortunately, one of the project's volunteers, a man named Walter 'Whitey' Whiteside, was an active hot-rodder and had raced with Mickey Thompson on the California dry lakes several years earlier. He supervised the purchase of a Pontiac Bonneville convertible capable of pulling the 1,000lb plywood M2-F1 at speeds over 100mph – which was, coincidentally, just fast enough to get the aircraft and NASA test pilot Milton O. Thompson airborne.

Whiteside sent the car to Mickey Thompson, where he finely tuned the engine, added roll bars, installed radio equipment, turned around the right passenger bucket seat to face aft, and removed the rear seats, installing another bucket seat for a second observer facing sideways. The slightly irreverent but enthusiastic group also arranged for the car to be painted with racing stripes and a NASA logo on the side. With Whiteside at the wheel of the Pontiac, the M2-F1 completed its first ground tows on 5 April 1963 and made forty-five others by the month's end.

Mickey Thompson's speed trials with *Challenger I* on Rosamond Dry Lake in 1959 earned him a reputation with the test pilots at Edwards. He could often be found with these fly boys at the nearby Happy Bottom Riding Club, owned by the legendary aviatrix, Pancho Barnes, where the talk was of ultimate speed 'upstairs' and on the deck.

By 1968 Thompson was back at Bonneville with an all-new contender, the exquisite *Autolite Special*, sponsored by the Ford Motor Company. The *Autolite Special* was powered by two 427-cubic-inch Ford single overhead cam engines, one aspirated; 810hp drove the front wheels, and a second

AUTOLITE SPECIAL

Length:	29ft 7in
Width:	34⅞in
Height:	27in, rising to 34⅞in above the cockpit canopy
Wheelbase:	195in
Track (front):	21in
(rear)	23ft
Weight:	5,400lb
Ground Clearance:	3in
Engine:	Two 427-cubic-inch Ford overhead cam engines. Front engine – normally aspirated: 810hp. Rear engine – supercharged 7-litre: 1,260hp
Engine Weight:	859lb
Transmission:	Two three-speed modified automatics
Chassis:	Tubular steel; spaceframe construction
Body Shell:	Reynolds lightweight aluminium sheeting, flush riveted over chassis
Wheels:	23¾in diameter; 19in tread on rear, 24in tread on front, supplied by Goodyear. Design speed: 600mph
Braking Systems:	Ventilated disc brakes on all four wheels, three-plus-one set of Deist safety parachutes; a 2ft pilot chute; one 7ft high speed chute and a 16ft final braking parachute
Steering Lock:	¾ turn of the wheel
Turning Circle:	¼ mile
Max Output:	2,070hp
Speed Capability:	500mph

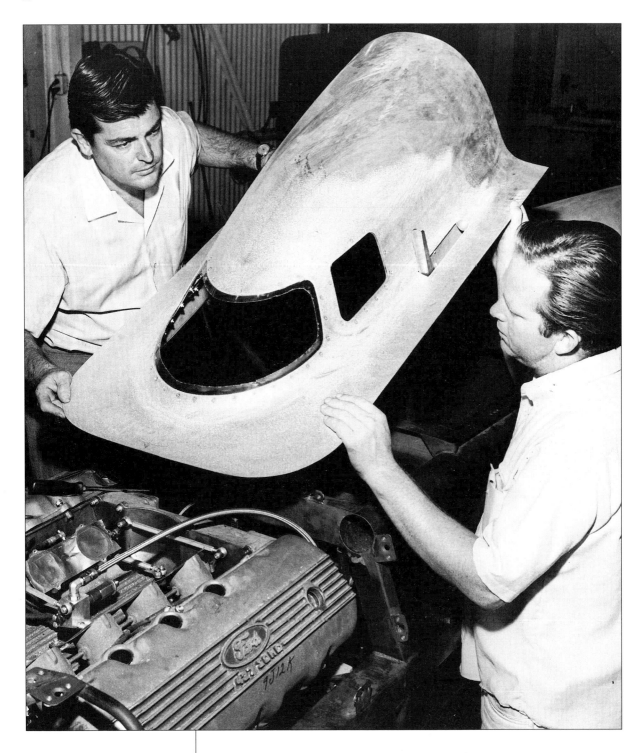

Mickey Thompson (left) and assistant Pat Foster fit the aluminium cockpit canopy into place on Thompson's land speed record car, the Autolite Special. *In the foreground is one of the two 427 cubic inch Ford single overhead cam engines that powered the car. (Mickey Thompson)*

engine, behind the driver was a supercharged 7-litre unit producing 1,260bhp and turning the rear wheels. The 5,400lb streamliner measured 29ft 7in long, 34in wide and was only 27in high at the nose and 37in above the cockpit canopy at the rear. The chassis was of tubular steel, space frame construction, covered with a lightweight body shell. All four wheels were fitted with 23¾in diameter Goodyear tyres, 19in tread on rear, 24in tread on the front, with ventilated disc brakes on all four wheels. In addition, the *Autolite Special* was fitted with a three-plus-one set of Deist safety chutes; a 2 ft pilot chute, a 7-ft high speed chute and a 16ft final braking parachute.

By the time Thompson reached the salt flats in late October 1968, the course was wet with sporadic rains, so with veteran drag racer Danny Ongais as his co-driver, he pushed a Ford Mustang around a 10 mile circuit gunning for Ab Jenkins' old endurance records. It kept his new sponsors happy until he could try for the wheel-driven record.

Despite the threat of further rain approaching from the Stansbury Mountains to the east, Thompson hurtled the *Autolite Special* across the salt to 425.03mph (683.01kph) before the rains came to rob him of a chance of a return run at the record within the permitted hour. Thompson ran the car twice more in 1969. On the first pass he clocked 360mph (580kph) and on the second 442.625mph (712.03kph) was claimed before chute failure denied him the record once again. The *Autolite Special* came to a stop a few hundred feet from the USAC tower and timekeeper Joe Petrali. The car was crated and returned to Los Angeles for a checkover. Sadly, however, Thompson's principal sponsors throughout the *Autolite Special* years, the Ford Motor Company, pulled out of the land speed record business soon after and he was forced to give up.

On 11 March 1969, Senator Joseph M. Kennick ordered the Senate of the California legislature to honour its native son Mickey Thompson for 'becoming the first man to travel on the ground at a speed in excess of 400 miles per hour, and for his many contributions to the automobile industry of the United States of America, and to the youth of the State of California and the Nation'.

His outstanding record of accomplishments included 485 national and international speed and endurance records. Mickey Thompson had international fame and recognition, and his ability to turn a passion for speed into a multi-million dollar industry made him a highly respected and wealthy entrepreneur, a feat almost without precedent in the field of World Land Speed Record breaking. Yet, despite this acclaim, the one thing he had always wanted above all else had eluded him for more than a decade: breaking the land speed record for wheel-driven cars. A purist record of 409.277mph (658.636kph) was set on 12 November 1965, by fellow Californian, Bob Summers in the *Goldenrod*, a record that has remained unbroken for over thirty years.

Thompson did drive again – on 9 July 1971 on the runway at March Air Force Base in Riverside, California, topping a 23-year-old record established by a German car. In his vehicle, the 550hp dash car *Tempest*, Thompson averaged 112.088mph (180.387kph) on a two-way kilometre run in the international Class D competition. The old record of 177.34kph (110.20mph) was set by Rudy Caracciola on the Avus track in Berlin in the Hitler-sponsored Mercedes in 1939.

In 1973 Thompson sold the *Autolite Special* to Don Alderson, who intended to run the car at Bob Summers record using his own Milodon-built Chrysler Hemi engines with Kelly Brown as driver, but lack of funding robbed Alderson and Brown of a shot at the title. In 1983 Thompson repurchased the vehicle, renamed *Conquest I*, and planned another attempt on the record with either himself or his crew chief son Danny at the wheel. The car was to use a significantly more potent fuel mix of 40 per cent nitromethane and 60 per cent hydrogen peroxide. For Thompson this attempt was to be the last in a golden era of wheel-driven cars, before the mighty jet-powered projectiles scorched their way into the record books. It was unsuccessful.

Mickey, and his wife Trudy, met a tragic death in 1988 when they were murdered in front of their home in Bradbury, California. Mickey's son, Danny, now runs the family business.

SUMMERS BROTHERS – THE FORGOTTEN HEROES

Bob 'Butch' Summers (top) driver of the Goldenrod and brother Bill, the remarkable duo who applied their purist experience to engineer the most remarkable vehicle to ever appear at Bonneville, taking the World Land Speed Record for wheel-driven vehicles – a record that has remained unchallenged for 34 years. (Author's collection)

The Summers brothers' *Goldenrod*, now on tour for special showings at car shows and exhibitions throughout the world, holds a very special place in automotive history, shared by only the most innovative creations built since the beginning of the century. In simplest terms, *Goldenrod* is the fastest automobile of all time. With an official World Land Speed Record of 409.277mph (658.636kph) set on 12 November 1965, *Goldenrod* has travelled faster than any other wheel-driven vehicle before or since. While faster times have been recorded by free-wheeling jet and rocket-propelled designs they have never been recognized as automotive records by the purist, since the power was not driven through the wheels.

The *Goldenrod* represents the culmination of the combined racing and mechanical engineering efforts of Bill and Bob Summers, which began in the mid-1950s. Also playing a major role in the $108,000 project were such sponsors as the Champion Spark Plug Co., the Chrysler Corporation, Firestone Tire & Rubber Co., Hurst Performance Products and the giant Mobil Oil Company. They were all attracted to the Summers brothers' plans for recapturing the land speed record for the United States on the basis of their progressively successful showings at the annual Bonneville Nationals held at the Bonneville Salt Flats in Western Utah.

Bob 'Butch' Summers was born on 4 April 1937 in Omaha, Nebraska. As children he and his older brother Bill moved to Auburn, California, with their parents. After getting their automobile feet wet with a 1936 Ford coupé (which Bill Summers characterized as a flop), the Summers brothers became perennial winners with every new machine they put together. From 1955 until they began the *Goldenrod* project in 1963, the pair always took first place in their respective category and almost always established a new national class record.

Their initial success came with a 1929 Ford Model A roadster that achieved 175mph (282kph), and they eventually worked their way up to a front-engined streamliner, which their competitors nicknamed the 'Pollywog'. The unorthodox streamliner was a wide-fronted vehicle of all-composite construction, tapering back to a tail section so narrow that its two rear wheels were set one in front of the other. It was débuted at Bonneville in 1961 where it clocked a very impressive 302.317mph (487.01kph), and the following year Bob drove it to a Speed Week record for a single-engined car – 323mph (520.02kph). On 10 October 1963, he set a new national and international Class C record of 279.4mph (450.03kph) for the mile and kilometre on the same course.

The success of the 'Pollywog' convinced the Summers brothers that a design concept incorporating more power was not as important as a narrower profile. At that time, Britain's Donald Campbell held the officially recognized World Land Speed Record of 403.1mph (648.728kph) set at Lake Eyre, and Bill and Bob concluded that they might as well use the momentum of their past efforts to go for the big one and bring the prized record back to America.

While they were confident that they possessed the technical knowledge and operating skills, there was always the matter of the vast financial support required for such an ambitious project. They accordingly directed their energy to acquiring such resources, and soon came up with a healthy financial package and some very valuable support. Firestone Tire & Rubber Co. agreed to provide a portion of the funds along with developing the special tyres required to ensure safety at speeds in excess of 400mph. Financial assistance also came from the Mobil Oil Co., which had a long history of underwriting past land speed record efforts, as well

Bob Summers assumes his supine driving position in the Goldenrod. *(Author's collection)*

The cockpit of Goldenrod. Instrumentation is dominated by four independent gauges, enabling Bob Summers to monitor the oil pressure of each of the four pushrod ohv, 6.9-litre, 608bhp, Chrysler V8 Hemi engines at a glance. (Author's collection)

as George Hurst, President of Hurst Performance Products. Hurst also furnished the complicated gear changing mechanism needed for the sleek, four-engined, four-wheel drive *Goldenrod*, and the special wheels. Adding credibility to the project was the much needed support of Ray Brock, then publisher of the Los Angeles based *Hot Rod Magazine*, now part of the famed Petersen Publishing Company. The basic package was rounded out with the all-important contributions of the Chrysler Corporation in the form of four brand new 426 cubic inch V8 Hemi engines. The Summers brothers had always relied upon the early style Chrysler Hemi-heads for their previous record-setting efforts at Bonneville, and the afternoon that the big truck came to their shop in Ontario, California, to unload the four crated engines was one that they still remember vividly.

After exhaustive wind-tunnel tests had been completed at Cal Tech, it was determined that the lowest, narrowest shape possible would offer the best chances of breaking Campbell's 403mph record. Accordingly, the four pushrod ohv, 6.9-litre, 608 bhp Chrysler V8 Hemi engines were mounted in-line and coupled in pairs, back to back, the front pair driving the front wheels, the rear pair driving the rear wheels. Engine rpms were synchronized between pairs by a mechanical coupling. Except for dry sump, a lubrication and fuel injection (required for low overall height) system was utilized instead of conventional carburettors. Engines were to stock specifications throughout – bore and stroke of 4.25 × 3.75in and rated at 6,600–6,800rpm each engine. Driver Bob Summers was placed right behind these powerful engines and a lightweight Harvey aluminium alloy 3003, 0.064in thick body was formed around this long and streamline shape for maximum aerodynamic efficiency. The streamliner measured 32ft in length, 48in wide, 42in high at the top of the tail section and a mere 28in to the top of the engine hood. All four wheels were fitted with 6.5 × 16 Firestone tubeless

The 6.5 × 16 Firestone tubeless Nylon tyres on the Goldenrod *were coupled to Hurst-designed 16in diameter × 6½in wide aluminium wheels forged by Harvey Aluminium. (Author's collection)*

Bob Summers inspects one of the four pushrod ohv, 6.9-litre, 608bhp Chrysler V8 Hemi engines that powered Goldenrod. *(Bill Summers)*

Nylon tyres – a special low-profile treadless design. Width of tread contact area was 4in, static diameter, 23in; inflation, 150psi, with a design speed of 600mph. Braking was completed by Airheart triple spots mounted on front and rear pinion gear coupler flanges for use at 100mph and below. There were Deist parachutes for high speeds: a pilot chute of 8ft diameter for first stage braking at maximum speeds; a 24ft final chute for 250mph and below; and an emergency 8ft chute. Automatic systems had manual override.

Construction of the car began on 1 January 1965 at the Summers brothers' shop. Just seven months later, the completed *Goldenrod* moved under its own power for the first time during a series of shakedown tests at the nearby Riverside International Raceway. After making the final necessary adjustments, the Summers brothers trailered *Goldenrod* to Bonneville in September 1965 and made four successful runs. Instructed by all involved to 'take it easy' on the first pass (in other words, not to exceed 100mph), Bob Summers more than slightly exceeded this limitation with a clocking of 250mph (403kph) on the *Goldenrod*'s first voyage across the salt. 'I felt so good that I just didn't see any reason to lift the throttle,' Bob later explained to newsmen. 'I took it to 3,500 rpm, and shifted through the gears, and it worked perfectly,' he said. Three more runs were made, the best of which was 390mph (628kph) on petrol(!) and it was a pair of encouraged brothers who took their racing machine back to their Ontario workshop to prepare for the final record breaking assault.

Goldenrod was back at Bonneville in October, and things looked especially good as Bob pushed the vehicle past the 400mph barrier on his first run at the record. With a chance to break the record now well within their grasp, the Summers brothers experienced what was to be the first in a series of frustrations as one of the engines separated from the drivechain, causing it to over-rev and produce internal component damage. By the time that the wounded motor was replaced, rainstorms had soaked the salt to the point where record run attempts could not be made, and chief steward Joe Petrali closed the course. To make matters worse was the fact that the Summers brothers were allotted a limited number of days on the Bonneville Salt Flats. Before the conditions could improve, their course reservation had run out.

With all hopes of setting the record now apparently postponed until the next season, they reluctantly towed *Goldenrod* back to Ontario. But on 7 November, an unexpected telephone call from Wendover, close to Bonneville, gave hope of yet just one more shot at the record. Land speed jet veteran Art Arfons had the salt booked for that week, but he had set his own record for jets in the *Green Monster* on the first day. A publicity man from Firestone, Jim Cook, who was also working with Arfons, told the Summers brothers to get back to Bonneville to use the remaining track time.

The bright golden streamliner was rolled off its trailer on to the hard, bleached white surface of Bonneville at 2.30 p.m. on 1 September 1965. Two hours later Bob 'Butch' Summers squeezed into the cramped cockpit, while crewmen fastened down the rear quarter panel that enclosed him. (Author's collection)

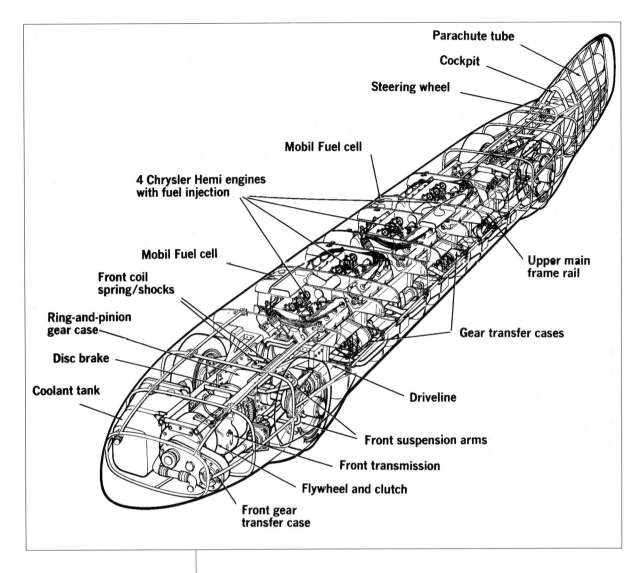

Parachute tube

Cockpit

Steering wheel

Mobil Fuel cell

4 Chrysler Hemi engines
with fuel injection

Mobil Fuel cell

Front coil
spring/shocks

Ring-and-pinion
gear case

Disc brake

Coolant tank

Upper main
frame rail

Gear transfer cases

Driveline

Front suspension arms

Front transmission

Flywheel and clutch

Front gear
transfer case

This longitudinal section of the
Goldenrod *reveals how the four
pushrod ohv, 6.9-litre, 608bhp
Chrysler V8 Hemi engines, and two
four-speed gearboxes driving all
four wheels, were accommodated in
the streamlined vehicle.*

Goldenrod, *without body panels, is
prepared for a run on the salt. The
vehicle was push-started at
Bonneville by Bill Summers in the
family station wagon. (Author's
collection)*

GOLDENROD

Length:	32ft	Final Drive Ratios:	May be varied. Anticipated: 0.95:1 to 1.05:1
Width:	48in	Chassis:	Mild steel. Lower rails: 2 × ⅛in
Height:	28in, rising to 42in at top of tail fin		diameter wall. Upper rails: 2 × 6in
Wheelbase:	207in		diameter rectangular tubes. ⅜in wall
Track (front):	32in		tubes mounted vertically for maximum
(rear)	33in		rigidity
Weight:	5,500–6,000lb (estimated)	Body Shell:	Harvey Aluminium; alloy 3003, 0.064in
Ground Clearance:	5in		thick
Frontal Area:	9 sq ft. Coefficient of drag: 0.117	Wheels:	Four 16in diameter × 6½in rim width,
Engine:	Four Chrysler Hemi V8s, mounted in-line and coupled in pairs, back to back, front pair driving the front wheels, rear pair driving the rear wheels. Engine rpms synchronized between pairs by mechanical coupling. Except for dry sump, lubrication and fuel injection (required for low overall height) engines are to stock specifications throughout		Hurst designed, hand forged Harvey Aluminium
		Tyres:	6.50 × 16in Firestone tubeless nylons; special low-profile treadless design. Width of tread contact area: 4 in. Static dia: 23in. Inflation: 150psi. Design speed: 600mph
Bore and Stroke:	4.25 × 3.75in	Braking Systems:	Airheart triple spots mounted on front and rear pinion gear coupler flanges for
Displacement:	426 cubic inch each engine		use at 100mph and below. Deist
Fuel:	Mobil racing gasoline, 105 research octane		parachutes for high speeds: pilot chute; 8ft diameter first stage for maximum
Fuel Supply:	5 gallons per engine in 4 tanks		speeds; 24ft final chute for 250mph
Transmissions:	Two five-speed Spicer units, utilizing top 4 gears		and below; plus emergency 8ft chute. Automatic systems with manual
Ratios:	2nd – 2.6:1		override
	3rd – 1.5:1	Suspension:	Fully independent, all 4 wheels via
	4th – 1.19:1		upper and lower A-arms. Upper arms
	5th – 1:1		pivot on frame, act on 4 special
	Simultaneous synchronized shifting via special Hurst shifter		Monroe coil spring/shock units mounted inboard
Clutches:	Two Schiefer double-disc, hydraulically actuated	Steering:	Chrysler, hydraulically actuated, 10° limit
Ring-and-Pinion Ratios:	1:1, locked rear ends	Max Output:	2,432hp
		Speed Capability:	450–500mph

Conditions were still somewhat damp on the course, and it took two 'push cars', one right behind the other, to get *Goldenrod* fired. But if the salt wasn't perfect, *Goldenrod* certainly was: Bob Summers hit 417mph (672kph) on his first run and then produced another successful effort on the return, back-up pass, netting a new official World Land Speed Record of 409.277mph (658.636kph). That record was set on Friday 12 November 1965. The following day, an unofficial one-way run was made and this produced for Bill and Bob Summers a clocking of 425mph (686kph), the fastest speed ever attained by a wheel-driven vehicle.

Bob Summers was still sitting in the cockpit when Joe Petrali's timing slip reached him at the end of the track. The crew pulled him out, hoisted him up on their shoulders and danced with joy. It was the first time ever in

Shielded from the glare of the salt'n'sun, Bob Summers prepares for the first of two runs through the timing beam that would cement a record that still stands today . . . some thirty-five years later. (Author's collection)

the modern history of the record that a crew had built a car and set a new World Land Speed Record all in one year.

It has now been over thirty years since this achievement was recorded at Bonneville and the passage of time certainly makes for an interesting perspective. According to Bill Summers, the cash contributions from the associated sponsors totalled about $108,000 and product development costs boosted the overall tab to over $250,000. To reproduce that effort in today's inflationary times would result in costs that would stagger the imagination. On the other hand, the still well-preserved *Goldenrod* is certainly capable of making another attempt today and subtle implementation of current state-of-the-art engine technology and weight reduction could easily result in speeds approaching 500mph. Hard as it may be to believe, *Goldenrod* produced the record with engines that were factory standard except for the induction system and exhaust.

Even more interesting is the fact that the Summers brothers received absolutely no financial rewards or endorsements for their outstanding efforts at Bonneville.

We were able to support ourselves during the construction of the vehicle and hire some additional help with the sponsorship money, but we took home only $150 a week each, and there was nothing to come after we set the record. All we ever wanted was the recognition. Looking back now, we probably should have worked out something

for additional financial incentives, performance fees, bonuses for breaking the record, and all that. These things are so commonplace now in most forms of automotive competition and the big contracts that you see in other professional sports.

But it did give us a national reputation for our technology and expertise, and with that as a springboard, we founded Summers Brothers, Inc., now a major manufacturing enterprise specializing in drivetrain components for high performance applications. We have a lot of customers that first started getting interested in racing when *Goldenrod* set the record for wheel-driven cars and a lot of other clients heard about it from their older friends. The reputation that we established with that one project is very much with us today.

And so, *Goldenrod*, having moved under its own power for the first time more than three decades ago, now tours the globe as a great attraction to the world's motorsport enthusiasts. Luring large crowds wherever it goes, *Goldenrod* has been just as successful as a showpiece as it was in its original competition assignment on the Bonneville Salt Flats in 1965. But one can only speculate as to just what might happen if a big truck were to pull up at the Summers brothers shop and start unloading four new aluminium 426 Hemi engines today. . . .

Nothing is permanent in the land speed record business. New efforts were mounted to break the Summers brothers record. The late Mickey

On 12 November 1965 the tranquil-looking hills of western Utah became alive with the sound of music when the Goldenrod, *the longest, narrowest and lowest package of piston-horsepower ever to run on the Bonneville Salt Flats, roared through the measured mile. (Author's collection)*

Thompson tried in 1969 with a twin-engined streamliner utilizing narrow, low profile lines similar to *Goldenrod*'s. Bonneville Speed Weeks veteran Bob McGrath, in partnership with Jack Lufkin of Ak Miller Garage fame, and drag racer Bill Hielscher, were preparing the twin-Chevrolet streamliner *Olympian*, an even lower and narrower car, to slice through the thin Utah air in an attempt to top the 500mph barrier, while Dean Moon's *Moonliner* was to have been run by Gary Gabelich. Craig Breedlove also explored the possibility of taking Donald Campbell's *Bluebird-Proteus CN7* out of mothballs for an attempt at the Summers brothers' wheel-driven record. Britain's Richard Noble has even toyed with the idea, and indeed Malcolm Olley in his dragster *Pink Panther* ... but both have met with little financial success.

One thing is certain: should the record be taken away from Bill and Bob Summers, they have more than enough technical knowledge and experience to snatch it right back. The Summers brothers welcome challenges and invite others to go ahead and set a new record. And besides, unless somebody breaks Bob's record, it is doubtful whether we will ever see the sleek golden lines of their remarkable *Goldenrod* on the Bonneville Salt Flats again.

Although not always recognized by the purist, unlimited-class World Land Speed Records – that is to say records established by land-bound vehicles or projectiles powered by jet or rocket engines – are now recognized by the FIA (Fédération Internationale de l'Automobile) the world governing body for motorsport and record-breaking since the Second World War. However, the history and development of pure thrust and rocket propulsion technology in a land-bound vehicle date back much further ...

SIX

THE DAWN OF
THE ROCKET AGE

In 1927 an apparently innocent letter arrived at the Rüsselsheim works of Opel, innocent in that the mere slip of paper led to one of the most bizarre episodes in the history of any of the world's automobile companies. The letter was written by Herr Max Valier, an Austrian-born author, university lecturer and enthusiastic advocate of the development of rocket propulsion for flights into space. Then thirty-two, Valier addressed his letter to Fritz von Opel at the suggestion of his wife, Hedwig, who thought that the indefatigable von Opel would be just the man to provide the financial backing, sought in vain by her husband for years, to support a programme of rocket research and development. Not long after the letter arrived in Rüsselsheim, so did Valier.

In their first meeting at the Opel works in July 1927, Valier learned that the Opel heir was interested in aviation and at that time was taking flying lessons at Rebstock near Frankfurt. Von Opel learned something of Valier's background: early study of physics and astronomy, experience as a test pilot in the First World War, and an association of several years with Professor Hermann Julius Oberth, the Romanian-born rocket pioneer from Hermannstadt who did so much to stimulate European interest in reactive flight. Studying the sharp-featured Valier through his horn-rimmed glasses, von Opel realized that the demonstration of a rocket-powered car – which

Behind closed doors at the Rüsselsheim works of Adam Opel AG, the birth of a legend in the form of Fritz von Opel's RAK 1, is seen for the first time in a rare photograph of the early stages of construction. (Author's collection)

Valier was willing to help build – would be a fantastic publicity coup without precedent in the automobile industry and of far greater value than its modest cost. Von Opel agreed to finance a series of tests.

Valier had to find a source for ready-made rockets. He turned to Freidrich Wilhelm Sander of Wesermünde, a respected manufacturer of compressed-powder rockets for marine use in signalling and line-throwing. Valier devised a simple thrust-measure and in January 1928 he and Sander started experimenting with different versions of his largest rocket. By mid-February the two men had prepared a report which they posted to von Opel. Von Opel reacted fast to the receipt of this information. He wired Sander and Valier that he wanted a meeting and demonstration at Rüsselsheim on 11 March, surprisingly soon. Not wanting to risk the possibility of failure in front of their sponsor, Valier urged Sander to contribute his little Opel sedan to the cause for static firing tests. Sander, however, fearing for his learned reputation and respectability as a founder member of the VfR (Verein für Raumschiffahrt or Society for Space Travel), was not willing to go quite that far in the interests of advancing rocket-propulsion in land-bound vehicles.

The 'honour' of taking the wheel of the first rocket car, RAK 1, was delegated by Fritz von Opel to Ing Kurt C. Volkhart, thirty-seven, a former Dürkopp designer who was also active throughout the 1920s as a racing driver. He owned three Bugattis during the period. (Author's collection)

They arrived at the Opel plant on the specified day, shipping their rockets there by road because the Deutsche Bundesbahn railway refused to carry them. Opel had begun the conversion of an old racing car to serve as a test facility for the rockets, but the vehicle wasn't ready, so a simple passenger car chassis was fitted with a wooden frame, not unlike a wine rack, to hold the twelve rockets, and a steel bulkhead to offer the driver some protection.

The 'honour' of taking the wheel of the first rocket car was delegated by Fritz von Opel to Ing. Kurt C. Volkhart, thirty-seven, then employed by Opel. Volkhart was a former Dürkopp designer who was also active

throughout the 1920s as a racing driver, owning three Bugattis during the period. With the brave young Volkhart at the controls, Opel mechanic Carl Lutzmeyer lit the fuses hanging from the rockets and then ran for cover. In seconds the rear of the car was enveloped in a cloud of hissing smoke and it was seen to lurch forward at a walking pace, no more.

This pathetic performance subjected the two pioneers to a barrage of derisive remarks. Their reply was a further series of tests culminating in the development of a special Opel rocket car or 'RAK', short for Rakete (the German word for rocket).

The first moment of truth for the Opel *RAK 1* came on 10 April. Only six rockets were used in the first test, in which the car reached 44mph (71kph) from a standing start. In a second test with eight rockets the Opel *RAK 1* went 6mph faster in spite of a misfire by one closely bunched complement of rockets. This was encouraging enough for Fritz von Opel to invite the press to a public demonstration the following day, 11 April 1928. For the first time the vehicle was equipped with all twelve of the high-thrust rockets, which were wired so that the accelerator lit a pair of them with each downward thrust. Von Opel hoped this would be enough to drive *RAK 1* all the way round the almost 1-mile Opelbahn.

Sadly, the rockets did not produce sufficient thrust, propelling the car to no more than 60mph (100kph), however, the rumbling progress of the car down the track was sensational enough to warrant headlines in the German newspapers the following day, blaring forth the news, 'Germany builds the world's first rocket vehicle', even if they did offend the serious German rocket researchers who considered the Valier-Opel-Sander venture to be no more than a promotional stunt, a problem that also faced Bill Fredrick and Hal Needham's controversial *Budweiser Rocket* car in 1979.

The curious rear aspect of RAK 1, which made its first run secretly on the Opelbahn at Rüsselsheim on 11 April 1928. Powered by twelve dry powder rockets – of which five failed to ignite – it zoomed from zero to 60mph in less than eight seconds. (Author's collection)

On 11 April 1928, Kurt C. Volkhart depressed the accelerator of RAK 1, electrically igniting seven of the full complement of twelve rockets to launch him down the almost 1 mile Opelbahn at a terminal speed of more than 60mph. (Author's collection)

The RAK 2 was deservedly the most famous of the Rüsselsheim rocket cars. It had an ultra-low chassis with semi-elliptical springing, and a bullet-shaped, black bodyshell with room at the rear to accommodate twenty-four rockets. Two extremely large down-thrusting canard fins were fitted to both sides of the fuselage, forward of the driver, and their angle of attack could be adjusted by hand lever inside the cockpit. (Author's collection)

Shoehorned into a marvel of motion engineering Fritz von Opel, alone in RAK 2, prepares to ignite the awesome power of the twenty-four 550lb-thrust rockets that would launch him into history. It was a thrilling sight for those who lined the Avus Speedway in Berlin's Grunewald, including the relatively unknown graduate from the Berlin Institute of Technology called Wernher von Braun, seen here approaching the vehicle from the left. (Author's collection)

Smoke billows behind the Opel RAK 3 as it dashes along the 3.2-mile stretch of railway track at Rebstock near Frankfurt, 23 June 1928. The car, with a far from willing cat as passenger and with electric remote-control ignition, achieved the remarkable speed of 180mph. (Author's collection)

Many claim the Fredrick-Needham Project Speed of Sound team did not conform to the official FIA rules governing world land speed records, citing that their vehicle, driven by Hollywood stuntman Stan Barrett and financed by corporate America, was little more than a 'stunt'.

Still more attention was accorded the next Opel demonstration, which took place on 23 May 1928 before a crowd of some 2,000 reporters, photographers and invited guests, including a young and relatively unknown graduate from the Berlin Institute of Technology called Wernher von Braun.

The driver was Fritz von Opel and the car, a completely new vehicle, the Opel *RAK 2*. This fabulous-looking vehicle was deservedly the most famous of the Rüsselsheim rocket cars. It had an ultra-low chassis with semi-elliptical springing, a bullet-shaped, black bodyshell with room at the rear to accommodate twenty-four rockets. Two extremely large down-thrusting canard fins were fitted, one to each side of the fuselage, forward of the driver. Their angle of attack could be adjusted by a hand lever inside the form-fitting cockpit. There was some thought of using *RAK 2* for an attack by Volkhart on the World Land Speed Record, which at that time was held by American, Ray Keech in the *White Triplex* and stood at 207.552mph (334.022kph); and if looks alone could do it, *RAK 2* had the record in the bag.

It was a thrilling sight for those who lined the Avus Speedway in Berlin's Grunewald. A report in the *Berliner Zeitung* detailed the event: 'The car started with a terrific roar, emitting a ball of flame and a billowing cloud of yellow, acrid smoke as the rockets ignited. The mighty machine gradually gained momentum as one rocket after another, all of uniform power, were fired – the car taking a lunge forward every time one ignited.'

All twenty-four of the special 550lb-thrust rockets fired properly, and von Opel is said to have reached speeds of 130 to 145mph while covering a distance of 1¼ miles. Over one section of the track he was alleged to have attained an unheard of speed of 240mph (390kph) for a few seconds, although this was not timed. At the highest speeds the nose of *RAK 2* started to lift menacingly; the canard fins weren't angled sufficiently but von Opel was too busy keeping the car under control to spare a hand to operate the adjusting lever. It must have been quite a ride, even for an experienced driver like von Opel, and as the illustrations show, *RAK 2* had no windshield in any shape or form to protect him!

Rockets in some form or other have been on man's agenda since the Chinese discovered gunpowder in AD 1200. The Chinese found out how to make a rocket weapon by putting gunpowder in a tube of tightly packed paper and attaching the tube to a stick. They called this weapon an 'arrow of flying fire' and used it to repel Mongols who besieged the Chinese stronghold of Kai-fung-fu in 1232. Later, a perhaps legendary account tells of a Chinese mandarin, Wan Hu, who in the year 1500 conceived the notion of using rockets to propel a vehicle through the air. Connecting forty-seven of the largest rockets in China to the framework of a chair, Wan Hu then had himself strapped to it. Two large kites attached to it were supposed to let the vehicle glide gently to earth at the journey's end. Coolies obediently set fire to the rockets. Wan Hu and his vehicle departed to his ancestors in a cloud of black smoke. But in spite of his spectacular suicide, he should probably be credited with having built the world's first jet aircraft.

Europeans, when they learned about paper skyrockets, used them only for display and signalling. By Western standards, this type of rocket was too weak to be a weapon of war. However, when the British fought in India against Raja Hyder Ali of Mysore in 1780, they ran into something new. The Raja had rockets of iron tubes, not pasteboard, ranging up to 12lb in weight and travelling up to half a mile. Since his rockets were no more accurate than those the Chinese had invented, Hyder Ali compensated by firing them in hundreds. His barrage drove the British off the battlefield at Guntur in 1780. Reports of this defeat reached William Congreve, an artillery colonel in the British Army, and stimulated him to make a serious study of the rocket as a weapon. After years of work Congreve was able to build a long-range, comparatively inexpensive and easily portable rocket weapon. Used successfully against Napoleon's fleet at Boulogne on 8 October 1806, Congreve's rocket was established as a weapon of swift destruction. Eight years later during the British attack on Fort McHenry, Baltimore, Congreve's rockets made a 'red glare' famous enough to become a part of America's national anthem.

Even Congreve found no cure for the inaccuracy of the rocket and by 1900 the military forces of the world had abandoned it as a weapon. But rockets were still used as fireworks, as signals and as lifeline launchers, uses that had been developed by numerous inventors in England and Germany during the 1820s.

When rocket research began again it was not inspired by war. The invention of the aeroplane had rekindled the old dream of escaping the

Fritz von Opel 1899–1971. The grandson of Adam Opel, founder of the famous Rüsselsheim motor manufacturing concern, and pioneer of rocket propulsion in a land-bound vehicle, sponsored a series of two cars, RAK 1 and RAK 2, in 1928. (Author's collection)

Fritz von Opel in white coat and Freidrich Wilhelm Sander of Wesermünde without hat, pose behind RAK 3, *the last of their land-bound experimental rocket vehicles. (Author's collection)*

bonds of gravity into space. In 1927 a group of men in Germany, drawn together through curiosity and excitement about rocket propulsion and space travel, founded the Verein für Raumschiffahrt. One of this group, science writer Max Valier, succeeded in interesting Fritz von Opel, grandson of Adam Opel, in the possibilities of a rocket-powered automobile.

Inspired by his success with *RAK 2*, Fritz von Opel went on to develop yet another vehicle, *RAK 3*, but this time he wasn't so eager to sit behind the wheel. He experimented with an unmanned rocket vehicle on a section of disused railway line at Rebstock, near Frankfurt, with a far from willing cat as passenger. Brake rockets in the nose of the vehicle ignited automatically to stop it at the end of the run. These brake rockets and the ignition were triggered by an electric clockwork device. The stretch of track was chosen because it was perfectly straight and level. A top speed of only 155mph (250kph) was attained, the brake rockets failed to perform properly and the vehicle coasted to a stop. Retrieved and towed back to the starting point, it was charged with a battery of thirty rockets in the hope of breaking all existing speed records – 248mph was the goal. Sadly, after attaining a staggering speed of 180mph, the vehicle was thrown off the track and destroyed by the violent thrust of its rockets.

The fate of the Opel *RAK 4* was similar. A rocket exploded and a splinter from a railway sleeper short circuited the ignition system, causing the remaining rockets to go off at once. *RAK 4* jumped the track and was demolished. Von Opel promised a *RAK 5* – also to be a track-bound vehicle built along the purposeful lines of *RAK 2* – but grumbling railroad officials prohibited further trial runs that might cause further damage to their track.

Despite the ultimate failure of both *RAK 3* and *4*, von Opel felt there was practically no limit to the speed that could have been reached by his earlier rocket car. However, the brilliant inventor never pursued the coveted World Land Speed Record and turned his efforts to flight, eventually realising his dream of building and flying the world's first rocket-powered aircraft – the HATRY-Flugzeug *RAK 1*.

On 30 September 1929 the rocket-powered glider was readied at Frankfurt-Rebstock for its first flight. Fritz von Opel sat at the controls in his bid to furnish proof that rockets could propel aeroplanes. Like a speeding bullet the aircraft slid along the 10 metre length of rail that served as a runway and was soon airborne. The flight lasted about ten minutes and reached a speed of about 100mph. However, the wings caught fire, the aeroplane was badly damaged on landing and could not be flown again. Miraculously von Opel escaped without injury. This was his final attempt at rocket research.

It wasn't until 1965 that a rocket-powered car took aim at the World Land Speed Record. However, American Walt Arfon's *Wingfoot Express II*, propelled by twenty-five rockets and driven by Bobby Tatroe, lacked the sustained thrust to grasp the record. Despite the failure, the land speed record era of thrust and rocket-powered vehicles had come of age.

Five years later, another rocket-propelled car attempted to succeed where the *Wingfoot Express II* had failed. It was *The Blue Flame*, driven by Gary Gabelich. On 23 October 1970, Gabelich became the fastest man on wheels when he drove the 35,000hp, liquid fuel rocket-powered *The Blue Flame* to a new World Land Speed Record of 622.407mph (1,001.664kph) at the Bonneville Salt Flats. The propulsion concept was inspired by the exploits of Fritz von Opel and his team experimenting with their vehicles some forty-two years earlier in Berlin. While the experiments made by Opel were not scientifically successful, his vision and determination to succeed earned him a place among the pioneers of rocketry and helped take land-bound vehicles to the sound barrier and beyond.

SEVEN

A JET IS POISED

DR NATHAN OSTICH – THE FLYING DOCTOR

Pausing for a moment from their work constructing the world's first jet-powered land speed record car Flying Caduceus, *are, left to right: Ak Miller, Dr Nathan Ostich, Ray Brock and Allan Bradshaw. Before them is the General Electric J47, 7,000lb thrust turbojet power unit already* in situ *within the tubular steel framework of the car. (Author's collection)*

The first man to race a jet car successfully at Bonneville will not be familiar to most readers and lay disciples of land speed record breaking. The name of Dr Nathan Ostich, a physician from the east Los Angeles barrio, doesn't appear in the record books, but certainly not for the want of trying. For three years, he waged a battle with the elusive record on the great salt stage, in his sleek 28ft jet car, the *Flying Caduceus*. Powered by a General Electric J47 turbojet unit from a surplus Boeing B36 bomber, the *Flying Caduceus*, boasting a 7,000hp punch, was some two years in the making 'between patients' in the garage behind the Doc's surgery.

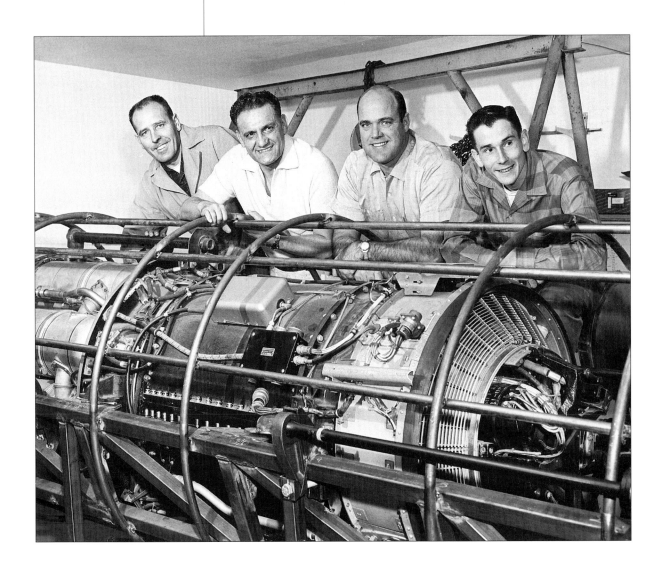

THE JET ENGINE

Over the course of the past half a century, jet-power has vastly changed the way we all live. However, the basic principle of jet propulsion is neither new nor complicated. In AD 100, Hero, a Greek philosopher and mathematician, demonstrated jet power in a machine called an 'aeolipile'. A heated, water-filled steel ball with nozzles spun as steam escaped. Why? The principle behind this phenomenon was not fully understood until 1690 when Sir Isaac Newton formulated the principle of Hero's jet propulsion 'aeolipile' in scientific terms. Newton's Third Law of Motion stated: 'To every action force there is an equal and opposite reaction force.'

Jet propulsion for aircraft did not become practical until the mid-1940s; however, various examples of jet propulsion preceded that date. In 1908, René Lorin, a French engineer, proposed using a piston engine to compress air that would then be mixed with fuel and burned to produce pulses of hot gases that would be expelled through a nozzle to generate a propelling force.

During the early 1930s, the Italian Caproni monoplane actually flew with a similar system but was woefully inefficient due mainly to the poor compressor and its source of power. It remained for Sir Frank Whittle and Hans von Ohain, a German, to successfully integrate the compressor driven by a turbine principle for a jet engine that could be used to power an aeroplane.

The piston engine and the gas turbine develop power or thrust by burning a combustible mixture of fuel and air. Both engines convert the energy of the expanding gases into propulsive force. The piston engine does this by changing the energy of combustion into mechanical energy, which is used to turn a propeller. Aircraft propulsion is obtained as the propeller imparts a relatively small acceleration to a large mass of air. The gas turbine, in its basic turbojet configuration, imparts a relatively large acceleration to a smaller mass of air, and thus produces thrust or propulsive force directly. Hence, the selection of turbojet power as a means of reaction propulsion for many successful land speed record vehicles.

The engine is started by rotating the compressor with a starter and then igniting a mixture of fuel and air in the combustion chamber with one or more igniters that resemble automobile spark plugs. When the engine has started and its compressor is rotating at sufficient speed, the starter and the igniters are turned off. The engine will then run without further assistance as long as fuel and air in the proper proportions continue to enter the combustion chamber and burn.

The reason why a turbojet will run as it does lies in the compressor. The gases created by a fuel-and-air mixture burning under normal atmospheric pressure do not expand enough to do useful work. Air under pressure must be mixed with fuel before gases produced by combustion can be used to make a piston engine or turbojet engine operate.

Finding a way to accomplish the compressing of air was the biggest challenge for designers during the early years of turbojet engine development. Recall that Frank Whittle solved the problem by using a centrifugal compressor similar to those employed in superchargers for aircraft piston engines. Whittle provided the power required to turn the compressor by mounting a gas-driven turbine immediately to the rear of the engine's combustion chamber in approximately the same manner used today.

Designed by Ray Brock, publisher of *Hot Rod Magazine*, Ak Miller and Allen Bradshaw, the 6,985lb car was built by a team of no fewer than twenty-one volunteers, including five of the doctor's patients, a lawyer and three reporters from the designer's editorial team, at a cost of $100,000 dollars and 10,000 man-hours.

The almost spherical body cross-section tested well in the wind tunnel facility at California Poly Tech. Overall chassis strength was achieved by combining heavy horizontal members of rectangular tubing with machine-bent hoops of heavy-gauge round tubing. The frame was of chrome moly, electrically welded, and the outer skin of the body shell was finished in aluminium. Shod with special high-speed Firestone tyres inflated to 200psi, the wheels were outrigged and unstreamlined.

Conventional GM truck suspension, A-arms, torsion bars and steering units comprised the running gear, and as the driving force was thrust only, there was no transmission or differential. Halibrand spot brakes on all four wheels supplemented a double-action speed-retarding Deist chute, which was fired from a tube in the vehicle's tail, just above the jet 'stove-pipe'. The chute first opened to a diameter of 4ft, then a delayed action fuse in the reefing shroud lines exploded 6 to 8 seconds after the initial deployment and allowed the chute to expand to 8ft in diameter for the final braking phase.

Ostich had caught the land speed bug in 1949 and was no stranger to the Bonneville Salt Flats; he had raced there for ten years in a wide variety of exotic propulsion systems, including a '56 Chrysler 300B, turning 141.579mph (228.03kph) for a D/Coupé–Sedan class win, and later clocked a mean 189.9mph (305.54kph) in a modified road car.

Poor salt conditions in 1959 virtually eliminated all attempts to break John Cobb's record of 394.2mph (634.267kph), established in 1947; thus all efforts to regain the World Land Speed Record for the United States were shelved until the following year. Pre-season publicity by the Southern California Timing Association heralded 1960 as a banner year, with no fewer than ten contenders – including seven jet cars. The cast of competitors included Mickey Thompson, Art Arfons, Bill Johnson, Bob McGrath, Bill Fredrick, Dr Nathan Ostich, Glenn Leasher, Ermie Immerso, Craig Breedlove, Bob Knapp and Bob Funk. In addition, the *City of Salt Lake* – the car that later carried Athol Graham to his death and was already known to have turned a surprisingly easy 344.761mph (554.829kph) the previous December, nearly equalling Mickey Thompson's flying mile record – was being prepared for its ill-fated run.

No sooner had Ostich and his team arrived at Bonneville on 5 August than things began to go wrong. Air supply for the vehicle's jet engine was ducted from slots on each side of the cockpit proboscis. While the split ducting system was engineered and designed from recommendations made by General Electric – the engine's manufacturer in Cincinnati, Ohio – the laminated fibreglass reinforced with square mesh steel was not strong enough to stand the air pressure differential between supply and demand at near full power settings, and the intake ducts, not packed out as normal by ram air, collapsed. A hasty all-night repair job did not prove to be strong enough and the *Flying Caduceus* was returned to Los Angeles where the crew constructed new ducts of honeycomb-section fibreglass.

On 5 September the car returned to Bonneville and progressively increased its speed from the low 200s to 324mph. Ostich was now ready to attack the record. Approaching a speed of 331mph (533.02kph), 7

Athol Graham, the Salt Lake City garage owner, kneels before his $2,500, V12 Allison-powered, City of Salt Lake, *sponsored by STP and Firestone, shortly before the run at the mile in which he lost his life. (Author's collection)*

miles down range, the car suddenly veered to the left in a terrifying slide. The left-hand front wheel buckled and snapped from its bearing. Fighting to regain control the 52-year-old driver fired his Deist safety chute and the *Flying Caduceus* remained stable before finally coming to a shuddering halt at the end of the salt. 'I had trouble pulling it back on course and then started shutting off power. It still wouldn't come back so I popped the chute. I felt the car spinning and I thought I was going into a roll. I did everything automatically – the things I had learned in numerous practice runs. I didn't know I lost the wheel until I felt the car go down.' Ostich had only one thought to share after that high-speed slide across the salt flats. 'I didn't want to burn. That was the one thing on my mind and I remember grabbing for the extinguisher overhead.' Although Ostich wasn't injured, the car had suffered considerable damage and the doctor and his crew returned to Los Angeles.

Ostich explained to the press soon after his return to LA, 'At high speed it is impossible to steer the car with wheels at speeds between 319 and 324mph, it handled perfectly, but if you get the least little bit out of line, say only two to three degrees, there's 19,000 pounds of pressure pushing on one side of the fuselage. There's simply no way to hold it, the wheels develop a form of gyroscopic co-efficiency. At such speeds the only thing you can do is control it with the rudder.' Then why the spin? 'The left front wheel spindle had broken off, causing the wheel to come loose. As a result, the excessive transfer to the left front of the car when it began slipping sideways caused the break,' he explained.

Ostich returned to Bonneville for a third crack at the record in 1963 and on one 324mph run into the mile, spun the car out of the timing trap while decelerating. He was travelling at only 75mph when he finally lost control, relying on friction alone to halt the car.

Wind tunnel tests of the car prior to his attempts at the record showed the *Flying Caduceus* to have a speed potential of 500mph, but in practice the vehicle never surpassed a terminal velocity in excess of 331mph. While the *Flying Caduceus* failed in its attempt to capture the record for the United States, the jet era had been officially launched.

Following the death of Athol Graham on 1 August 1960, Otto Anzjon, a seventeen-year-old mechanic from Salt Lake City persuaded Graham's widow Zeldine to let him rebuild the *City of Salt Lake* for another crack at the record in 1962. The very idea of breaking the land speed record had come to Graham in a dream one night in 1957, at his home in Ogden, near Salt Lake City.

In 1958, Graham turned his dream into a reality, in the form of a car named for his beloved Mormon State capital. For the engine, Graham came up with a 3,000hp USAF surplus supercharged V12 Allison aero-engine, which came from William E. Boeing Jr's unlimited hydroplane *Miss Wahoo*, piloted by Jack Regas in the 1957 Gold Cup on Lake Washington. Graham mounted the powerplant in the rear of the car, driving the rear wheels.

The streamlined body shell of the *City* was fabricated around a drop tank taken from the belly of a Second World War Boeing B-29 Superfortress bomber, cut into three sections, forming the nose, centre and sandwiched tail section, aft of the engine housing and propellant tanks. The chassis was engineered from 12in deep aluminium, incorporating stock Cadillac components throughout.

Most experts, including Mickey Thompson, were of the opinion that Athol Graham simply accelerated too hard on that ill-fated run down the Bonneville course, causing the left rear wheel hub to shear off under the load of the tremendous torque transmitted during the start of the run.

Dr Nathan Ostich, the Los Angeles physician who introduced the jet era to land speed racing with his $100,000 General Electric J47 turbojet-powered Flying Caduceus. *(Author's collection)*

Concerned by the *City*'s unfortunate history, Joe Petrali, Bonneville's wise elder statesman counselled the inexperienced Otto Anzjon regarding a number of design changes he considered mandatory for a fresh attempt at the record, but with very little funding, and as it transpired, very little time, it was agreed the car could be run with a small device to measure the loads on the troublesome rear axle.

'The idea of rebuilding the car was all Otto's,' said Zeldine Graham. 'I would never have asked him to race but he has expressed a strong desire to fulfil Athol's lifetime dream.'

'I guess I should be scared but I'm not,' the young Anzjon told Petrali. 'My parents say its OK and I'm most eager to drive the car.'

Anzjon attained an impressive 254mph (409kph) on his first one-way pass across the salt flats, and Zeldine quickly applied to Joe Petrali for a record attempt sanction. Anzon roared past the timing beam in excess of 200mph (322kph), when the left rear Firestone tyre suffered a blowout, and the *City of Salt Lake* once again, pitched, turned and crashed its way into the realms of the unrecognized and unlucky in pursuit of the record.

Otto Anzjon was robbed of another opportunity to drive the *City of Salt Lake* for in the winter of 1962 he died of leukaemia in Tooele Hospital where, by way of an ironic preamble, Zeldine Graham worked and her courageous husband Athol had died, two years earlier.

The *City of Salt Lake* was rebuilt again and on 12 October 1963 driver Harry Muhlbach hurtled the car down the Bonneville course at an estimated 395mph (636kph), when again the car veered out of control, pitched violently, turned and crashed to a halt after sliding upside down for over 1,000ft. Muhlbach survived the crash, but the *City*'s reputation didn't, and both STP and Firestone withdrew their support.

ART ARFONS AND THE GREEN MONSTER

The dream of the Bonneville Salt Flats is a door to the outer limits – a place of strangeness where almost anything can be imagined and almost anything achieved. Hot as the Sahara in the summer and extremely cold in the winter, this huge basin of mineral residue left by prehistoric Lake Bonneville has stood as a natural barrier to travellers since the opening of the US western frontier. Animals avoid it like the plague; birds who fly over it usually perish. But there is one animal that returns religiously to the vast saline plain year after year: the modern speed addict, who finds in the hard, smooth surface the world's most perfect speedway.

John Cobb's 1947 record with the *Railton-Mobil-Special* stood for no fewer than sixteen years, by far the longest tenure by any one man with one car. Apart from the sporadic international class records and the 24-hour endurance races, the opening of the salt flats in 1949 with the first Bonneville National Speed Trials saw the genesis of an era that culminated in the greatest confrontation in the celebrated history of the World Land Speed Record.

From the end of August each year – when the salt is dried out by the hot summer sun – until the November snows, a steady stream of speed enthusiasts flock through Wendover, the only town within 80 miles of Bonneville, with their cars, motorcycles and other exotic vehicular monstrosities. Each one is bent on breaking some kind of world record. Foremost among them is the legendary Ohio hot-rodder, Art Arfons.

The Art Arfons story reads like a chapter from the book of the American dream. It is the story of an Ohio kid with a self-taught

Art Arfons shortly after cementing a new record of 536.71mph (863.71kph) on the hallowed salt flats. (Author's collection)

knowledge of aerodynamics and jet-turbine propulsion systems; a kid who forged an innovative concept into a workable, winning machine – a machine that realized a dream of ending thirty years of British dominance of the World Land Speed Record.

He was born Arthur Eugene Arfons on 3 February 1926 in Akron, Ohio. As a boy, growing up in the pleasant Akron community, the young Arfons' two loves were aeroplanes and hot-rods. He was bright, inquisitive, and his curiosity for all things mechanical was wholly encouraged by his parents. He seemed to have a natural mechanical ability from the beginning. He tore down his first engine at the age of eleven. While a student at Springfield High School, Arfons enrolled for special classes in welding and aircraft mechanics.

In 1943 – aged only seventeen – he persuaded his parents into letting him enlist in the US Navy. After initial training in diesel mechanics, he sailed for the Pacific. In 1945, he piloted a landing barge during the Battle of Okinawa – the largest of the Ryukyu Islands held by the Japanese Imperial fleet. But Arfons' barge was different. He rigged up a motor on the deck so none of his winchmen would be exposed to enemy fire.

After the Second World War, Arfons returned to Akron and the family feed mill. He married June LaFontaine on 14 June 1947. One Sunday afternoon seven years later, Art and June were out for a leisurely drive when they happened upon a drag strip in Akron, Ohio, and his life changed. Arfons' days were now filled with news about such heroes as Art Chrisman, Don Garlits, Dick Griffin and the now legendary Bean Bandits.

Not all drag racing was being done at Muroc Dry Lake, El Mirage or on the salt flats at Bonneville. The wide streets of Los Angeles were a constant temptation, and it wasn't long before the hot-rods were getting the wrong kind of attention. Wally Parks, who later became editor of *Hot Rod Magazine* and founder and president of the National Hot Rod Association, was one of those who realized that for drag racing to survive it needed to improve its image and be self-policed. In 1937 the Southern California Timing Association was formed. Within a year the SCTA had its own paper, the predecessor of *Hot Rod Magazine*. With Muroc, an air base, and Bonneville 800 miles away, drag racing, to stay in business, was forced to move from streets to private strips. The first drag strip opened at Goleta Airport near Santa Barbara, California, in 1948.

When Art Arfons returned home from that Sunday afternoon drive he told his brother Walt about the drag races, and Walt, older by ten years, became just as enthused. Within a week, the Arfons brothers had begun working on their first dragster. First, they acquired the front end of a wrecked 1940 Oldsmobile, fashioned a set of rails and installed an engine. Coupled to this was the rear end of a '37 Packard. The car was completed by the incorporation of a surplus Second World War aeroplane wheel welded to the chassis.

That chance happening upon the hot-rods rumbling down the runway at his local drag strip had a strange effect on the 28-year-old Art Arfons. Within a week, the Second World War veteran entered his first drag race in the three-wheeler, now sporting a covering of green tractor paint. The *Green Monster* as it was dubbed by the race announcer, proved to be a disappointment for the Arfons brothers. On its first run, the dragster shut down halfway down the strip, attaining a mere 85mph on its second try.

The following year, the Arfons brothers *Green Monster No. 2* was hitting speeds in excess of 100mph in Detroit, running against the likes of Otis Smith and George Montgomery in the Middle Eliminator and Little Eliminator titles. Going that fast gave them the confidence they needed to enter the World Series of Drag Racing in Lawrenceville, Illinois. By the

Art Arfons and the Green Monster *at Bonneville, shortly after he cemented his third World Land Speed Record on the morning of 7 November 1965, with a speed of 576.553mph (927.829kph) in two consecutive runs. His faster time during the mile was a fantastic 577.386mph (929.21kph) in the second run, averaging 575.724mph (926.529kph) in the first. He returned the crown to Ohio. (Author's collection)*

In the summer of 1960, Art Arfons left for the Bonneville Salt Flats, with a new car bearing a remarkable resemblance to John Cobb's 1947 Railton-Mobil-Special. Powered by a V12 Allison aero-engine, Arfons' Anteater attained 260mph (419kph) on the salt before gear trouble forced him to retire and return to Ohio. (Art Arfons)

A revealing side view of Art Arfons' Anteater shows the location of the mighty V12 Allison aero-engine in situ atop the massive backbone chassis. (Art Arfons)

time the World Series was over Art had attained a menacing 132.25mph (213.01kph) with the dragster. A further three vehicles followed, before, in 1956, Art and Walt Arfons decided to go their separate ways, leaving the car-building to Art and his boyhood friend, Ed Snyder. Together, Arfons and Snyder turned out *Green Monster No. 6*, which secured Art his third straight World Series victory, but of perhaps greater importance, the Ohio hot-rodder became the first drag racer to break 150mph in the quarter mile in Great Bend, Kansas.

Arfons continued to travel faster and faster, progressing with distinction until 1959 when the National Hot Rod Association moved their Nationals from Oklahoma City to the Motor City's own backyard, the Detroit Dragway. The fastest time of the meet went to Art Arfons in his *Green Monster No. 11* at 172mph (278kph), powered by a V12 Rolls-Royce Merlin 61 aero-engine, originally designed for the North American P-51 fighter plane.

By the summer of 1960, Art Arfons was at the Bonneville Salt Flats with a new car that bore a remarkable resemblance to John Cobb's 1947 *Railton-Mobil-Special*. Powered by a V12 Allison aero-engine, Arfons' *Anteater* attained 260mph (419kph) on the salt before gear trouble forced him to retire and return to Ohio. Arfons did return to Bonneville in 1961, in the hope of some additional shakedown runs. The course was much too short for the *Anteater*, and once again mechanical problems forced him to retire. Nevertheless, he did make a couple of test runs – the best being an otherwise unheard of speed of 313.78mph (505.09kph) for the class in the mile.

To break John Cobb's 1947 record, Arfons, like Dr Nathan Ostich, chose jet power rather than a piston engine. In the winter of 1961, he bought a surplus General Electric J47, 5,200lb thrust turbojet power unit, producing an estimated 8,000hp, and his first jet car, *Cyclops*, was born. The *Cyclops* was quite a crowd-puller with its one 'eye' light piercing the darkness as it reached terminal speeds of 240mph on the drag strips. But the new lance was more than just a dragster. *Cyclops* was also a serious contender for the land speed record.

Arfons added an afterburner and took the car to Bonneville in August 1962. He fell short of the record, but posted the fastest time at the Bonneville National Speed Trials that year with a run of 343.88mph (553.32kph).

To break John Cobb's 1947 record, Arfons, like Dr Nathan Ostich, chose jet power rather than a piston engine. In the winter of 1961, he bought a surplus General Electric J47 5,200lb thrust turbojet power unit, producing an estimated 8,000hp, and his first jet car, Cyclops, was born. He posted the fastest time at the Bonneville National Speed Trials the following year with a run of 343.88mph (553.32kph). It was the fastest anyone had travelled in an open-cockpit car but was short of the record. (Art Arfons)

It was the fastest anyone had travelled in an open-cockpit car. A year later he broke the world quarter mile acceleration record by running 238mph (384kph) at Wingdale Raceway, New York, in the now legendary *Cyclops*.

Art Arfons was an established drag racing celebrity when, in November 1962, while competing in Denver, Colorado, he learned from a dealer that there was a slightly damaged J79, 15,000lb thrust jet power unit for sale for $700 in Florida. Built by General Electric at an original cost of $250,000, the 17,500hp powerplant was intended for use in the Convair B-58 Hustler supersonic bomber and Lockheed F-104 Starfighter aircraft and was capable of air speeds in excess of 1,400mph.

The manufacturers would just as soon have broken it down for scrap, because a large wedge of steel had been run through the impeller blades, and the engine was believed to be worthless. What they hadn't considered was the mechanical genius of racing veteran/inventor Art Arfons. He hung the enormous engine aloft in his workshop in Pickle Road, Akron, Ohio. He and Ed Snyder painstakingly removed the sixty-seven blades one by one, shaping them with a hand file. Those blades damaged beyond repair they discarded, and many good blades were removed to balance the engine. It took them ten days to complete the task, but Arfons now had at his disposal the most powerful engine to hit the Bonneville Salt Flats. Without the cooperation of the manufacturer in supplying spare parts, Arfons and Snyder had worked around the clock and, to the embarrassment of the United States Air Force who discarded it as scrap metal, rebuilt the engine to fine working order.

The Sunday afternoon in South Akron when Arfons first ignited his new engine is still talked about today. Art had put the J79 powerplant in his latest *Green Monster* car upside down, and anchored the car to two

A schematic view of Art Arfons' Green Monster 17,500hp jet engine.

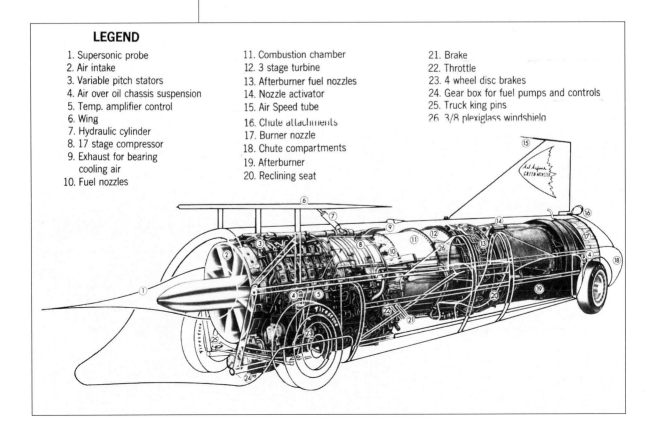

LEGEND

1. Supersonic probe
2. Air intake
3. Variable pitch stators
4. Air over oil chassis suspension
5. Temp. amplifier control
6. Wing
7. Hydraulic cylinder
8. 17 stage compressor
9. Exhaust for bearing cooling air
10. Fuel nozzles

11. Combustion chamber
12. 3 stage turbine
13. Afterburner fuel nozzles
14. Nozzle activator
15. Air Speed tube
16. Chute attachments
17. Burner nozzle
18. Chute compartments
19. Afterburner
20. Reclining seat

21. Brake
22. Throttle
23. 4 wheel disc brakes
24. Gear box for fuel pumps and controls
25. Truck king pins
26. 3/8 plexiglass windshield

GREEN MONSTER

Length:	21ft
Width:	74in
Height:	7ft 2in (from ground to top of tail fin)
Wheelbase:	14ft 2in
Track (front):	65in
(rear)	68in
Weight:	6,500lb
Fuel:	Kerosene
Fuel Tank:	110 gallon capacity. Consumption: circa 68 gallons a minute
Engine:	General Electric J79 turbo-jet power unit with multi-stage afterburner
Chassis:	Chromoly steel tubing, spaced-tubed frame
Body Shell:	Aluminium and carbon fibre
Wheels:	Forged aluminium manufactured by Firestone Steel Products Company
Tyres:	Firestone 7.00–18 'Bonneville'. Inflation: 200lb + psi. Design speed: 750mph
Brakes:	Disc brakes, two 16ft diameter drogue parachutes for added drag at braking phase
Suspension:	Oleo-pneumatic (air over oil) front suspension, unsprung rear axle
Thrust:	15,000lb
Speed Capability:	650mph (1,047kph)+ with afterburner
Max Output:	17,500hp at sea level with afterburner, at 7,800 rpm

trees in his backyard. Directing the exhaust towards the swamp behind his workshop, he ignited the 17,500hp engine. His chicken shed was incinerated in a blinding flash; trees, shrubs and a freshly painted fence were disintegrated. Even without unleashing the four-stage afterburner, the menacing roar of the potent engine rattled windows for over half a mile. The police and fire department responded to emergency calls from the neighbour-hood; converging on Arfons' yard expecting to find a house destroyed by a mysterious explosion, they discovered a smiling Art Arfons testing his latest racing machine.

The *Green Monster No. 14* was a truly massive device, characterized by the demands of a large jet engine and its insatiable appetite for huge quantities of air. In essence the driver became an 'outrider' placed in an aerodynamically inconvenient position either side of the powerplant. The vast frontal intake was interrupted only by a central supersonic proboscis. The vehicle – 21ft in length and 7ft 2in high at the top of the tail fin at the rear – had no rear suspension, simply a 2-ton Ford truck solid axle, with a 1937 Lincoln beam axle incorporating 1951 Dodge truck stub axles at the front, sprung by aircraft-type oleo-pneumatic (air over oil) suspension, with a steering system from a '55 Packard. A large aerofoil was located above the nose, forward of the powerplant to eliminate flight characteristics.

Having designed a jet car around his new engine, Arfons went to his local tyre dealer, which by way of coincidence just happened to be Firestone, asking them to sponsor the wheels. With initial reluctance, Bill

McCrary, head of Firestone's race tyre sales, agreed to provide the wheels and tyres, inaugurating one of the largest single engineering projects in the company's history. Upon completion, Arfons had a $10,000 jet car sitting on $500,000 worth of tyres and wheels. The wheels were of solid forged aluminium, shod with Firestone 7.00–18 'Bonneville' tyres, inflated to 200+lb psi with a design speed of 750mph.

Some twelve months and 5,000 man-hours later, the *Green Monster* was rolled out and the stage was set for the greatest speed duel in automobile history. The contenders were Craig Breedlove, Art Arfons and Tom Green, a young engineer from Wheaton, Illinois, driving Walt Arfons' Westinghouse J46 jet-powered, four-wheeler *Wingfoot Express*. Green was a last-minute replacement at the wheel of this jet car for the owner, 47-year-old Walt Arfons, had suffered a heart attack watching the *Wingfoot Express* crash during trials at a drag strip earlier that year.

On 2 October 1964, Tom Green set a new World Land Speed Record of 413.02mph (664.95kph) on runs of 406.5mph (654kph) and 420.07mph (676kph) for the mile at Bonneville. Three days later, Art replied on his first run through the mile with 394.34mph (635.01kph). On the return run across the salt flats, twenty-five minutes later, he gunned the *Green Monster* to a scorching 479mph (771kph), attaining an impressive 434.02mph (698.455kph) and a new record – using only 60 per cent of the car's potential power.

Two days later, Arfons decided to raise his own record, mindful that Breedlove was waiting in the wings for a crack at the title. On 7 October, Art was roaring through the mile at a staggering 500mph when a right

The Green Monster, *its afterburner blazing, scorches a path towards the timing traps at Bonneville. (Author's collection)*

rear tyre blew. Fighting for control, he managed to bring the car to a halt at the end of the course. Upon inspection, the Firestone engineers found that the pressure of the tyre coupled with engine torque had dug up a stray bolt somewhere on the course, shooting it towards the tyre. Arfons was forced to return to Akron for vital repairs.

In the meantime, Craig Breedlove turned up on the salt with the controversial three-wheeled *Spirit of America* and bettered Arfons' record by 34mph with an average speed of 468.72mph (754.296kph). Forty-eight hours later Breedlove upped the record to an astonishing 526.28mph (846.926kph), before the tricycle lost its drag chute, coming to a water halt in a brine ditch at the end of the salt flats.

Arfons was back at Bonneville by 25 October. Two days later he regained the record with a 536.71mph (863.71kph) average, but the sortie was not without its mishaps. On the return run through the mile, Arfons saw the air-speed indicator dancing around the 600 mark, when he heard an almighty bang. He had blown another rear tyre. He fired his first braking chute, but the tow-line broke. Reducing speed to 400mph he released the second chute and that shredded, leaving him only the foot brake to bring the car to a halt at the end of the course. He was to hold the record for a year.

On 2 November 1965, Breedlove regained his record with a new car, dubbed the *Spirit of America – Sonic I*, averaging 555.483mph (893.921kph). His record lasted only five days. Arfons returned on 7 November and pushed the *Green Monster* to an average speed of 576.553mph (927.829kph) in two consecutive runs. His faster time during

Art Arfons' mighty 17.500hp Green Monster *with braking chute deployed roars out of the speed trap on the Bonneville Salt Flats after cementing a new record of 576.553mph (927.829kph). Eight days later – 15 November 1965 – Craig Breedlove raised the record to 600.601mph (966.528kph) in the* Spirit of America – Sonic I *. (Author's collection)*

the mile was a fantastic 577.386mph (929.21kph) on the second run, averaging 575.724mph (926.529kph) in the first, returning the crown to Ohio. Eight days later – 15 November 1965 – Breedlove hurtled *Spirit of America – Sonic I* to a new World Land Speed Record of 600.601mph (966.528kph).

On his return to Bonneville on 17 November 1966, Arfons made a further run to try to beat Breedlove's 600mph. Using full afterburn he was clocked through the measured mile at 589.597mph (948.862kph), with a terminal speed of more than 615mph. Coming out of the flying mile, wheel failure once again took Arfons' fate beyond his control. The solid forged aluminium right rear wheel held up, but a bearing in the offside front wheel broke, snapping the spindle, and that wheel flew away from the speeding car. The *Green Monster* listed to the right, dug into the salt, and catapulted down the course for more than a mile, scattering wreckage all over the salt. One wheel off the car bounced high in the air and miraculously passed directly through the rotor blades of a press helicopter hovering overhead without hitting anything. Another wheel flew over the United States Automobile Club timing shack. It was later found 4 miles from the scene of the crash. The crew, timekeepers, indeed every soul of the Bonneville contingent, jumped into every available car and truck and converged on the wreckage of the jet car strewn over 3 miles of the course.

Arfons' right-hand man, lifelong friend and project associate, Ed Snyder, wandered aimlessly through the carnage of twisted metal, weeping for his friend, 'Art, Art!' From amidst a pile of tangled wreckage, a blood-stained head emerged and answered, 'Ed, I'm all right!' With that Art Arfons lapsed into unconsciousness. He was found strapped snugly in the seat of the cockpit and to this day credits the central location of the seat and the outrigged cockpit with saving him. It had rotated with the cartwheeling car.

Arfons was flown to St Mark's Hospital in Salt Lake City, 110 miles away. On arrival a doctor in the ambulance shook his head. Here was a man who had crashed at 600mph, but appeared only to have a severely cut face. 'It's amazing,' said Dr Albert Martin who treated Arfons at the hospital. 'He's not as badly off as an average driver in a rear-ender.' The doctor said there were no major fractures, although he thought Arfons might have cracked a cheek bone. Nursing supervisor Jalene Green said he had two small cuts on his face, plus bruises and salt burns. Within an hour of arrival at the hospital Art was taking a shower in his private room when his wife June telephoned. They had called her from the hospital and said, 'It's unbelievable, he's in taking a shower.' June replied, 'Well, if he can take a shower, he can call me on the phone.' Twenty-four hours later Art Arfons, having survived the fastest and most violent crash in automobile history, was on an airliner flying back home to his family in Akron.

As a driver, Arfons realized the risks involved in his sport and these were made all too clear in 1969. Three years after Arfons' near fatal crash at Bonneville, a young driver named Garth Hardacre was killed at a drag strip in Pennsylvania, driving one of Arfons' dragsters.

Arfons' appearance at Dallas, Texas, in October 1971 was to be his last. He had hoped to run the quarter-mile distance at 300mph in his latest jet car – *Green Monster Super Cyclops*. Instead, a tyre blew during a run. The car veered violently out of control, smashing through a safety barrier and into a crowd of spectators, killing three people.

On 15 January 1969, Arfons had triggered his latest *Green Monster* to a new world quarter-mile record from a standing start to 267.05mph (429.774kph) on Firestone's 7-mile high-speed test track facility at Fort

Stockton, Texas. In November of the same year, he hit 273.55mph (440.23kph), with an elapsed time of 5.5 seconds for the quarter-mile, at the Rockingham Speedway, North Carolina.

Arfons planned to return to Bonneville for another crack at the record and in 1975 began working on a revolutionary new vehicle. This was to be a three-wheeled, 5,000lb thrust rocket car, *Firestone Mach 1*, which he believed would carry him past the 1,000mph barrier. However, it never ran and was succeeded by *Green Monster No. 27*, powered by 4,5000lb thrust jet engine.

No sooner, it seems, had Arfons returned home from Bonneville to recuperate from his 1966 crash, than he also made plans for an assault on the World Water Speed Record. He wasn't at home on water and admitted 'I don't like boats really, but I want to prove my theory.' He built an 8,000hp jet boat, the *Green Submarine*. After a relatively short period of water trials in January 1967, on a chemical lake behind Firestone's Akron plant, he abandoned his bid, citing lack of sponsorship.

Art Arfons' contribution to the World Land Speed Record industry did not pass without recognition. On 8 November 1965, he was presented with Utah's first Distinguished Service Medal by Governor Calvin L. Rampton. In making the presentation, Governor Rampton explained that the medal had been created for presentation to 'out-of-staters' who had contributed significantly to Utah's prestige and recognition.

The tangled wreckage of the Green Monster, *shortly after Art Arfons survived a terrifying crash at over 600mph (950kph). Coming out of the flying mile, wheel failure once again took Arfons' fate beyond his control. The right rear wheel held up, but a bearing in the offside front wheel broke, snapping the spindle, and that wheel flew away from the speeding car. The* Green Monster *listed to the right, dug into the salt, and catapulted down the course for more than a mile, scattering wreckage all over the salt. (Art Arfons)*

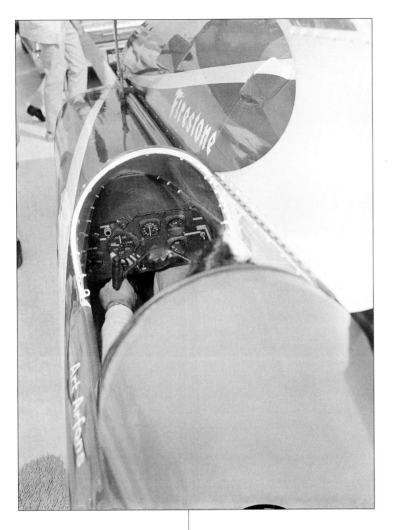

The Green Monster's *shape is characterized by the demands of a large jet engine and its insatiable appetite for huge quantities of air. In essence the driver becomes an 'outrider' placed in an aerodynamically inconvenient position either side of the main 'tube' – a design concept later adopted by Richard Noble in* Thrust 2. *(Author's collection)*

Since then, Arfons has concentrated his efforts on drag racing and competition tractor pulling. His Anheuser-Busch sponsored, jet-powered tractor, also called the *Green Monster* soon became a featured attraction as well as an extremely potent competitor at tractor pulls across the United States. Like his land speed record cars and dragsters, the tractor utilized Firestone tyres, in this case, two monstrous 30.5–32 Firestone All Traction Field & Road Puller tyres on the rear, and two Firestone Champion Guide Grip tyres on the front.

In addition to ranking among the nation's top ten tractor pullers, Arfons and the *Green Monster* won the 12,000lb unlimited national championship of tractor pulling. Unlike fellow competitors at the meet, Arfons' inventive mind, coupled with his flair and initiative, was a contributing factor in his decision to select a jet engine for the tractor: on this occasion, a 3,000hp, Lycoming T-55 powerplant, taken from a surplus Hughey helicopter, reminiscent of his earlier success in the repair and adaption of government-surplus propulsion systems.

In 1978 Arfons, now heavily committed to competition tractor pulling with son Tim, sold the *Green Monster* record car, rebuilt after the 1966 crash, to drag racing veteran and jet-propulsion experimentalist, Slick Gardner of Santa Ines Valley, California. Gardner made a number of modifications to the vehicle, including the emplacement of two horizontal canard fins mounted either side of the fuselage, forward of the driver cockpit. In addition, the vehicle was equipped with Cragar solid forged aluminium wheels, tested to 1,000mph.

For sponsorship, Gardner approached the Los Angeles-based Andersen Company, who, by way of product marketing association, insisted the vehicle should bear their corporate identity. This Gardner conceded and the famed *Green Monster* was renamed *Andersen's Pea Soup Monster*.

Following a series of trials at El Mirage dry lake, California, Gardner took the vehicle to Bonneville with high hopes of eclipsing Gary Gabelich's record of 622.407mph (1,001.664kph) set in 1970. Sadly, however, neither man nor machine was up to the task, and a disappointed Gardner returned to California with the vehicle in tow.

In 1985 Australian speedsters Rosco McGlashan and Loyd Coleman of Mullaloo, near Perth, Western Australia, approached Gardner, as they were contemplating hiring the *Andersen's Pea Soup Monster* for an all-out assault on Australia's then official land speed record of 403.1mph (648.728kph) set by Donald Campbell at Lake Eyre in 1964, but the $500,000 rental Gardner was asking left the duo 'gasping for air', McClashan told this author in 1986. Undaunted, Rosco McGlashan would return for the Australian record in 1994 with his own car, *Aussie Invader 2*, powered by a mighty SNECMA Atar turbojet engine.

In 1984 Arfons was joined on the competition tractor pulling circuit by his daughter Dusty, in the *Dragon Lady*. For the previous 5–6 years Arfons has been competing without a sponsor in a new twin-engined T-64 powered tractor. Then in 1989 Arfons arrived at Bonneville with *Green Monster No. 27*. The new vehicle took four years to construct with the help of his son Tim. It started out as a two-wheeled motorcycle. During test runs on the salt Arfons punched it a little too hard and the vehicle became airborne. At approximately 350–375mph the two-wheeler lifted, spun for about 30ft in the air, landed on its side, and pinwheeled along the course. The bruised and sore Arfons returned to Akron, Ohio, for repairs and returned to Bonneville the following year with a modified *Green Monster No. 27*, now sporting four Alcoa solid forged aluminium wheels in a three-wheel configuration, in that the two 26¼in high front wheels were closely paired. The 16in high rear wheels were outrigged and had a 6½ft wide track for roll stability. Arfons made three passes on the salt and attained a top speed of 359mph (578kph). However, the vehicle developed engine screech problems and Arfons was forced back to his workshop for further modifications.

Arfons returned to Bonneville in 1991 and made two passes on the salt, but every time he hit the burner the car would veer to the right, and with only three degrees of steering, he could not make enough correction. Further attempts at the record were abandoned due to bad weather.

In 1985 Art Arfons received the Glenn Davis Memorial Puller of the Year Award from the United States Hot Rod Association, in recognition of his outstanding contribution to competition tractor pulling. Arfons' son Tim switched to Funny Car pulling in 1984, and is now running jet-powered quads and a radical jet-powered bar stool.

But of Art Arfons, will he return to the land speed record arena with a new bid? Citing Britain's triumphant supersonic run in 1997 with Squadron Leader Andy Green in Richard Noble's *Thrust SSC*, Arfons told this author in 1999, 'I'm afraid you guys [the British] have put the record way out of reach.'

WALT ARFONS – THE FORCE BEHIND THE WINGFOOT CARS

Having parted company with brother Art in 1956, Walt Arfons went on to build a number of cars of his own. He built his first dragster, the jet-powered *Avenger* in 1962, driving the machine – the world's first jet dragster – more than 600 times at speeds well in excess of 200mph.

Walt's closest call with the *Avenger* came at a drag strip in 1963, when the dragster sliced through a cyclone fence, jumped two ditches, veered across a highway and ended up in a conifer plantation 75ft away. Fortunately, he was unhurt. The accident was triggered by parachute failure. His top speed in the quarter-mile with the car was 242mph (390kph), set at Miami, Florida, in 1961. Walt had hoped to set the World Land Speed Record himself, but a heart condition robbed him of a chance at the title.

Walt Arfons and Tom Green, a sales engineer with a Wheaton, Illinois, tool company, conceived the idea for their *Wingfoot Express* record car in the spring of 1962. Arfons built the frame and mounted the Westinghouse J46 triple-jet power unit, and then the car was transported to Green's garage in Elmhurst, Illinois, for completion.

Walt Arfons inspects the jet-pipe of the 6,200lb thrust Westinghouse J46 triple-jet power unit on the Wingfoot Express *shortly before Tom Green made his return run at the mile on Friday 2 October 1964. Within minutes, the record had fallen with a clocking of 420.07mph (676kph). The average speed for the two runs was calibrated at 413.02mph (664.95kph). (Author's collection)*

In 1963, Tom Green was knocked out of contention at Bonneville after only four runs when salt was sucked into the J46 engine intake behind the cockpit. The *Wingfoot Express* had turned a very smooth 250mph (403kph) run when the trouble developed. To prevent a similar occurrence, Arfons and Green added deflectors ahead of the intake to keep the salt spray away from the fragile engine compartment. In addition, canard fins were emplaced on the nose of the vehicle and a tail fin was fitted to improve stability and steering capabilities.

The slender *Wingfoot Express*, with ice cool Tom Green hard on the throttle, roared to a new World Land Speed Record of 413.02mph (664.95kph) on the afternoon of Friday 2 October 1964 on the desolate Bonneville speedway.

It was a tremendous victory for thirty-year-old Green and the car's owner, Walt Arfons, and it came as the lowering sun warned that time on the salt was running out for the duo. That Friday was the last day allotted to the crew of the *Wingfoot Express* to wrest the record from Craig Breedlove, who had achieved 407.45mph (655.696kph) on the same course the previous year in the General Electric J47 thrust jet-powered *Spirit of America*. 'We had to do it Friday because it was our last day on the salt,' a jubilant member of the working crew explained. 'And we did it. The runs on Friday were the fifteenth and sixteenth of the series. What a victory!'

Under instructions from Walt Arfons, at exactly 4.06 p.m. Green started on his south to north run through the measured mile that had dashed so many hopes in the past. The four-wheeled, jet-powered vehicle gradually increased speed and then roared into the measured mile and timing traps. It was clocked on the fifteenth run at 406.4mph (654kph) but the record still hung in the balance.

Without further ado Tom Green, Walt Arfons and the working crew swiftly refuelled, turned the machine around and prepared for the return run at the mile. At exactly 4.47 p.m., Green embarked on his greatest pass. Within minutes, veteran observers of the run sensed that the record had fallen and this was soon verified by the official USAC timers with a clocking of 420.07mph (676kph). The average speed for the two runs was then calibrated at 413.02mph (664.95kph). 'Don't try to arrive at that figure by taking an average of the times on both runs,' Clyde Schetter, the Goodyear publicist explained. 'It won't work out. It's a complicated mathematical telemetry formula the timers use to arrive at the official record speed.'

Walt Arfons' jet car also set the kilometre record of 415mph (667.87kph) based on runs of 415.63 and 414.55mph (668.35 and 667.15kph) through the measured kilometre. 'We don't intend to argue structural design or other engineering matters,' Schetter said. 'It's a "jet-job" but as of right now it's the fastest vehicle in the world.'

Green had carried out four runs over the course prior to the record dash, all of which were made without the additional thrust of the jet-car's afterburner, but he couldn't produce enough power, for his fastest clocking was 297.72mph (479.13kph). With this factor in mind, and knowing time was running out, Arfons ordered the use of the afterburner, and the result . . . a new World Land Speed Record.

Green's wife Patricia and Walt Arfons were the first to greet the triumphant driver as the *Wingfoot Express* rolled to a halt at the far end of the north to south run. 'Everyone was yelling and crying,' Schetter reported. They had a right to yell, for the success was the culmination of three years of research and development, construction and numerous trials on the salt.

The *Wingfoot Express* was powered by a 10,000hp Westinghouse J46 triple-jet power unit, developing an awesome 6,200lb of thrust, with additional power from the afterburner. Weighing in at 42¾cwt and 24ft long, it was a true streamliner, with a partly transparent, tapering nose for maximum observation from an enclosed cockpit, and located at the rear, high above the great maw of the engine unit, was a now familiar sight on the Bonneville Salt Flats – a vertical tail fin. With oleo-pneumatic sprung suspension on all four, curiously small diameter wheels mounting Goodyear tyres, the vehicle skimmed across the salt with a clearance of only 3 in. It would be a year before Walt Arfons returned to Bonneville, this time with a delta-shaped car in which he harnessed the power of rocket propulsion.

In the meantime, Arfons had to be content with helping to achieve the women's World Land Speed Record. Returning to Bonneville in November 1964, he uncrated not only the record-setting *Wingfoot Express*, but also his jet-powered dragster *Avenger*. Paula Murphy, a 29-year-old mother from the San Fernando Valley, California, drove the STP sponsored dragster to a new women's record of 226.37mph (364.02kph), eclipsing her old record of 169.32mph (273.01kph) set in Andy Granatelli's piston-engined *Hawk*. That record was later broken by the intrepid aviatrix Betty Skelton in brother Art Arfons' *Cyclops* jet dragster, and then by Lee Breedlove, Craig's second wife, in the *Spirit of America – Sonic I*.

Turning to a new and revolutionary source of propulsion, Walt Arfons went on to design a massive 5-ton projectile in the form of the *Wingfoot*

Express II, with which he intended to exceed the speed of sound. 'In the span of less than 23 seconds,' Walt said, 'the rocket-propelled car would unleash it's full 28,000 horsepower to demolish the existing record, held by Craig Breedlove in the new *Spirit of America – Sonic I*, a massive jet with twice the power of his badly damaged three-wheeler.' The new *Spirit* boasted 15,000hp from its General Electric J79 thrust jet engine, with a three-stage afterburner.

The *Wingfoot Express II* was undoubtedly the world's first rocket-powered land speed record vehicle. The 28ft, sky blue car was built under sponsorship of the Goodyear Tire & Rubber Company and Arfons announced that it would be driven by Bobby Tatroe, twenty-eight, of Grand Rapids, Michigan, who had driven many of Walt's earlier jet and steam-powered dragsters, including *Neptune* and *Avenger*, on the drag racing circuit across the United States.

Although the *Wingfoot Express II* was designed to break the sound barrier, Arfons said the immediate project objective would be to top the new World Land Speed Record of 536.71mph (863.71kph) posted the previous year by Walt's brother Art in the 17,500hp *Green Monster*. International rules demand that a record must be exceeded by at least one per cent, in this case 5.367mph (8.365kph), which meant the *Wingfoot Express II* would have to average a speed in excess of 542mph (873kph) within two runs through the measured mile. The two runs must be made in opposite directions within the hour.

The earliest Arfons and Tatroe could run on the salt was 19 September in the 1965 season. Walt reserved the saline track for three separate weeks: 19–25 September, 17–23 October and 31 October–6 November.

The previous October Walt Arfons' *Wingfoot Express* had established a new world's record, a record that stood for only three days before a new high was set by his brother. Walt was determined to snatch the record back and was convinced rocket power was the answer to compete successfully with the mighty jet-powered cars of Breedlove and brother Art.

Ultimately, Walt Arfons disclosed, the new *Wingfoot Express II* would attempt to break the sound barrier, which, at Bonneville's altitude would be approximately 750mph (1,207kph). (The speed of sound varies according to altitude and atmospheric conditions.)

Powered by a complement of fifteen Aerojet JATO (Jet Assisted Take-Off) solid fuel rocket 'bottles', the car had a potential power output of 28,800hp. The combined thrust of the rockets totalled 15,000lb, which, it was hoped, would guarantee rapid acceleration at high speeds from transonic to low supersonic. The 35in high tyres had been designed by skilled engineers at the Goodyear laboratories in Akron, Ohio, to perform safely at supersonic speeds, although the reputation of Goodyear was on the line; no one really knew what would happen to

The tyres on Walt Arfons' rocket-powered Wingfoot Express II *were similar to those on Breedlove's* Spirit of America – Sonic I. *These were hand-made 8 × 35in Goodyears of bias-belted construction, with wafer-thin treads, inflated with compressed dry air to 350lbpsi .(Author's collection)*

conventional rubber tyes at such speeds. (As this book will later reveal, no one ever put the concept to the test, it being believed that conventional tyres would simply disintegrate; thus followed the development of solid-forged aluminium tyres in the late seventies by Bill Fredrick of Chatsworth, California.) Goodyear also designed the wheels, brakes and braking parachute system for the new rocket car.

From the tip of the air speed pitot tube on the nose to the top of its bold, vertical tail fin, which towered 9ft in the air, the car was an outstanding example of the aerodynamic design of the day. Although it had four wheels, the sleek projectile had a definite triangular appearance. The two front wheels were paired very close together, and the covered rear wheels were set 13ft apart, with a wheelbase of 15ft 5in and a ground clearance of 15 in.

During the record runs with the *Wingfoot Express II*, Arfons planned to have Tatroe ignite the solid fuel rockets in five stages, with one stage being ignited every two seconds. Arfons estimated that firing the rockets in his car would take no more than 23 seconds for each run.

The car was steered through the front wheels, and a canard fin placed on the nose would add to the stability at high speeds. Most of the bodyshell was constructed in tempered aluminium, although the frontal area, forward of the cockpit, was covered in fibreglass fitted over a robust frame of welded steel.

The new rocket-powered car was tailor-made for Tatroe. To preserve its aerodynamics, the cockpit was built with the interior shaped to Tatroe's own body dimensions (clearly evident in the photographs). Even the reclining seat was form-fitting to the broad-shouldered driver.

Bobby Tatroe sits poised in the cockpit of Wingfoot Express II, *the first rocket-powered land speed record car, before igniting the fifteen Aerojet JATO rockets in the tail, supplemented by five more in each side, to launch him across the desolate Bonneville Salt Flats. The steering was through the front wheels and a canard fin mounted on the nose. The power pack, however, could not deliver sufficient thrust to break the record – a particularly disappointing start to a new era on the salt. (Author's collection)*

Alex Tremulis of Ann Arbor, Michigan, the brilliant designer and aerodynamicist, served as consultant to Walt Arfons during the construction of the car, and it was Tremulis who later rigged the extra rockets on the outside of the vehicle.

Reminiscent of the Chinese mandarin Wan Hu's spectacular ride in a rocket-propelled vehicle in AD 1500, Walt Arfons débuted the world's first rocket-powered land speed record car in a publicity run down the Akron-Canton Airport runway on 15 September 1965. Leaving a trail of fire and blanketing the runway with billowing smoke, the car attained a disappointing speed of 120mph (193kph) propelled by just two of its fifteen rockets. Arfons predicted the unlimited World Land Speed Record was within his grasp. Sadly, he was far from success as the following sequence of events will reveal.

The *Wingfoot Express II* arrived at Bonneville in October 1965, with its team of experimentalists, Walt Arfons and driver Bobby Tatroe, and within two hours the delta-shaped car was ready for its assault on the sound barrier. Tatroe unleashed all fifteen JATO rockets, but only managed a terminal velocity of 247.59mph (398.45kph) from a standing start, clocking a speed for the last 2,000ft of the mile of 406.4mph (653.89kph). Down, but not out, Arfons conceded. 'We'll break the sound barrier yet,' he vowed, and returned to Akron to consult with Alex Tremulis.

Within weeks Arfons returned to Bonneville with ten additional JATO rockets bolted in position either side of the car, igniting at a 30° angle. Because the rockets had a short firing life, it was decided not to ignite them all at the same time. Tatroe was instructed to fire the side rockets first and then to leave an interval of 8 seconds before igniting the rockets at the rear of the car. Bobby Tatroe was literally surrounded by rockets in the tiny cockpit, packing some 50,000hp.

After a delay of 35 minutes caused by heavy rain and high winds, the *Wingfoot Express II* lurched forward slowly at first, overcoming the inertia of nearly 5 tons of weight. To the horror of Alex Tremulis and Walt Arfons, one of the rockets worked loose and fell out of the car, prematurely igniting seven other rockets within the fuselage. Tremulis had expected to see rockets fire out of the rear, instead, the arrow-shaped car was trailing a plume of fire from the top and underside, turning the projectile into a potential fire-ball.

From inside the vehicle Tatroe looked out in disbelief to see he was surrounded by a blazing inferno. The air-speed indicator showed he was travelling in excess of 400mph (644kph), and timing equipment inside the flying mile recorded a terminal velocity of 510mph (821kph). Tatroe managed to maintain control of the car until he could fire the braking chutes. The car came to a halt some 38ft short of the end of the course, looking as if it had been scorched by re-entry into the Earth's atmosphere; but this rocket was launched horizontally. 'When I reached the car,' Tremulis said, 'Walt and Bobby were there together, crying like babies. Their beautiful car was a charred mess. I took one look and started crying too.'

The *Wingfoot Express II* was rebuilt for another try at the record, but in the meantime Craig Breedlove had increased the mark to 555.483mph (893.921kph), and Goodyear cancelled all further runs of the rocket car. Alex Tremulis remained undaunted. He presented a bizarre plan to Goodyear that would make the revolutionary rocket car a symbol of ultimate speed for posterity. 'If we launch her vertically,' he began, quite seriously, 'it has enough thrust to reach a speed of 380 miles an hour at burn out. By that time the car would be 4,000 feet up and would coast to 7,500 feet. On the way down, with that needle-nose configuration it would turn over and return to earth nose-first, impaling itself in the salt.

Where the car lands it would remain forever, to become a most impressive monument to high speed,' he explained, 'much like Robin Hood.'

It was thought by many that the *Wingfoot Express II* saga would see the end of rocket propulsion systems at Bonneville, but while Arfons was counting the cost of his high-speed foray across the salt flats, a team of three young engineers was already working on another rocket-powered car with land speed record potential in downtown Chicago. This was the Institute of Gas Technology-sponsored *The Blue Flame*.

Walt Arfons continued racing for a spell. In 1967, his J46 powered Dodge Dart *Rebellion*, capable of speeds in excess of 200mph in less than 8 seconds, maintained his credibility on the drag racing circuit.

Having introduced the rocket age to land speed racing in 1965, Arfons envisaged another rocket car or steam-powered vehicle. A prototype steam-powered Grand Prix car had already demonstrated tremendous speed potential but was not recognized by the FIA, the world governing body for motor sport and record-breaking. It was hoped Walt's 39-year-old son Craig, of Bradenton, Florida, would pick up the gauntlet, but in 1989 he was killed piloting his *Rain-X Challenger* drag boat on Lake Jackson in Sebring, Florida, in an attempt on Ken Warby's long standing World Water Speed Record of 319.627mph (514.39kph) set on 8 October 1978 on the Blowering Dam Lake at Tamut, New South Wales, in the Speedo-sponsored unlimited hydroplane *Spirit of Australia*.

Last minute instructions are given by owner Walt Arfons to driver Bobby Tatroe as he prepares to pilot the rocket-powered Wingfoot Express II *en route to a place in history. (Author's collection)*

For Walt Arfons, the new vehicle would not only have enabled its owner to invest in the future of land speed record-breaking, but would have rewarded him with the dividend of conceiving it, and, if Walt's son Craig had survived to pick up the gauntlet and race into the future, the force behind the *Wingfoot* cars would have left an indelible mark upon the present.

CRAIG BREEDLOVE – 'THE SPIRIT OF AMERICA'

Craig Breedlove was born on 23 March 1937 with speed in his blood or so it must have seemed when at thirteen years of age he decided he did not want a Christmas present, instead he wanted $35 to purchase a scrap 1934 Ford coupé. He had already saved $40 and his father agreed.

Within two years the young Californian had built his first classic street rod – a chopped and channelled, five-window coupé with a blown flathead V8 and four Stromberg carburettors – that was typical of the engines running on the dry lakes of Muroc and El Mirage in the early days, although Breedlove would have to wait two years until he could hit the streets around the tranquil coastal community of Mar Vista, California. Street racing was the 'in thing' in Southern California. On any given night in the dazzling postwar era hundreds of 'hot-rods' could be found in the drive-ins around Los Angeles. Picadilly's drive-in was one of the first and most popular in the Los Angeles area at the end of the war. It nestled in the corner of Washington Place and Sepulveda Boulevard and at the witching hour, it resembled the present day pits of a major drag race meeting.

When Breedlove was sixteen he took his hot-rod to the Bonneville Salt Flats and achieved a mean 154mph (248kph) on alcohol, taking his neighbourhood car club, the Igniters, into eighth place with 112mph (180kph) in the quarter mile.

Breedlove graduated from Venice High School, California, majoring in drafting and machine shop, 'so I could build parts for my racing cars'.

Craig Breedlove's pride and joy – a chopped and channeled, five-window '34 Ford coupé he built himself before he was old enough to drive it. (Craig Breedlove)

Fresh out of school, he spent his time around the drag strips and the legendary dry lakes of Rosamond, Harper, Buckhorn and Muroc, high in the Mojave Desert region of Southern California – places well known to all associated with the sport of hot-rodding. But Craig Breedlove was eventually to aim for much faster cars than the cut-down Fords, Chevys and Mercurys so beloved of the hot-rodders.

In the years following his departure from high school, Breedlove took a job with the Douglas Aircraft Corporation, where he learned the skills of structural engineering as a technician. Then in 1960, he changed tack and joined the Costa Mesa fire department, where as a fireman he found excitement and worth:

> I didn't think I was accomplishing anything at Douglas. I wanted to do something more important, more exciting. I began thinking that a lot of young Americans were just as good at designing and building cars and souping up engines as were the racing teams of Europe. I became convinced that we could build a car that would capture the unlimited World Land Speed Record for the measured mile. After all, we lacked only backing.
>
> These ideas gradually jelled into the *Spirit of America* project. Deciding on the car's name was easy; the name tells the whole story.
>
> But it wasn't easy for a 22-year-old guy with no college education to go to a company and get them to believe in your idea.

Meanwhile, Breedlove's plans for such a vehicle were gradually forming. His first thoughts were of a conventional, piston-engined streamlined racing automobile, when he happened upon a surplus General Electric J47 engine in a crate in the loading bay of the firehouse. The engine was up for sale and Breedlove could not resist the $500 asking price, knowing that he could buy lots more horsepower for more or less the same price in a jet engine. Furthermore, a jet-powered car would be simpler and far more efficient at the high speeds he had in mind.

Breedlove drew up plans for such a car but realizing his limitations as a designer, he turned to experts for help. Through his enthusiasm, he enlisted Rod Shapel, an automobile designer and aerodynamicist at the Task Corporation, for the blueprints, Walt Sheehan, a jet-propulsion engineer with Lockheed, and Art Russell, a model builder for Revell, who carved a ⅛ scale model of the car out of pine for wind-tunnel tests. More than 100 wind-tunnel tests were carried out at Cal Tech for specific design analysis and improvement.

At this point in time, two years after the start of the project, Breedlove's meagre resources ran out. Married at seventeen, he was divorced at twenty-two, the father of three young children. 'My wife didn't understand what was burning inside me to do these things. Everybody wants to do something. People who haven't any drive never get anything done.' However, Craig's second wife, Lee (they were divorced in 1968) understood exactly what he wanted. She had two children by a previous marriage and shared his passion for speed. She was just the kind of encouragement Breedlove needed to fulfil his dreams.

Breedlove tried to interest many major companies in the *Spirit*, but met with little success, until the October of 1961. Casting about for potential sponsors, he walked into the Santa Monica district office of Shell. Under one arm he carried a project brochure, under the other was a box containing Art Russell's scale model of his unique racer. The rest is history, as he recalls. 'I showed up at the Santa Monica district office of the Shell Oil Company and asked to see the manager. I waited for about

40 minutes, when I heard the receptionist call "Mr Breedlove . . . Mr Lawler will see you now." I then went in.' Thinking Mr Breedlove was a member of the company's corporate board of directors, district manager Bill Lawler offered to give him 10 minutes, which in terms of the LA business philosophy of 'time is money' meant that Lawler expected the visitor from head office to take no more than 5 minutes.

Two hours later Craig Breedlove emerged from the office with a smile on his face and a sponsorship pledge from a man he had never met before, let alone discussed corporate funding with. Lawler, by now realizing this was not the Breedlove he had expected, was so impressed with the young Californian's fluent knowledge of aerodynamics, structural analysis and metallurgy that knew he would be backing a winner. Within months he had convinced his peers that the possibility of backing a jet-powered car of unbelievable power to attack the British grasp on the coveted World Land Speed Record was not only a viable investment, but of national interest. Within three months, the Goodyear Tire & Rubber Company was enlisted as co-sponsor and agreed to design and build the 48-in tyres, wheels and brakes.

Breedlove's partly-completed machine was moved from the garage behind his home to the shop of a leading builder of custom racing cars. For months the work continued. . . .

Then in August 1962, the $250,000 *Spirit of America* was loaded on to a trailer and brought to the desolate Bonneville Salt Flats. Accompanying the vehicle was an expert working crew of more than twenty men and women, equipped with everything from a complete machine shop to spare parts. Breedlove had incorporated theories in the design of the car that had yet to be proven on the salt. The *Spirit of America* weighed nearly 3 tons, stood 6ft 2in high at the top of the cockpit canopy, was 35ft in length and 11ft wide. It resembled a grounded jet fighter with its tricycle undercarriage down and its wings removed. It was supported by only three wheels, the single front wheel was partly recessed under the nose, and the rear wheels, outrigged on a faired dead axle, were fully

A schematic view of Craig Breedlove' three-wheeled Spirit of America, *showing the aft location of the General Electric J47 5,200lb thrust jet power unit. It resembles a jet fighter without wings.*

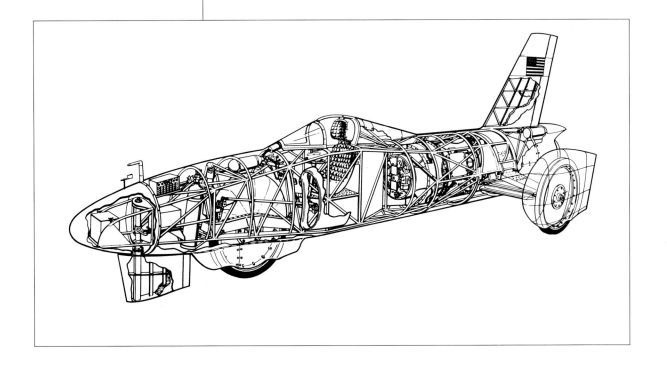

streamlined. All were non-steerable. Breedlove planned to steer by braking the two rear wheels independently from floor-mounted pedals at speeds up to about 150mph. From then on a canard fin under the nose was expected to provide enough bite in the slipstream to provide control via a conventionally mounted steering wheel. All braking was by parachute.

Breedlove did not seem concerned that the *Spirit* was a pure jet-driven three-wheeler and thus would not comply with the Fédération Internationale de l'Automobile's stipulation that a successful land speed record vehicle must have at least four wheels, two of them driven, to get official recognition. Ironically, Breedlove would later condemn Bill Fredrick and Hal Needham's *Budweiser Rocket* car as a 'publicity stunt', complaining that their three-wheeler, driven by Stan Barrett in 1979, had 'roared through the rulebook'. He added, 'I don't like the public relations campaign to adjust the format to fit the effort.'

The *Spirit of America* began its low speed trials on 19 August 1962. Here, on this table-flat, dried-up bed of Lake Bonneville, Breedlove drove his new thoroughbred to an estimated 300mph (483kph) but, as could be expected, numerous bugs showed up. Light crosswinds caused the car to veer from the marked course and the differential braking on the rear wheels was unable to correct the veering.

The only recourse was to go 'back to the drawing board'. New technical engineering expertise was called in. The *Spirit of America* was modified in various ways: the front wheel was made steerable through 2° in each direction; a 6ft high vertical tail fin was added to increase stability and move the centre of pressure to the rear (this also helped to counteract yaw tendencies); the Goodyear industrial-tyre disc brakes were rigged to work from a single brake pedal; the throttle linkage was arranged for either hand or foot operation, where formerly it was operated only by hand, thus leaving Breedlove to steer the massive jet-car with only one hand during operation.

Late in July 1963 the *Spirit of America* and her crew were back at the Bonneville Salt Flats. Numerous test runs and minor adjustments were made and after a week of teething problems the car was ready. Shortly before dawn on the morning of 5 August 1963, Craig Breedlove climbed into the cramped cockpit, closed the canopy, depressed the throttle to a setting that represented approximately 90 per cent of its maximum 4,000lb thrust, and the *Spirit* moved slowly forward down the carefully graded 8 mile long, 100ft wide course. At that moment, he had driven the car no fewer than 200 miles in a series of twenty-two separate runs.

That first run through the measured mile was made at an official speed – timed by the United States Automobile Club – of 388.47mph (625.18kph). Quickly the car was turned around, refuelled and started on its return run. This time Breedlove set the throttle at 95 per cent of power. He roared through the measured mile at an unbelievable 428.37mph (689.39kph). The average for the two runs, calculated from the elapsed time of the two, was 407.45mph (655.696kph). The young Craig Breedlove had broken the World Land Speed Record, set sixteen years before by John Cobb. . . . He was the fastest man on wheels!

In the timing stand were officials of the Fédération Internationale Motocycliste (FIM), which is the official European and world governing body that sanctions all two and three-wheeled World Land Speed Record competitions, and which was prepared to accept Breedlove's three-wheeled jet record. All previous records were set by conventional four-wheeled vehicles, and ratified under the rules of the FIA, who did not recognize Breedlove's record.

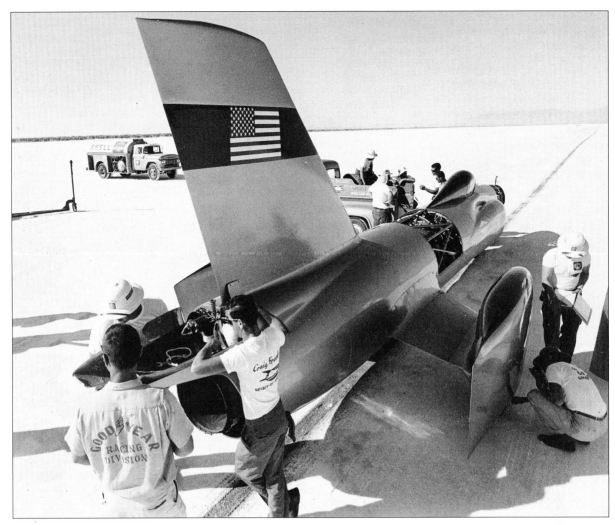

Final preparations: the crew of the Spirit of America *makes a final check shortly before the record-breaking run at Bonneville on 5 August 1963. Riggers double-check the drag chute installation above the great maw of the jet exhaust, while Goodyear tyre engineers make sure the 4ft-tall tyres have exactly 250psi inflation. (Author's collection)*

Above: *Craig Breedlove enters the cockpit of* Spirit of America *prior to setting a new World Land Speed Record of 407.45mph (655.696kph) on the 5 August 1963. At that moment, he had driven the car no fewer than 200 miles in a series of twenty-two separate runs. (Author's collection)*

Opposite: *Shortly before dawn on the morning of 5 August 1963, Craig Breedlove climbed into the cramped cockpit of* Spirit of America, *closed the canopy, depressed the throttle to a setting that represented approximately 90 per cent of its maximum 4,000lb thrust, and the* Spirit *moved slowly forward down the carefully graded 8-mile-long, 100ft-wide course. (Author's collection)*

Indeed, to this day, one of Craig Breedlove's most cherished possessions hanging on the wall in his office at Spirit of America World Land Speed Record Team Inc., in Rio Vista, California, is a gold medal presented to him at the Autumn Congress of the FIM in London in 1963. The inscription reads: 'Craig Breedlove – World Record – Fastest on Wheels'. In addition, Breedlove has often said, 'I would take the car out again tomorrow if there was any question as to the validity of the record.'

As far back as 1954 Captain George E.T. Eyston had predicted that the next holder of the record would be an American hot-rodder who learned his craft during the Bonneville National Speed Trials. As it transpired, he was right, for Craig Breedlove was the holder who succeeded John Cobb. But Breedlove was not satisfied. He had his eyes firmly set on that magical mark of 500mph. 'I don't think the limit has been reached yet. I think I can go faster,' he said. 'The course was bumpy, but the car held up well under the punishment.' He convinced Shell and Goodyear that such a speed was attainable with the *Spirit of America*.

So, late in 1963, after the furore over his controversial achievement had subsided, Breedlove and his team of experts went back to work on their creation. The *Spirit* was given a new General Electric J47 engine with 5,700lb of thrust – an increase of 500lb more thrust over the 5,200lb produced by the previous unit. The nose was given a more streamlined configuration. New wheels and tyres were installed, though not because of wear, for the previous set had been used throughout his earlier runs. They were taken out of service by his sponsor for historical and exhibition purposes. The braking pressure was also increased.

Meanwhile, in Paris, the FIA declared the *Spirit of America* was not an automobile and referred all questions concerning recognition of the record to the FIM in Geneva, Switzerland, who welcomed the sudden attention. Having sanctioned the *Spirit of America* at Bonneville, the FIM promptly created a turbine class to accommodate the three-wheeler.

In the meantime, others had their sights set on the Breedlove record. Walt Arfons of Akron, Ohio, prepared to run his Goodyear sponsored *Wingfoot Express*. His brother Art was ready again with the *Green Monster*. Heavy rains on the Bonneville Salt Flats delayed the 1964 speed attempts for months . . . a problem all too familiar to land speed record contenders. Not until late September was the course in shape for trials.

First to attack the record was Walt Arfons and his *Wingfoot Express*, driven by Tom Green of Elmhurst, Illinois, who raised the record to 413.02mph (664.95kph) on the afternoon of Friday 2 October. Three days later, Art piloted his famous *Green Monster* twice through the measured mile, averaging 434.02mph (698.455kph) using only 60 per cent of the car's potential power.

His 1963 record exceeded twice in three days, Breedlove arrived back on the salt with his working crew on 11 October. Around-the-clock testing and tuning made the *Spirit of America* ready for its initial timed trials on 13 October. Repeating his procedure of 14 months previous, Breedlove climbed into the cockpit, fastened his helmet and safety harness; he watched as the cockpit canopy was closed above him. Alone he sat, waiting to regain his cherished record.

This year he had one more factor working in his favour. The hydraulic pressure on the Goodyear brakes had been increased so he could hold the car motionless while he primed its mighty jet-engine to the required acceleration speed. With the brakes released, the *Spirit of America* hurtled down the course toward the distant measured mile, 4½ miles away. Through the timing traps it roared at ever-increasing speed. Once past the second marker in the mile, Breedlove released the drag chute, which pulled

his speed down to around the 150mph point where he could begin to apply his foot brake by means of a slow pumping action until the car came to a gentle halt at the end of the glistening salt. His speed – 442.59mph (712.27kph).

While the Shell special turbine fuel was poured in for the return run, Breedlove made a number of minor adjustments to the car, in particular the throttle setting. This time he launched the *Spirit* through the timing traps at 498.13mph (801.66kph). His average speed – again calculated on the time required to make the two runs – 468.72mph (754.296kph). Breedlove was once again the fastest man on wheels! But neither he nor his crew was satisfied. He hadn't used the full power available from his jet engine. The track was very rough and needing additional grading. With several minor adjustments, and given the right track and weather conditions, the *Spirit of America* team was certain Breedlove would top the elusive 500mph barrier.

For 48 hours, almost without pause, the team of experts and mechanics laboured over the *Spirit*. It was tuned to absolute micrometric fineness. Early on 15 October, Breedlove's all-out assault was made. Down the course he raced, roaring toward the electronic timing equipment each side of the measured mile. Faster than man had ever gone before he sped past the markers. His speed – 513.33mph (826.12kph). Again came the fast turnaround, the refuelling, and the resetting of the throttle to an even

A parking problem for Craig Breedlove at his home in Costa Mesa, California, shortly before setting off for Bonneville to regain his title as the fastest man on earth in the first Spirit of America. *(Author's collection)*

The Spirit of America *braking safely with the assistance of its drag parachute after the first run through the mile at Bonneville. (Author's collection)*

On 15 October 1964, Craig Breedlove broke his own record at 526.28mph (846.926kph), only to lose his braking parachutes, which robbed the car of its essential braking power. Spirit of America demolished two telegraph poles in a 6 mile skid, leapt into the air and finished up in a brine ditch at the end of the salt flats. Climbing out of the submerged car, Breedlove quipped bravely, 'What a ride . . . For my next trick I'll set myself afire!' (Author's collection)

greater speed level. This was surely it! Equal or exceed his timed speed on the first run, and he would be the first man ever to establish a 500mph record in a land-bound vehicle.

To the spectators and project working crew posted far back from the race course, it appeared he was 'in the groove', speeding faster than any man before him. As he rocketed past the marker at the end of the measured mile, they watched for his drag chute to billow out behind the hurtling jet-car. But it didn't. Breedlove was reducing speed when, at 500mph (800kph), the Deist braking parachutes broke away, robbing the hurtling car of its essential braking power. The *Spirit of America* demolished two telegraph poles in a 6 mile (9.6km) skid. Breedlove opened the cockpit canopy seconds before the car nose-dived into a brine ditch at the end of the vast salt flats; he swam to the shore unhurt. Whether Breedlove had set a new World Land Speed Record or not was forgotten. The brave young man and his safety was the only concern. . . .

What happened? Let Craig Breedlove tell you in his own words:

I felt the car start to slide in the measured mile and knew that I had to stop as soon as possible. When I saw the sign at the end of the mile, I hit the drag chute button.

The chute ripped right off and I immediately hit the emergency chute button. This chute came loose just as fast. My first reaction was to hit the brakes. At 500mph they didn't begin to slow the car. [Those brakes were designed to stop the car after it had been slowed down to a velocity of 150mph (240kph) by the drag chutes; they burned out in seconds at 500mph (800kph).]

I knew I was in serious trouble. Then I saw a telegraph pole right in front of me. . . . I was running out of track. . . . I knew I couldn't miss it. That pole shattered like a toothpick.

When I didn't flip then, I said to myself, 'I've got another chance.' Then I ploughed through a quarter mile of shallow water and through an 8ft-high dirt bank at the end of the salt flats.

The car hurtled through the air and into an 18ft-deep pool of brackish water on the other side of the dyke.

To go through all of this and then drown really scared me. I pushed hard on the car's cockpit canopy. It flipped off and I was able to swim out of the cockpit, now filling with water, to safety. Thank God the car and its tyres held up through all that, or I'd have been a goner for sure.

Climbing out of the submerged car, Breedlove quipped bravely, 'What a ride . . . For my next trick I'll set myself afire!' Craig Breedlove was no stranger to the performing arts. His father, Norman, was a motion picture studio special effects man. His mother, Portia, worked at the studios as a dancer, performing with the likes of Fred Astaire and Ginger Rogers.

The speed through the measured mile on that radical return was an incredible 539.89mph (868.86kph). The official speed for the required twin runs was 526.28mph (846.926kph), equal to the cruising speeds of the newest, most sophisticated jet airliners.

In the autumn of 1965, Breedlove showed up again on the salt stage, with a new car: a 4½-ton monster named *Spirit of America – Sonic I*, at first thought to be capable of travelling faster than the speed of sound. Its rocket-like configuration, Breedlove explained, was designed to slice

Flame blasts from the afterburner of the General Electric J79 15,000lb thrust jet power unit of the Spirit of America – Sonic I *at full power on a test bed. (Author's collection)*

through the shock waves that build up as a car approaches the sound barrier (720mph, 1,158kph at Bonneville's altitude). The new *Spirit of America* was powered by a General Electric J79 thrust jet engine, the same unit used in the Lockheed F-104 Starfighter aircraft. Breedlove picked it up as government surplus in Charlotte, North Carolina, for $7,500. New, it cost the US government a staggering $175,000.

With the help of some friends, Breedlove had designed the car around the 15,000lb thrust jet power unit and supervised its construction in six months. Once again, confident of his success, Goodyear agreed to foot most of the bill, which was close to $200,000. Before the 1965 season drew to a close, however, the costs to Goodyear had risen beyond $500,000.

To satisfy the FIA, the new *Spirit* had four wheels with a diameter of 25in at the front and 39in at the rear, shod with special Goodyear low-profile tyres with a design speed of 850mph. The front axle was a tubular beam with torsion bar springing, while the rear suspension was independent, also sprung by torsion bars. The single-disc, caliper-type braking system was developed by the Aviation Products Division of Goodyear, and the disc brakes were of forged steel, ⅝in thick and with a diameter of 18in. There were two calipers per brake, each with two friction surfaces. Braking was complete by a Hemis-Flo drag parachute also developed by Goodyear.

The vehicle's waisted centre later earned it the nickname 'the Coca-Cola bottle', regardless of the superior engineering and otherwise streamlined appearance. The new *Spirit* was clearly designed from the ground up for unlimited speed. Its rectangular body form, smoothly clad in fibreglass and machined aluminium, commenced at the taper nose with a supersonic probe and culminated at the tip of a sharply raked tail fin, riding high above the vast expansion skirt of the J79 exhaust outlet at the rear. Breedlove's form-fitting cockpit was slightly forward of the front wheels under the intake of the jet power unit. Steering was by pistol-grip instead of conventional wheel.

The car had bugs in it from the start. At speeds over 500mph (800kph), the aluminium panels rippled as if they wanted to tear off. Wheel wells twisted and buckled, once nearly blowing out a rear tyre. 'We're just going to have to bullet-proof the whole damn car,' Breedlove announced when a 534mph run put a man-sized dent in the front cowling, and it was all Breedlove could do to keep the car on the ground. Once on a record run, the front of the car went airborne at more than 600mph and the new *Spirit of America – Sonic I* veered off the Bonneville speedway out of

Craig Breedlove and a technician from the Aviation Products Division of the Goodyear Tire & Rubber Company, discuss the single-disc, caliper-type braking system of the Spirit of America – Sonic I. *The disc brakes were of forged steel, ⅝in thick and 18in in diameter. There were two calipers per brake, each with two friction surfaces. In the background, the fibreglass air intake duct to the General Electric J79, thrust jet power unit takes shape. (Author's collection)*

Above: *High speed stress shows both in the* Spirit of America – Sonic I *and the face of driver Craig Breedlove. Breedlove explains to newsmen and fellow land speed record driver Bobby Tatroe (far right) the state of the damage the car suffered during a run of 534mph. The stress caused the top seams to buckle slightly, as seen in the foreground. Tatroe drove the rocket-powered* Wingfoot Express II, *built by Walt Arfons of Akron, Ohio, under Goodyear sponsorship. (Author's collection)*

Right: *Craig Breedlove and his crew worked around the clock after the* Spirit of America – Sonic I *was damaged at Bonneville in 1965. 'We're just going to have to bullet-proof the whole damn car,' he announced when a 534mph run put a man-sized dent in the front cowling. Breedlove is seen here applying fibreglass to the damaged air-duct that leads to the intake of the jet engine. (Author's collection)*

In the autumn of 1965, Craig Breedlove returned to the Bonneville Salt Flats, with a new car – a 4½-ton monster named Spirit of America – Sonic I. *At first thought to be capable of travelling faster than the speed of sound, the Goodyear-sponsored car carried him past the 600mph barrier on 15 November 1965, with a two-way average speed of 600.601mph/966.528kph in the mile and the kilometre. (Author's collection)*

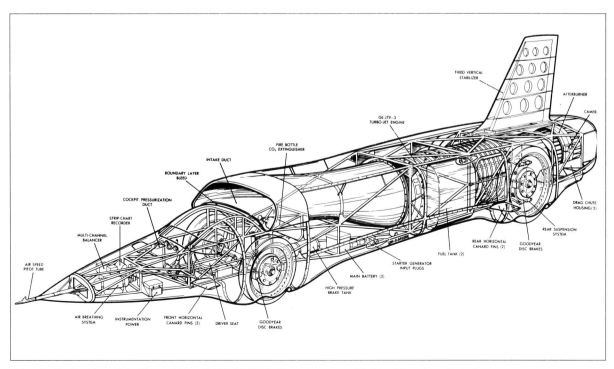

A longitudinal section of the General Electric J79 15,000lb thrust jet-powered Spirit of America – Sonic I.

control. Both braking parachutes were torn off the car, but Breedlove managed to pump his brakes and bring the car to a stop just 300ft from the brine ditch where he had dunked the first *Spirit of America* in 1964. Unnerved by his second hair-raising experience, Breedlove fastened two large aerodynamic spoilers on the nose of the car to keep it on the ground at high speeds. Back on the salt stage on 2 November 1965, Breedlove raced to a two-way average of 555.483mph (893.921kph). He had got his record back!

The record didn't stand long. Art Arfons hurried back to the salt flats, set up camp on the morning of 7 November, and before one o'clock in the afternoon, had upped the speed to 576.553mph (927.829kph) in two wild death-defying runs through the measured mile. Coming out of the measured mile on the last run, Arfons' car, the *Green Monster*, blew a right rear tyre. The explosion was heard for miles across the Bonneville Salt Flats. Some spectators at first thought Arfons had broken the sound barrier. The blow-out ripped out a huge chunk of the right rear cowling, much of the wheel well, blasted loose the entire parachute braking system on the right-hand side – casing and all – and embarrassed Arfons' sponsors, the Firestone Tire & Rubber Co., who had earlier said in a public announcement that the tyres were good up to 800mph. It was the third blow-out for the *Green Monster* in three record runs in 1964 and 1965. Each time it was the right-hand rear tyre.

'It sounded like a bomb going off,' said Arfons. 'I knew that it was all right. I've heard that sound before.' Now on three wheels and a rim, the *Green Monster* careered down the speedway, crashed into a steel-pipe track marker, popped its emergency chute, and rolled to a stop. Arfons climbed out of the cockpit and walked in a daze around his car. He swore! His working crew and spectators arrived. 'How are you, how do you feel?' asked a visibly shaken reporter. 'I feel fine,' Arfons said, 'but I seem to have broken my car.'

He had the record once again, but this time his supremacy lasted exactly eight days. With winter storms already pushing across the Rocky Mountains, Craig Breedlove and his crew were back with the *Spirit of America – Sonic I*, this time with just about every panel in the car reinforced with structural aluminium. Breedlove set up camp in a drizzling rain and then waited for a break in the weather. It came on 15 November. At 8.10 a.m. the United States Automobile Club gave Breedlove track clearance. He fired up the powerful jet engine, closed the canopy over his now familiar star-spangled helmet, and roared down the carefully graded track, leaving behind the eye-burning orange and red flame of his afterburner and a ghostly spray of white salt. The *Spirit* screamed through the measured mile in just over 6 seconds at an average speed of 593.178mph (954.02kph) in the mile and 597.03mph (960.12kph) in the kilometre – faster than Arfons' record, but a little shy of the 600mph (965kph) goal that Breedlove had set for himself.

Coming out of the mile, Breedlove popped his braking chute. It held momentarily, then filled up with salt water on the wet north end of the salt flats and collapsed, but the driver once again was able to stop with his brakes, just short of the red flag marking the end of the salt and the beginning of the soft, crusted mud flats of Lake Bonneville.

With 20 minutes left in the hour time limit, Breedlove and crew refuelled the *Spirit of America*, turned it round, and towed it to the 11½ mile mark on the speedway. This would give him a 5½ mile speed build-up before the first timing light, a half mile more than on the first run. Once Breedlove fired up the jet disappeared down the track trailing a plume of salt behind. This time he streaked through the mile in just under

6 seconds at an amazing 608.201mph (978.478kph) in the mile and 604mph (971.328kph) in the kilometre. The two-way average, 600.601mph (966.528kph) in both the mile and the kilometre, made him the first man in the world to crack the 600 mark. He was also the first over 400 and 500mph. The early Beach Boys album 'Little Deuce Coupe' immortalized Craig Breedlove in the song 'Spirit of America', in which the lyrics of Brian Wilson crowned him the 'King of All Cars'.

When asked what the ultimate speed would be, Breedlove said that by using maximum afterburner his car could go in the high 600s, 'but it'll never break the sound barrier,' he admitted. 'We're a long way from that. It's going to take something entirely different in the basic design and overall configuration of the car to go that fast.'

Within three days, Lee, the 28-year-old wife of Breedlove set a new women's World Land Speed Record of 308.56mph (496.57kph) at the Bonneville Salt Flats. Lee Breedlove drove the *Spirit of America – Sonic I* to the record during runs of 288.02mph (463.52kph) and 332.26mph (534.71kph) through the measured mile. The run, marking the first time a woman had travelled faster than 300mph in an official measured mile, eclipsed the previous timed record of 277.15mph (446.02kph) set earlier the same year by Betty Skelton in Art Arfons' *Cyclops* jet dragster.

From Akron, Ohio, Arfons conceded that the *Green Monster* wouldn't be repaired until December '65, and couldn't be raced until January 1966 at the earliest, but few veteran Bonneville racing buffs thought there could be any racing on the salt flats in midwinter, when the water table on the speedway is at its highest and winter storms blast across the Great Basin

Spirit of America – Sonic I thunders across the salt flats at Bonneville, with Craig Breedlove at the controls. In two runs through the measured mile – one at 593.178mph, and the second at 608.201mph – Breedlove established a new World Land Speed Record of 600.601mph (966.528kph). (Author's collection)

with unpredictable, icy fury. From all indications it looked as though Craig Breedlove was now the undisputed Land Speed King of the World.

For a while he had fame and glory, but the tides of time and destiny began to turn on the dashing, patriotic champion of the American people. In the years that followed, Breedlove's personal life fell to pieces. He lost a lucrative contract with the American Motors Corporation, and as if that wasn't enough for the young Californian, a torrential storm and ensuing flood destroyed his entire workshop in Torrance, near Los Angeles, the birthplace of the two *Spirits*, destroying just about everything he owned and cherished, including two prized jet-turbines. Breedlove lost almost everything, but not his gusto and fighting determination. He gathered what remained of his tattered life and embarked on a new career in property. Over a period of time he rebuilt his workshop, made a number of successful investments in Baja, California, and began working on a rocket dragster.

Breedlove knew that another crack at the record would require rocket propulsion to deliver the required thrust. To test his theory he called on Jerry Elverum and Ron Gardner, whose experience of rocket propulsion and telemetry would prove invaluable in the engineering and design of a prototype liquid-fuel rocket system for the dragster. Within a year, Craig Breedlove realized his dream of driving his own rocket dragster, the *English Leather Special*, on the famed Bonneville speedway. The year was 1973.

Craig Breedlove explains the controls of the jet-powered Spirit of America – Sonic I *to his 28-year-old wife, Lee. She drove the car to a new women's World Land Speed Record of 308.56mph (496.57kph) during runs of 288.02mph (463.52kph) and 332.26mph (534.71kph) through the measured mile at Bonneville. The run, marking the first time a woman had travelled faster than 300mph in an official measured mile, eclipsed the previous timed record of 277.15mph (446.02kph) set earlier the same year by Betty Skelton in Art Arfons'* Cyclops *jet dragster. (Author's collection)*

Above: *By the end of September 1981, with the team behind it full of hope and optimism,* Thrust 2 *was shipped out to the hallowed Bonneville Salt Flats. The team was intent on breaking Gary Gabelich's long-standing record. Driving the gold, white and red machine on its aluminium wheels across the salt proved to be an 'utter nightmare' for the indefatigable Richard Noble. (Author's collection)*
Below: *Nine years after he dreamed the impossible dream, Britain's Richard Noble sped across the Nevada desert at near supersonic speed to notch up a new record of 633.468mph (1,019.465kph) after nineteen years of American dominance. (Castrol International)*

Above: *Designed by Ron Ayers, Thrust SSC had to be a research vehicle long before it became a record breaker. (Castrol International)*
Below: Thrust SSC *was a tribute to Ron Ayers' design genius, as the sleek lines of the car reveal. It is seen here being refuelled for the second leg of the supersonic record run, 15 October 1997. (Castrol International)*

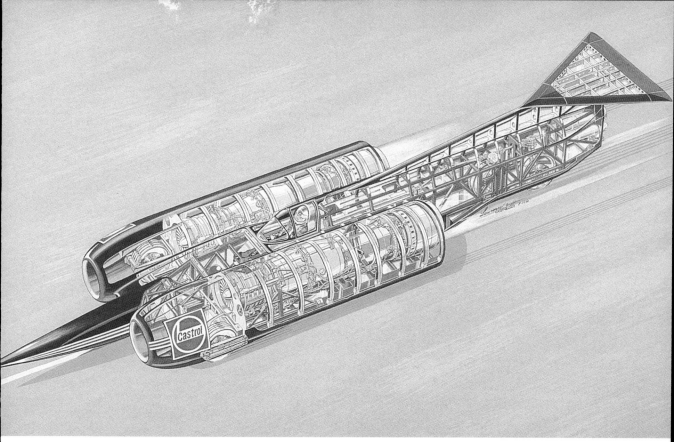

Above: *A cutaway section of Thrust SSC showing the location of the two Rolls-Royce Spey 202 engines. Producing 110,000hp, and yielding a combined afterburn thrust of around 50,000lb, the powerplants were slung well forward of a central monocoque fuselage, housing the cockpit. (Castrol International)*

Below: *The cockpit of Thrust SSC. Andy Green played a key role in designing the layout of the instruments and controls, now familiar to him at speeds of up to 771mph. (Castrol International)*

On 15 October 1997 Andy Green, *shoehorned into a marvel of motion engineering, roars towards the sound barrier in Richard Noble's* Thrust SS

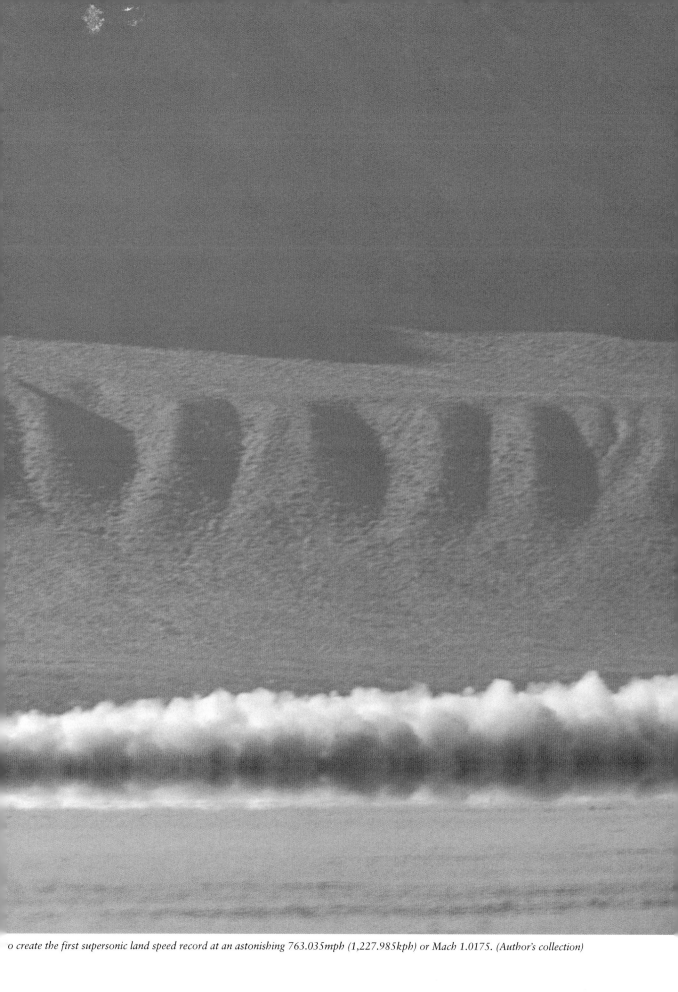

o create the first supersonic land speed record at an astonishing 763.035mph (1,227.985kph) or Mach 1.0175. (Author's collection)

Andy Green emerges from the cockpit of Thrust SSC *shortly after taking Richard Noble's thirteen-year-old record from 633.468mph (1,019.465kph) to a staggering 714.144mph (1,150kph), consuming fuel at the rate of 4 gallons per second. He shattered Gary Gabelich's 630.338mph kilometre record, which Noble had just missed with* Thrust 2. *(Castrol International)*

'The Fastest Men on Earth' – a remarkable photograph by Peter Brock of the exclusive '600mph CLUB' at Gerlach, Nevada, shortly after Andy Green set the first supersonic land speed record. Left to right: Richard Noble, Craig Breedlove, Andy Green and Art Arfons. (Peter Brock)

Above: On 6 October 1997 Craig Breedlove ran the Spirit of America – Sonic Arrow *at 531mph (855kph) in an attempt to regain the record from Andy Green, then standing at 714.144mph (1,150kph). The exquisite lines of Breedlove's new lance are more than evident in this shot of the car at full speed on the Black Rock Desert. (Peter Brock)*

Below: *A schematic view of the new, third-generation* Spirit of America – Sonic Arrow. *The vehicle is an all-composite structure powered by a modified General Electric J79 GE-8D-11B-17 jet engine, developing an awesome thrust output of 22,650lb, 48,000hp.*

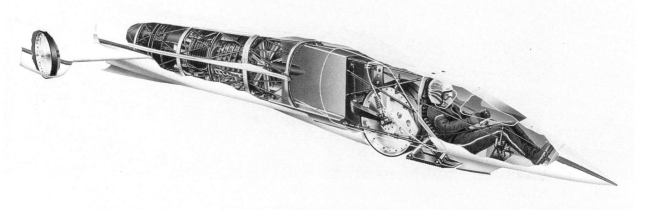

Craig Breedlove's third-generation Spirit of America – Sonic Arrow *rests under a setting sun on the beautiful Black Rock Desert, Nevada, in 1997. The car is an all-composite structure powered by a modified General Electric J79 GE-8D-11B-17 jet engine from a US Navy F4 Phantom, developing an awesome thrust output of 22,650lb, 48,000hp. (Peter Brock)*

It was a successful venture for Breedlove and his team, for not only did it mark his return to the salt after an absence of 8 years, it served admirably as a marketing tool for his lifelong ambition to engineer and design the first car to exceed the speed of sound. Only three years before the *English Leather Special* he had lost the opportunity to the Institute of Gas Technology-sponsored *The Blue Flame*, when, from a short list of no fewer than five selected candidates – including Art Arfons and Mickey Thompson – Breedlove was pipped to the post to drive the first rocket-powered car to set an official World Land Speed Record by his lifelong friend, the late Gary Gabelich.

From 1973 on, Breedlove and his company, Spirit of America Enterprises grew from strength to strength. The rocket dragster was modified and renamed the *Screaming Yellow Zonker*, and soon Craig was joined by his grown son, Norm, to work on the final chapter of the Craig Breedlove story, the *Spirit of America III – Sonic II*, with which they were going for the ultimate record – the speed of sound on land.

In 1979, however, Stan Barrett became the first man to exceed the speed of sound on land at the wheel of the controversial *Budweiser Rocket*, with a staggering 739.666mph (1,190.377kph) or Mach 1.0106. Breedlove ignored the success of the *Budweiser Rocket*, claiming that the Project Speed of Sound did not attempt to meet the requirements for FIA recognition of a land speed record attempt – a procedure Breedlove also ignored in 1962. Unlike Breedlove, however, the team never did set out to break a record, simply Mach 1, and as Brigadier General Charles E. 'Chuck' Yeager explained to this author shortly after Barrett made his historic run in 1979, 'When I flew the X-1 back in '47, there were no rules for breaking the speed of sound, and there are none for this thing going supersonic on the deck.'

Four years later Britain's Richard Noble drove the Rolls-Royce Avon 302 jet-powered *Thrust 2* to an official FIA World Land Speed Record of 633.468mph (1,019.465kph), bettering Gary Gabelich's long standing record by 11.061mph. Moreover, and perhaps even more impressively, *Thrust 2* had eclipsed Craig Breedlove's existing jet car record by 32.867mph.

Now, at the age of sixty-two Craig Breedlove, the courageous man who grasped the World Land Speed Record for the United States in the 1960s after thirty years of British dominance, is set to regain the record yet again, in a ferocious 48,000hp jet car, dubbed *Spirit of America – Sonic Arrow*.

Breedlove has already attained speeds in excess of the 600mph regime with the new *Spirit*, on the vast Black Rock Desert, Nevada, in a duel with Britain's Andy Green, driving Richard Noble's *Thrust SSC*.

On 15 October 1997, Squadron Leader Andy Green smashed through the sound barrier to create the first supersonic land speed record at an astonishing 763.035mph (1,227.985kph) or Mach 1.0175. It is Green's mark with *Thrust SSC* that Breedlove hopes to eclipse with the *Spirit of America – Sonic Arrow* and secure the return of the record to the United States.

The two vehicles that established Breedlove's earlier records are now on permanent display in the United States. The 1963/4 *Spirit of America* stands sentinel in the Museum of Science and Industry, Lake Shore Drive, Chicago, Illinois, and the 1965 *Spirit of America – Sonic I* at the Indianapolis Motor Speedway, Hall of Fame Museum, Indianapolis, Indiana.

For Craig Breedlove, the *Sonic Arrow* is not a conservative prospectus, but rather one that elegantly repudiates automotive conformity and convention. . . . For Breedlove the technology will be a triumph not merely of engineering excellence, but engineering innovation. To wit, he is confident of success!

EIGHT

NEW POLITICS AND A NEW TECHNOLOGY

GARY GABELICH – A LEGACY OF SPEED

On 23 October 1970, Gary Gabelich became the fastest man on wheels when he drove the 35,000hp, rocket-powered *The Blue Flame* to a new World Land Speed Record of 622.407mph (1,001.664kph) at the now famed Bonneville Salt Flats.

Gabelich was born on 29 August 1940, in San Pedro, California, the son of Mexican-born Rachel Padilla and Yugoslav Mhel Gabelich, a deputy US marshal. When selected to drive *The Blue Flame*, he was far from being a speed novice. In his long career on the drag strips and dry lakes of Southern California he drove with the team of Lee Vest and Monte Bowers. Their car was a Crosley-bodied competition-altered hot-rod on Model T rails powered by a stock Cadillac engine with eight carburettors. He went on to drive almost every piece of exotic racing equipment on the market, ranging from gas and top fuel Funny Cars to the powerful jet dragsters.

Gabelich drove the mighty jet car *Untouchable I*, owned by drag racing veteran Romeo Palamides, and later handled another jet-powered racing machine owned by Mickey Thompson and Art Malone. In the summer of 1963, Gabelich achieved the ultimate dream of all top drag racing drivers, outduelling the national champion 'Big Daddy' Don Garlits in the first United States Drag Racing Association meeting at the Indianapolis Raceway Park, Indiana.

Gary Gabelich had worked for a spell with the giant North American Rockwell Corporation, undergoing long environment tests in space capsules under simulated zero gravity conditions in parabolic streaks across the sky, and making protracted parachute falls over the Pacific Ocean during which he photographed the simulated re-entry of space capsules for the early NASA Mercury project. Only when it became apparent he had no chance of being selected for astronaut training himself did Gabelich quit his job and become a full-time drag racer. All of this richly qualified him to drive the prestigious rocket car *The Blue Flame*.

The dream of engineering a liquid-fuel rocket-powered car capable of beating Breedlove's 1965 record of 600.601mph (966.528kph) started with Ray Dausman, a slightly rotund and jovial young research technician with the Chicago, Illinois-based Institute of Gas Technology (IGT). Dausman was far from impressed by the speeds attained by conventional nitro-burning dragsters and Funny Cars. At the very most they were clocking in the low 200mph regime. Dausman was thinking in faster terms, and discussed highly ambitious plans with Dick Keller, a friend and

colleague at the IGT. The partners devised a three-phase initiative that would commence with the development of a small-scale, 25lb thrust prototype rocket motor to demonstrate their theory and their ability to construct such a powerplant. The unit was successfully ignited, and performed to specification with a 6-second burn. Having established the viability of their small-scale engine, the pair advanced to stage two, with the help of Pete Farnsworth, a professional dragster driver and automobile technician who had served briefly on the Don Garlits crew. The trio formed a partnership in the form of Reaction Dynamics Inc., of Milwaukee, Wisconsin and, with their own funds began building a rocket-powered dragster – the now legendary *RD X-I* or *Rislone Rocket*.

The dragster's engine was a slight variation of the 25lb thrust prototype, producing 2,500lb thrust, equivalent to approximately 2,800bhp at full throttle. Indeed, compared with a solid-fuel rocket engine, which is simply ignited and burns under full power until it has spent its energy, the liquid-fuel rocket can be controlled by step-throttling, not unlike an internal combustion engine.

A series of extensive trials proved not only the state-of-the-art engineering capabilities of the team, but the overall success of the *RD X-I* on drag strips throughout the United States. This enabled it to secure the vital corporate sponsorship from both the Institute of Gas Technology and the Goodyear Tire & Rubber Company for stage three of their project, the development of a rocket-powered land speed record vehicle, which would run on liquified natural gas (LNG), in combination with hydrogen peroxide – *The Blue Flame*.

But Officer . . . I thought you were Breedlove, otherwise I would have stopped! Sgt Bill Lane of the Utah Highway Patrol gives Gary Gabelich a mock citation for speeding on the salt flats. (Author's collection)

The *RD X-I* was retired soon after construction of *The Blue Flame* began. It was eventually sold to Snow Pony, a division of the Studebaker-Worthington Corporation, manufacturers of snowmobiles. On 14 February 1970, with Ky Michaelson at the wheel, the *RD X-I*, appropriately renamed *Sonic Challenger*, set a world snowmobile drag racing record of 114.57mph (184.38kph).

While Gary Gabelich was carving out a drag racing reputation on the West Coast with his *Beach City Chevrolet* top fuel Funny Car, the Reaction Dynamics team, now under the learned direction of project manager Dean Dietrich, had reached the point of negotiations with James McCormick of the Engineering Design Services Co., of Buffalo, New York, who agreed to join them in the development of the powerful rocket engine for *The Blue Flame*. Such was the prestige of the project, Bill Fredrick the former butcher turned rocket propulsion experimentalist from Woodland Hills, California, joined the Reaction Dynamics team as telemetry consultant, and some two years later débuted the first of his own rocket cars, a three-wheeled lance called *Courage of Australia*.

By now, some thirty specialists from the Institute of Gas Technology had joined the project alongside the Reaction Dynamics crew, and over seventy students of the Institute were able to participate in the design of the vehicle, including Shashi Kurani, Dr Carl Uzgiris and Monoj Adhikari.

The engine, designated the RD HP-LNG-22,000-V, followed the basic engineering principle of the smaller 25lb thrust prototype units, but the LNG, liquified by cooling to minus 258°F, passed from a helium-pressurized Alcoa aluminium chamber into the rocket motor: 75 per cent filtered through a central intake, with the remaining 25 per cent passing through a peripheral intake duct into a 'feathered' heat exchanger, while the hydrogen peroxide passed from a compressed air-pressurized stainless steel tank, through the outer jacket of the 22,000lb thrust motor to initiate the decomposition of the catalyst pack.

The subsequent superheated steam and oxygen flowed over the heat exchanger, converting the 25 per cent of LNG into gas which ignited as it joined the heated oxygen flow. The resultant reaction raised the temperature to the point where the remaining 75 per cent of LNG, injected as a liquid, ignited upon contact with the remaining oxygen. The resultant thrust produced from the 17in diameter annulus (throat), delivered a maximum 22,000lb, equivalent to a staggering 58,000bhp in a 20 second burn. For the record attempt, Dausman and Keller decided the thrust ratio was sufficient to keep the engine throttled back to produce only 13,000lb thrust, or an equivalent 35,000bhp.

Design considerations for the vehicle led to an ogive-shaped fuselage, which was adopted as the least resistant nose configuration, and a cross-section of the car's body was a rounded triangular shape. The two front wheels (racing specifications dictated a four-wheeled vehicle), were housed in the underside near the front of the vehicle, forward of the driver-controlled canard (stabilizing) fins. For high-speed stability, the rear wheels extended beyond the rear of the vehicle, and had a wide track for roll stability. The driver's cockpit was located aft of the propellant tanks and forward of the rocket engine – a driver preference. The semi-monocoque fuselage included ring-and-stringer construction in the central section of the car, and the rear of the vehicle had a welded nickel-steel tubular frame for additional strength because of the additional stresses of the powerful engine, wheel struts, tail-fin and parachute braking system housing. The bodyshell was constructed in tempered Harvey aluminium sheeting 0.064in thick (over 4,000 cs rivets held the outer skin to the chassis). The vehicle was shod with 8 × 25in Goodyear (hand-made) low-

Ray Dausman of the Chicago-based Illinois Institute of Gas Technology, with the 22,000lb thrust RD HP-LNG-22,000-V rocket motor used in The Blue Flame. *Design considerations favoured a rocket engine to reduce bulk required for comparable-thrust turbines and the vital power to weight ratio. The* Blue Flame *engine weighed only 770lb. (Author's collection)*

profile, bias-belted tyres, of a special high-speed treadless design, inflated to 350lbpsi with a design speed of 1,000mph. Steering was through the front wheels with a 91:1 ratio. The braking system was by Kelsey-Hayes 15in diameter discs on the rear with pinion gear coupler flanges for use at 100mph and below. There were also Deist 'ribbon' drogue parachutes for high speeds: primary chute, 7.3ft diameter for deployment below 650mph; secondary chute; 16ft diameter for below 250mph; and automatic reserve systems with manual override. The projectile – 38ft 2.6in long, 26in wide, 8ft 1.5in high at the top of the tail fin at the rear – had a ground clearance of only 9.5in and a wheelbase of 25.5ft.

Throughout the long and protracted history of rocket engine development, the principles of chemical combustion have been applied to increasingly efficient propulsion systems, based on the simple law, first

written down by Isaac Newton, that to every action there is an equal and
opposite reaction. From the Chinese firecracker of 1,000 years ago, to the
complex and demanding requirements of a modern high-performance
liquid propellant motor, the same basic principle has been employed by
weapons of war and tools for the exploration of space, but for all the
drama and pomp that surrounded early endeavours beyond Earth's
atmosphere, it is a sobering reality that Man has hardly stepped beyond
his own back door into the hostile void that spans the Universe. Travel
from earth to the most distant planets in the Solar System would require a
light-speed journey lasting four or five hours, while the nearest star is
more than four years away. For Gary Gabelich, the destination was nearer,
yet still so far away.

Many of the top names in high-speed driving were considered for *The
Blue Flame*, including Craig Breedlove, Art Arfons, Mickey Thompson
and Ky Michaelson, but the dashing hot-rodder from San Pedro,
California, was selected. Neither Gabelich nor his sponsors, the Institute
of Gas Technology and the Goodyear Tire & Rubber Co., planned to
attack the record head-on. Speeds would be steadily increased until all was
ready for full-throttle runs on the Bonneville Salt Flats.

On the morning of 17 September 1970, Gary Gabelich clocked a
leisurely 185.086mph (297.866kph) on his inaugural run, but during this
sortie an engine backfire caused a minor explosion in the combustion

chamber, melting the exhaust nozzle. 'We injected the fuel into the combustion chamber at too low a temperature,' explained project manager Dean Dietrich of the IGT. 'That caused the explosion, which doesn't appear to have seriously damaged any vital components.'

Three days later, 20 September, Gabelich was timed at 411.23mph (661.8kph) through the measured mile. 'It was a perfect run. This is the fastest I've ever travelled on land. It felt real good. It was out of sight,' Gary told the press soon after the run.

While *The Blue Flame* was recording speeds in the 400mph (650kph) range, for some reason the engine was producing only 11,000 of its 22,000lb of thrust capability. 'We're simply not getting the full thrust potential out of the car,' groaned Gabelich shortly after a 450mph (725kph) sortie. It was later discovered to be a malfunction in the fuel catalyst, damaged during the explosion on 17 September. The team returned to base on 25 September to await the arrival of a new catalyst pack from Buffalo, New York.

Two weeks later, they were back on the salt. With the replacement catalyst in position, *The Blue Flame* made two runs through the mile

With the assembly of the streamline body panels near completion, The Blue Flame *stands sentinel in the Milwaukee workshop of Reaction Dynamics, Inc. (Author's collection)*

THE BONNEVILLE SALT FLATS

At an elevation averaging 4,212ft above sea level, the Bonneville Salt Flats are the remnants of prehistoric Lake Bonneville which covered one-third of the state of Utah over 10,000 years ago. Located 120 miles west of Salt Lake City and 8 miles east of Wendover, the salt flats were originally 125 miles wide and twice as long. The fresh water lake slowly evaporated and drained internally, depositing concentrations of minerals in the lowest portion of the Great Salt Lake basin. Today, millions of tons of salt are spread over 40,000 acres of extinct Lake Bonneville. The salt flats are one of the most consistently flat areas on earth – the saline plain is so vast and expansive that when standing on the flats, one can clearly see the curvature of the earth.

The salt flats were named after the early American military explorer, Captain Benjamin L.E. Bonneville (1796–1878), and weren't penetrated until 1826 when Jedediah Strong Smith led the first known party of white men across the area. The stories he and his men told about their hardships were so well heeded by travellers that the region was avoided for two decades. The Donner-Reed party lost valuable time, wagons and animals crossing the salt on their way to California. Other travellers, including the Pony Express route and first telegraph stage lines, avoided the salt and went to the north or south of it. Not until 1906 did a permanent access route cross over the barren plain – the Western Pacific Railroad which connected Salt Lake City with San Francisco. Construction on the salt mud flats required three long years. Later, the last link in a coast-to-coast telephone hook-up was laid directly across the salt flats with the final connection or 'Wedding of the Wires' held in nearby Wendover on 17 June 1914. It was followed by construction of the Victory Highway between Salt Lake City and Wendover in 1925.

The flats' potential for racing was first recognized in 1896 by W.D. 'Bill' Rishel who was scouting a bicycle racecourse from New York to San Francisco. In 1911, he returned to organize bike races and, shortly thereafter, horseless carriage races.

The first record-breaking ever essayed at Bonneville was in 1914, when American Indianapolis racing star 'Terrible' Teddy Tetzlaff came to the salt flats to drive Ernie Moross's famed *Blitzen* Benz, the car that had gained its reputation in the hands of barney Oldfield and 'Wild Bob' Burman.

The history and legend of the area are unsurpassed. Bonneville had been the location for many land speed 'firsts', including man's first record for breaking the 300, 400, 500 and 600mph land speed barriers. The reason the Bonneville Salt Flats are uniquely suited to racing is quite simple: the area is flat and hard. Other dry, flat alkali playas are composed of mud and silt. Bonneville's salt holds up under the strain of wheeled vehicles better than mud.

In 1952, 8,927 acres were withdrawn from the general mining laws by Public Land Order 852. This order dictated that the Bonneville Salt Flats were to be administered by the Secretary of the Interior as an 'automobile racing and testing ground'. The withdrawn area only covers part of the straight race track. Most of the withdrawal covers the old circular race track, which is seldom used today.

The actual Bonneville Salt Flats International Speedway is 9 miles long and 80ft wide. In 1949, Bonneville Nationals, Inc. held their first annual 'Speed Week'. The event is sponsored by the Southern California Timing Association.

The significant climatic condition is a sparse rainfall. The recorded yearly high is 10.13in and the low is 1.77in. The average annual rainfall is 4.74in. Prevailing west to east winds are generally light but occasional gusts of 87mph have been recorded in Wendover. Each autumn, rains and mountain run-off flood further activities on the salt flats. The area appears to be a giant salt sea throughout the winter until spring winds and rising temperatures evaporate the water. Smoothness of the salt is maintained by winds moving the saline water solution back and forth until the waters evaporate and the salt is redeposited.

At one time the course covered over 100,000 acres and the salt depth was over 36in. Today, the salt flats are closer to 40,000 acres and the salt is 3 to 4in deep and in some places the mud shows through the salt.

The 40,000 acres of salt flats north of Interstate 80 have been managed by the Bureau of Land Management since 1946. Other parts of the Bonneville Salt Flats are owned by the State of Utah and by Reilly Industries Inc., which operates a potash plant near Wendover.

The old 'International' course was 13 miles long. Currently there are only 7 miles left to race on. The recently formed 'Save the Salt' campaign has been successful in that Reilly Industries has been ordered to start a resalting programme designed to replace 4in of salt on the racecourse each year.

attaining 462.321mph (744.031kph) and 478.77mph (770.503kph) burning only hydrogen peroxide. 'We were practically out of liquid nitrogen and we wanted to take no chances with the new catalyst pack,' said Dietrich. The runs, however, were not without incident. Halfway through the first solo run on the course, Gabelich fired his braking chutes prematurely. It turned out to be a necessary manoeuvre, for he became separated from his oxygen mask and was forced to hold the oxygen line to the face mask with one hand and steer the speeding vehicle with the other – a hurtling 35,000hp rocket car, loaded with high-octane propellants is not easy to control.

Two days later another mishap occurred. This time the braking chutes failed to deploy and Gabelich finally halted the rampaging car four miles past the designated finishing marker at the end of the Bonneville speedway. Gary estimated the car was approaching 550mph (885kph) when he released the safety chutes on *The Blue Flame*, but nothing happened. 'Apparently enough radiant heat was coming off the exhaust system to melt the nylon shield on the chutes' casing,' said co-builder Dick Keller. 'The drogue guns fired, but with the nylon shields destroyed it was like firing a blank shell.' The problem was overcome by the fitting of aluminium shields to protect the nylon ropes that held the chutes from the intense heat of *The Blue Flame*'s roaring exhaust.

Seconds before the cockpit canopy was sealed on Friday 23 October, Gary Gabelich knelt by the silver-blue, needle nose of *The Blue Flame*. He caressed the shining nose of his car and talked to it in a whisper. 'Let's do it together, baby. Give me a good ride. Let's go, baby. You can do it. We can do it together, baby.' At 11.40 a.m. Gabelich, the former NASA would-be astronaut adjusted his love beads and cradled his St Christopher medal in his hands. Gabelich, now alone in the confinement of his cockpit, began the countdown sequence. 'Ten, nine, eight, seven, six, five, four, three, two, one . . . Ignition!' He pushed down the

The sun sets on The Blue Flame *after a long day of trials at the famed Bonneville Salt Flats. The following day driver Gary Gabelich drove his lance to a new World Land Speed Record of 622.407mph (1,001.664kph). (Author's collection)*

Right: *On 23 October 1970, Gary Gabelich entered the land speed record sphere with a new rocket-powered car* The Blue Flame. *He is seen here waiting for his speeds to come through from the timekeepers. (Author's collection)*

Below: *Gary Gabelich is presented with the timing slip by USAC timekeeper Joe Petrali, just after setting the record. To the right of Petrali, Dean Dietrich of the Institute of Gas Technology. (Author's collection)*

accelerator pedal and could feel the rush of the fuel around him as it was forced toward the catalyst pack. He was forced back in the seat so hard he couldn't move his head to see the vital instrument panel and telemetry dials. In a split, ear-shattering second, the rocket car disappeared in a stream of white smoke as it streaked towards the deep-blue horizon and the target, almost 2 miles down range.

At about the same time all the vibration and noise vanished, as *The Blue Flame* roared across the hard-packed salt. Gabelich now experiencing the full effects of the high g-force, aimed the car and continued to accelerate in an eerie silence caused by the increasing pressure as the car generated its own shock waves, now approaching speeds in the high supersonic region. This time there were no problems on the salt as *The Blue Flame* blasted through the measured mile in 5.89 seconds – speed: 617.602mph (993.931kph). The car was refuelled, the Deist braking chutes repacked. Again the 31-year-old driver knelt by the car's nose, rubbing it fondly, his lips moving, 'That was far out, baby, but we're not through yet. We've got to do it one more time and do it better. We can do it. Just you and me. We can do it. Now, let's go and do our thing together, you and me, baby, you and me.' With 12 minutes remaining in the countdown, *The Blue Flame* flashed across the salt flats, accelerating

THE BLUE FLAME

Length:	38ft 2.6in
Width:	26in
Height:	8ft 1.5in (from ground to top of tail fin)
Wheelbase:	25.5ft
Track (front):	9in
(rear)	7ft
Weight:	6,608lb (with fuel)
Ground Clearance:	9.5in
Engine:	Reaction Dynamics HP-LNG-22,000-V pressure fed bio-propellant rocket system
Fuel:	AGA – 75/25% mixture of liquified natural gas and hydrogen peroxide
Oxidizer:	Hydrogen peroxide
Pressurant:	Helium
Burn Time:	20 seconds at 13,000lb thrust
Chassis:	20ft, semi-monocoque aluminium centre span with welded tubular steel nose and rear sections
Body Shell:	Harvey Aluminium sheeting 0.064in thick (over 4,000 cs rivets hold the outer skin to the chassis)
Tyres:	8 × 25in Goodyear (hand-made) bias-belted; special low-profile, high-speed treadless design. Inflation: 350lb psi. Design speed: 1,000mph
Braking Systems:	Kelsey-Hayes 15in diameter discs on the rear with pinion gear coupler flanges for use at 100mph and below. Deist 'ribbon' drogue parachutes for high speeds; primary chute, 7.3ft diameter for deployment below 650mph; secondary chute, 16ft diameter for below 250mph. Automatic reserve systems with manual override
Steering Ratio:	91:1 through the front wheels; ball-joint linkage with coaxial coil spring-cum-damper units
Steering Lock:	¾ turn of the wheel
Turning Circle:	¼ mile
Thrust:	Step throttling from 13,000 to 22,000lb (for the LSR run the engine was throttled to produce only 13,000lb thrust from a 17 in diameter annulus)
Max Output:	35,000hp
Speed Capability:	750mph

GARY GABELICH

ALTERNATE DRIVER
GERARD BRENNAN

Pictured just after setting the record, Gary Gabelich stands beside Reaction Dynamics' The Blue Flame. *(Author's collection)*

through the mile in 5.739 seconds. The even faster, 627.287mph (1,009.518kph) run cemented a new World Land Speed Record of 622.407mph (1,001.664kph).

The remarkable *The Blue Flame* was the last in a golden era of record-breakers at the Bonneville Salt Flats, which saw John Cobb's record of 394.2mph (634.267kph), set in 1947, rise to within sight of the sound barrier in a period of only twenty-three years.

Shortly after Gabelich set his record in October 1970, Dausman and Keller began working on a design concept for a new vehicle with Mach 1 capabilities. Basically a slender version of *The Blue Flame*, their new marvel of motion engineering, officially dubbed *The American Way*, would utilize a similar power system, packing some 21,000lb thrust, and once again Gabelich would drive. Sadly, however, Reaction Dynamics were unable to secure backing for another high-speed foray financed by corporate America, and a near strike among crew members, quelled by Gabelich himself, forced Dausman and Keller to shelve the project. It was the beginning of the end for the legendary team.

In January 1984, Gary Gabelich was killed in a motorcycling accident close to his home in Long Beach, California. He was travelling at high speed when a truck pulled out in front of him and, in an attempt to avoid collision, Gary laid the bike down trying to slide under it. He didn't make it. Gary wasn't wearing a crash helmet, and died instantly. He had survived speeds in excess of 600mph, only to lose his life on a freeway.

Gary Gabelich was one of the most likeable individuals in the record-breaking business and is missed by so many who return to the salt arena year after year in the wake of the true master of the art.

In 1986, *The Blue Flame* was donated to the Auto + Technik Museum in Sinsheim, Germany, by Gary Gabelich's widow Rae, where it is now on permanent display.

STAN BARRETT – AGAINST THE WALL

Less than 100 miles north-east of the bustling city of Los Angeles lies a barren, windswept landscape known as the Mojave Desert, the south-western corner of which is called Antelope Valley. It is an unfriendly environment known for blazing summer temperatures and bone-chilling winter winds – a place once described by Colonel Henry H. 'Hap' Arnold as 'not good for anything but rattlesnakes and horned toads'. The vast, hostile desert produces alfalfa, turkeys, fruit, almonds – and supersonic vehicles.

For all its desolation, the high desert also contains unique gifts. It offers unending days of piercing indigo skies, dawns and sunsets that bathe its rocky mountain sides with ethereal hues of colour. And while its arid landscape and dry lakebeds support little vegetation, for the past half century they have provided an ideal environment for pilots, researchers and engineers to test and explore new concepts in flight.

It was above this stark expanse of land that the notorious 'sound barrier' was finally broken; that innumerable speed and altitude records were set and quickly surpassed; that the first Space Shuttle proved it could land safely without power. It was here that the North American X-15 taught researchers valuable lessons about hypersonics and the threshold of space; that the F-8 Crusader, the first fully digital fly-by-wire aircraft was flown; it is the home of the B-1 strategic bomber, the SR-71 Blackbird; and it is where a brave young man successfully drove the world's first supersonic car. For over half a century, this desolate location, pragmatically dubbed by politicians as 'Aerospace Valley', has allowed innumerable technologies to be explored, improved upon, and given enough credibility for industry to accept and apply them – it is the legendary Edwards Air Force Base, California.

When Hollywood stuntman Stan Barrett stopped pretending to be someone else, he became the fastest man on Earth, and successfully pulled off the stunt of his life. He hurtled his controversial three-wheeled, 48,000hp rocket car, the *Budweiser Rocket* across Rogers Dry Lake at the US Air Force Flight Test Center at Edwards Air Force Base, to make history in becoming the first man to exceed the speed of sound on land. He reached a terminal speed of 739.666mph (1,190.377kph) or Mach 1.0106, with the help of a US Navy Sidewinder missile.

At exactly 7.26 a.m. on 17 December 1979, Stan Barrett turned a page in automotive history. The $1.2million £400,000 three-wheeler blasted off in a cloud of dust and, like a bright red needle with a huge ball of flame flying from its tail, scorched a path across the coffee-coloured dry bed of Rogers Dry Lake, high in the Mojave Desert. Barrett was 12 seconds into the run when, at an already staggering 612mph (984kph), he hit a button on the small butterfly steering wheel to fire the missile. 'I felt some real hard buffeting, then a period of smoothing out, and then it was like hitting a wall when the motors quit.' Barrett explained. 'I didn't know what had hit me . . . I thought I had lost my chute, I managed to purge the engine and fire the main chute, there was a jolt as the chute pulled then released the secondary chute to slow me down before applying the brakes.'

The cockpit of Bill Fredrick's Wynn's sponsored, 12,000hp rocket-propelled Courage of Australia, *driven by Vic Wilson and 'Courageous' John Paxson. (See colour plates between pages 152 and 153 for a view of the car.) (Author's collection)*

Some claim that there was a supersonic boom. Other observers, including this author, heard only a small rumble like distant thunder. Barrett covered the 5¾ mile timed section of the course in seconds before a series of Deist braking parachutes was deployed, bringing the arrow-like projectile to a controlled halt at the end of the immense Rogers Dry Lake.

Engineered and designed by Bill Fredrick of Chatsworth, California, the remarkable *Budweiser Rocket* began its assault on the sound barrier in September 1979 at the Bonneville Salt Flats, the home of high-speed racing. After achieving a terminal speed of more than 638mph (1,027kph) on 9 September, however, further attempts at Bonneville had to be abandoned because the crystalline salt was so rough the vehicle was rocking back and forth on its two rear wheels. On one occasion at Bonneville, five working crew members were sprayed with rocket fuel when a press helicopter, carrying a CBS television crew, swooped over the car at the end of the run while they were emptying hydrogen peroxide from its fuel reserve chambers. They were rushed to the nearby Wendover clinic where they received treatment for burns.

US Air Force permission to use the Edwards facility came two months later, and the *Budweiser Rocket* resumed its sound barrier attempts on the same site where Chuck Yeager became the first man to attain the speed of sound in 1947. At 10.22 a.m. on the morning of 14 October 1947, then United States Air Force Captain Charles E. 'Chuck' Yeager established aviation history by piloting the rocket-powered Bell X-1 through the 'sound barrier'. Dropped from the belly of a B-29 bomber at an altitude of 42,000ft Yeager relied totally on his four-chambered XLR-II rocket engines developing an awesome 6,000lb of thrust to launch the bright orange Bell X-1 *Glamorous Glennis* to a speed of 670mph across the sky. It is now over fifty years since Yeager, the man they said had 'The Right Stuff' broke the elusive 'sound barrier', an accomplishment that spawned supersonic flight and took man to the moon.

Bill Fredrick and car owner, film director Hal Needham had always dreamed of breaking the sound barrier on land. For ten years Fredrick prospered as owner of a chain of meat markets in Woodland Hills, California. With partner Fred Hartman, he worked on exotic propulsion systems as a hobby. He is now an aerospace industry consultant on rocket propulsion and, as head of The Shotmaker Company, is a technical advisor to the motion picture industry on the use of rockets and studio equipment for special effects.

In August 1962, Fredrick arrived at the Bonneville Salt Flats with his first car, the 23ft jet-powered *Valkyrie I* powered by a Westinghouse J46. Driven by Chuck Hatcher and a young Gary Gabelich, the car was a great disappointment for Fredrick as insurance problems following the death of Glenn Leasher in Romeo Palamides jet-powered *Infinity* robbed him of any serious runs on the salt. Subsequently, the car was sold to Mickey Thompson.

Fredrick began working on the speed of sound project back in 1972 when he débuted his first rocket car, the Wynn's sponsored, 12,000hp *Courage of Australia* driven by Vic Wilson and 'Courageous' John Paxson. Powered by a 6,100lb thrust Fredrickinetics monopropellant hypergolic rocket system, the 27ft dragster broke the timing beam at 311.41mph (501.01kph) in 5.107 seconds on 11 November 1971 at the Orange County International Raceway in Irvine, California.

'Courageous' John Paxson, co-driver of the Wynn's sponsored Courage of Australia *prototype. (Author's collection)*

In 1975, Fredrick was approached by Texan drag racer Billy Meyer, whose uncle offered to sponsor a new rocket car on the understanding that Frederick promoted the name of his company's product. Thus, the vehicle was to be known as the *Aquaslide'n'Dive Special*, and construction of the car began in earnest. It was initially planned to run the car in a side-by-side match race at Bonneville against Craig Breedlove in his proposed *Spirit of America III – Sonic II*. The event was to be sponsored by Top Rank. Fredrick was never happy with the idea of running two cars at supersonic speeds within a quarter mile of one another and cast about for a new sponsor.

Meanwhile, Billy Meyer's father Paul stepped in and offered to bankroll the project, and as founder and owner of the Success Motivation Institute in Waco, Texas, insisted the car should be rechristened the *SMI Motivator*. By the summer of 1976 the lance was completed. While supersonic aerodynamic theories had to be used, the vehicle was based on a simple design concept using computational fluid dynamics – a simulation technique culminating in the launch of an instrumented model of the car along the 35,000ft high-speed test track facility at the White Sands Missile Range, Holloman Air Force Base, New Mexico, under the watchful eye of Ray Van Aiken of the US Ordnance Test Station at China Lake Naval Weapons Center, California, who supplied the vital ground effects data relating to supersonic velocity – a pioneering experiment that would later be adopted by Richard Noble's brilliant aerodynamicist, Ron Ayers, for *Thrust SSC*.

On 19 March 1954, United States Air Force Colonel John Paul Stapp, a veteran of aviation medical research, rode a water-braked rocket sled to a record speed of 632mph (1,018kph). The 2,000lb sled, propelled by nine rockets unleashing 40,000lb of thrust, required just 5 seconds to complete its run down the 35,000ft high-speed test track at the United States Air Force Missile Center at the White Sands Missile Range, Holloman Air Force Base. Three days later, a driverless sled attained 2,075mph (3,339kph) over a 2-mile track. A monorail sled later reached 2,850mph (4,586kph) again unmanned. But could a car or wheeled projectile hold the ground at high subsonic to low supersonic speeds?

For the *SMI Motivator* Bill Fredrick also commissioned Joe Sargent, an ex-Northrop Corporation man who programmed NASA's computers for the Apollo II EVA lunar landing mission, to design and produce a radical computer system for the car. Fredrick was confident that the man who ran the computers for Neil Armstrong's moonwalk in 1969 would be capable of delivering his vehicle to Mach I with equal accuracy.

The form-fitting cockpit of the SMI Motivator. The driver was protected from impact and fire by being isolated within the vehicle, surrounded by 2in thick mineral wool firewalls with stainless steel bulkheads. The driver was firmly harnessed into a seat of energy absorbing foam and all controls, including the butterfly steering wheel, rocket arming valve and instrumentation, were easy to reach from the supine position. (See colour plates between pages 152 and 153 for a view of the car.) (Author's collection)

Design considerations for the vehicle led to an aerodynamic configuration for pure supersonic ground effects. The lower surface of the car tapered to a V to dissipate the enormous swell of pressure and boundary layer build-up approaching supersonic speeds. The centre of pressure was located aft of the centre of gravity to counteract the tendency to yaw and to eliminate flight characteristics through the emplacement of a sharply-raked stabilizing fin at the rear. An ogive shape was adopted as the least resistant nose configuration, and a cross-section of the vehicle's fuselage revealed a rounded, tear drop shape.

The vehicle – 41ft in length and 8ft 10in high at the top of the tail fin at the rear – weighed only 2,990lb dry and rode on a revolutionary new concept in high-speed tyre design of solid forged aluminium with a V-shaped tread and keel for lateral bite. Each wheel had a diameter of 32in and weighed 120lb – a pioneering concept that would later be adopted by other contenders. The steering was 28° lock-to-lock with a turning radius of ½ mile. A single front wheel was housed in the underside of the vehicle, forward of the in-board controlled canard fins. For high-speed stability, the rear wheels extended beyond the rear of the vehicle, and had a 12ft wide track for roll stability.

The driver's cockpit was located aft of the propellant tanks and forward of the rocket engine. The semi-monocoque fuselage ring-and-stringer construction in the central section of the car, and the rear of the vehicle, had a welded nickel-steel frame, utilizing square and round chrome moly tubing for additional strength to compensate for the stress of the engine, torsional flexing wheel struts, tail fin and a parachute braking system. The safety system included one 12ft diameter Deist drag chute for below 800mph, and a secondary ribbon drogue for speeds below 600mph was 16ft in diameter. All were pyrotechnically activated. The driver was firmly harnessed into a form-fitting seat of energy absorbing foam and all controls and instrumentation were easy to reach from the supine position. For the engine, Fredrick arrived at a hybrid design combining both liquid and solid fuel propellants, producing 24,000lb of thrust, 48,000hp.

Early in 1976 it was announced that Hollywood stuntman turned director Hal Needham had succeeded Billy Meyer as driver of the *Motivator*. Meanwhile, Kitty O'Neil, a 28-year-old part Irish, half-Cherokee Indian stuntwoman from Corpus Christi, Texas, was contracted to drive Fredrick's new rocket-powered tricycle, to shatter Lee Breedlove's long-standing women's record of 308.56mph (496.57kph) set at Bonneville in 1965.

If her fame was to become as short-lived as that of Stapp and Gabelich, Kitty was not the sort to worry. She had been tempered by adversity since childhood and now prospered in obscurity. She was born deaf but, tutored by a persistent mother, she learned to lip read and speak well enough to attend regular classes before she completed grade school. She was a promising 3-metre and junior Olympic platform diver in the early '60s, despite being crippled by spinal meningitis, and, in the years since, she had survived cancer thanks to two operations.

Kitty got to drive the *Motivator* because some years earlier she had made the right connections in Hollywood. In 1970, while racing motorcycles in cross-country events, she met and married a one-time bank vice-president, Duffy Hambleton who, realizing he was a daredevil at heart, had quit banking to become a stuntman. After several years living on an orange ranch serving as a housewife and a mother to Duffy's two children by a previous marriage, Kitty decided she wanted to get back into some kind of action herself. Duffy spent two years teaching her the survival techniques of his profession and in March 1976 she joined him in

Stunts Unlimited, a cooperative association that included many of the world's top stuntmen, including Hal Needham. Through her husband, Kitty met Bill Fredrick, who earned his living developing studio equipment for special effects.

Before Kitty O'Neil travelled more than a few cautious miles in the *Motivator*, John Paxson, the rocket car veteran, made four test runs in the car at El Mirage dry lake, California, and another pass at Bonneville. On the Bonneville sortie Paxson attained a respectable 360mph (580kph), but before he had passed midway in the timing trap, the car veered dangerously off the course, missing a protruding pipe by 4ft. On her only run at Bonneville, Kitty topped out at about 300mph (483kph), but wandered all over the marked course.

After the *Motivator* was bench-tested and remeasured, Fredrick concluded that its habit of wandering was not an inherent fault but had been caused by the slick and badly degraded course on the salt. As a result, the record attempt was shifted to the immense Alvord Desert in Oregon, a dry lake bed that was once restricted as an emergency landing strip by the US Air Force and was well known to Ray Van Aiken of the US Ordnance Test Station at China Lake Naval Weapons Center, who supplied Fredrick with the ground effects data.

On 3 December 1976, Kitty O'Neil made one short orientation run at Alvord, peaking out at a little more than 300mph (483kph). The next day she averaged better than 300 on three consecutive runs through the kilometre trap. On the third day she twice exceeded 400mph (644kph), and on the fourth she pushed the *Motivator* to a top speed of 524.016mph (843.323kph) in the second of two runs through the kilometre trap. On her second run she was slightly slower, but her two-way average was 512.71mph (825.126kph) and she probably touched 600mph (965kph) momentarily. Using less than 60 per cent of the hybrid's power, she had set a new women's land speed record.

Although Kitty O'Neil stood only 5ft 3in and weighed 97lb, her entry into the record books with Fredrick's lance was a minor victory in itself, because the form-fitting cockpit of the *Motivator* was barely large enough to accommodate a small child. Fredrick himself was fearful of such confinement, for as a child a brother had rolled him in a rug and pushed him off the roof of a barn.

Prior to every sortie in the *Motivator*, Fredrick began a 10 second countdown. Because Kitty was totally deaf, an assistant, Stan Schwanz, relayed the count to her by hand signals. When Schwanz signalled 'zero,' Kitty said a short prayer and depressed the throttle. Under a contract for which Duffy Hambleton paid $20,000 to get her the ride, Kitty was only supposed to drive the *Motivator* to a new women's record. By similar contract, Marvin Glass and Associates, a Chicago toy concern, paid $25,000 for Needham's ride as successor to Billy Meyer. Marvin Glass and Associates had developed a toy line featuring Hal Needham, 'Hollywood Stuntman' dolls, similar to 'Action Man', and sold it to Gabriel Industries, a New York company best known for its toy subsidiaries, Gilbert and Kohner. Including marketing and promotional expenses, Marvin Glass eventually paid more than $75,000 for Needham to try for the speed of sound.

The day after Kitty O'Neil set the women's record, the *Motivator* was being prepared for her to try to break Gary Gabelich's World Land Speed Record of 622,407mph (1,001.664kph) set at Bonneville in 1970, when Fredrick received several telephone calls from afar reminding him that he had a binding contract to let Needham try for the mark. So Kitty came out of the driver's seat and became a symbol of wronged womanhood across the land. To make matters worse, in the midst of the turmoil, John Radewagen – a Chicago-based spin-doctor paid to promote Needham and maintain a low profile for Marvin Glass and Associates – was falsely quoted as saying that it would be 'degrading' for a woman to hold the record. As a consequence, Marvin Glass and Associates lost their low profile, and Needham got a number of phone calls accusing him of male chauvinism and worse. Two weeks later Gabriel Industries was saying they did not want any publicity on their line of Hal Needham dolls. Thus it was that an enterprise of great pith and moment fast went to pot.

In 1977 Fredrick and Needham were at Mud Lake, near Tonopah, Nevada for further trials with their lance. No sooner had the team arrived on the dry lake than the ebb and flow of turmoil caught up with them. Needham had already attained a declared one-way pass of 619.99mph (997.02kph) at Bonneville on 14 October, when he ran overcourse on to the mud flats, and Kitty O'Neil's stuntman husband wasted no time in slighting Needham's ability to drive the car. Duffy Hambleton tried unsuccessfully for an injunction to prevent the *Motivator* running at at Mud Lake without his wife at the helm.

Bill Fredrick (right) working on the construction of the Budweiser Rocket. *The protruding tension pins 'clecos' enable frequent and easy removal of the body panels for access to the propellant tanks and inboard instrumentation during construction. (Author's collection)*

Hal Needham, owner of the Budweiser Rocket, *is a leading Hollywood film director. As a stuntman, he is without peers. In 1976 he drove the* SMI Motivator *to a staggering 548.9mph (883.02kph) on Mud Lake, near Tonopah, Nevada. (Author's collection)*

Needham, nevertheless, posted three test runs in Nevada Desert. On the third run he was travelling at an estimated 620mph (998kph) when disaster struck. As Needham later explained to this author, who was watching the run with Mickey Thompson, 'At 620 miles an hour my parachute failed to open, my brakes were unable to stop me. Thirty-four seconds, five and a half miles later, I came to, and ran off the end of the dry lake.' When he reached the end of the lake he was travelling at 200mph (322kph) when the car made a slight veer to the right of the course and ran into the sage brush, across a dry creek and took off for 165ft before nose-diving into the desert. He was lucky to be alive. Indeed, when this author interviewed him at the scene of the crash, he replied, 'I wanna tell you something, the last couple of hundred yards is a son of a gun' . . . and vowed never to drive the car again. Regardless of chute failures, the one-way peak speed was clocked at 548.9mph (883.02kph). As for the braking parachutes? Deliberate sabotage was suspected when it was discovered that acid had been poured over them. Predictably, the fingers of suspicion were pointed at Duffy Hambleton, and the atmosphere was further heightened by the suicide of the Needham doll inventor as he faced four murder charges in Illinois. For Fredrick and Needham 1977 was a bad year . . . and so the search began for a new sponsor and driver.

The new backer for Fredrick and Needham's Project Speed of Sound was billionaire August A. Busch III, head of the Anheuser-Busch empire out of St Louis, Missouri, famous for its Budweiser and Michelob beer brands. The sponsorship appropriately dubbed the vehicle the *Budweiser Rocket* car.

While supersonic aerodynamic theories had to be used, Fredrick explained the new vehicle was based on a simple design concept. 'You design for the smallest amount of frontal area and the largest amount of power available. That's why we had three wheels instead of four, nothing to do with breaking the rules, there are no rules for going supersonic, only a supersonic land speed record. Our design meant a smaller frontal area and it was more stable at high speeds.' Fredrick continued, 'The thing you begin with is the size of the human body.' As a result the car's fuselage section was only 20in wide and 24in high, and 39in high at the top of the cockpit canopy.' By comparison, Richard Noble's *Thrust SSC* required a width of 12ft to accommodate its two massive Rolls-Royce Spey 202 engines.

The *Budweiser Rocket*, 39ft 2in long and 8ft 10in high at the top of the vertical tail fin at the rear, rode on Frederick's pioneering high-speed tyre design of solid forged aluminium, now commonplace in all land speed record vehicles, including *Thrust SSC* and Craig Breedlove's *Spirit of America – Sonic Arrow*. At speeds in excess of 700mph, the wheels would be spinning at 9,200rpm and conventional rubber tyres would have disintegrated. Fredrick's confidence in solid tyres was proven in the prototype to the *Budweiser Rocket*, the successful *SMI Motivator*, which Kitty O'Neil and Hal Needham both drove to speeds of more than 600mph in 1976. 'We had four of them at $26,000 by the way . . . three to use and one spare,' Fredrick explained.

For the engine of the *Budweiser Rocket*, Fredrick used a hybrid Romatec V4 rocket system, combining both liquid and solid fuel propellants, producing 24,000lb of thrust, 48,000hp. Fredrick explains, 'The hydrogen peroxide filters through a silver catalyst pack and decomposes, giving you superheated steam and oxygen at temperatures well in excess of 1,370°F. That erodes the polybutadiene solid fuel rings which automatically ignite as soon as they become gaseous.'

In attempting to exceed the speed of sound, the main problems that faced the aircraft industry were designing for the airflow encountered at transonic speeds, and providing sufficient thrust for the aircraft to accelerate through the transonic region, with its attendant drag rise. The horsepower produced by a rocket varies with the speed. Power is thrust × velocity. At 1,000mph (1,690kph), 80,000hp would be produced by a rocket engine having a thrust ratio of 3,000lb. To go supersonic Fredrick added a further 12,900hp from a US Navy Sidewinder missile mounted in the tail of the vehicle above the hybrid Romatec V4 rocket engine.

As for fuel, the *Budweiser Rocket* burned a hydrogen peroxide monopropellant at Bonneville, which produced less than half the engine's potential power. For the sound barrier run, the hydrogen peroxide was used as an oxidizer for the polybutadiene, and the Sidewinder missile, approved for Stan Barrett's run by the Pentagon, gave a final jolt toward the sound barrier. A body-width increase of only 2in would have required approximately 2,000 more horsepower.

From a standing start, the *Budweiser Rocket* could accelerate from 0 to 140mph (225kph) in one second, and travelled 400ft in the first second. The vehicle attained a speed of 400mph (644kph) in 3 seconds, and used the equivalent of 650 gallons of fuel – 17 yards to the gallon.

No one had ever driven at more than 700mph. Stan Barrett's supersonic run was the culmination of three-and-a-half months and eighteen attempts, which began when he broke the previous timed speed on land – 622.407mph (1,001.664kph) set by Gary Gabelich in the Institute of Gas Technology sponsored *The Blue Flame*, on 23 October 1970.

The son of a Baptist minister and himself a devout Christian, Stan Barrett was a leading Hollywood stuntman, performing all the major

The Budweiser Rocket *rode on a revolutionary new concept in high-speed tyre design of solid forged aluminium now commonplace in all land speed record vehicles. Each wheel had a diameter of 32in and weighed 120lb. The author is pictured here with one of these wheels during trials at the Edwards Air Force Base, California, in 1979. (Author's collection)*

stunts in *Hooper*, the film in which actor Burt Reynolds played the role of an ageing stuntman. Barrett has doubled for Reynolds and Paul Newman in numerous films including *Smokey and the Bandit*, *Cannonball Run*, *Airport '77* and *When time Ran Out*. His career in motion pictures began in 1964 after four years in the US Air Force. Barrett entered the USAF after attending Roosevelt High School and Missouri Military Academy in Mexico, Missouri. He was just seventeen when he reported for basic training at Lackland Air Force Base, near San Antonio, Texas, and was later sent across town to the School of Aerospace Medicine at Brooks Air Force Base for additional schooling in the altitude chamber with partial and full pressure suits, and ejection seat training.

In December 1960, Barrett reported to Chanute Air Force Base, near Rantoul, Illinois, for duty as a physiological training specialist. 'I was in the business of teaching airmen and officers the techniques of survival at high altitudes,' he recalled. When he left the Air Force, Barrett wanted to continue his career in the medical profession. 'I went to the University of Oregon as a pre-med student. My work in the Air Force really gave me the interest for medicine as a career. But while in Oregon, I learned that a movie was being filmed nearby. I auditioned and got a small part in the Jimmy Stewart movie, *Shenendoah*, which led to my meeting Hal Needham and a career as a stuntman.'

Barrett is a private pilot and has raced motorcycles. Former Golden Gloves (undefeated) lightweight champion in his home town of St Louis, Missouri in 1959, he is a Black Belt in karate. Barrett was thirty-six when he drove the *Budweiser Rocket*, and lives on a ranch near Bishop, California, with his wife Penny, a former member of the US ski team, and their daughter Melissa. They have two grown sons, David and Stanton, who is also a Hollywood stuntman. Following Fredrick and Needham's Project Speed of Sound, Barrett drove the *No. 33 Circle K/Skoal Bandit* Chevrolet as team-mate to Harry Gant on the NASCAR Winston Cup circuit, owned by Burt Reynolds and Hal Needham.

The 48,000hp, hybrid design, Romatec V4 mono-propellant rocket motor of the Budweiser Rocket *nears completion in Bill Fredrick's Romatec Research Laboratory, Chatsworth, California.*

It is not a long drive by conventional car from the sprawling ranch home of Stan Barrett in Bishop, California, to the Edwards Air Force Base where the assault on the sound barrier was made. Walking relaxed, in the mountains high above his valley home, Barrett told this author:

Stan Barrett depressed the accelerator with his right foot, igniting the 48,000hp rocket engine and the Budweiser Rocket *blasted away from the line with a menacing roar. (Author's collection)*

When I was a youngster growing up in my home town of St Louis, I used to day-dream about guys such as Chuck Yeager and Charles Lindbergh and what contribution I might make to American history. Had I realized then how close my thoughts were to exactly what God had destined as my fate . . . Here I sat on that cold December morning in '79, strapped into the tiny cockpit of a multi-thousand horsepower rocket car about to ignite enough power to light a small city in an effort to go faster than any man on earth. I can remember very vividly as I peered over my instruments out of the windshield down the fuselage of the rocket to the vast dry lake bed in front of me as car designer Bill Fredrick and crew chief, Kirk Swanson, busied themselves with the task of arming the vehicle for its sternest test. When we got into the countdown, that was a time that I said a prayer. 'Lord, into Thy hands I commit myself.' Usually that's about on the count of 2, 1, then away I went. That's a moment that I felt close to the Lord.

To prepare his body for the tremendous g loading that he would encounter in the car, Barrett was tested in the centrifuge at the University of Southern California. Inside the *Budweiser Rocket* he accelerated faster than any other human being ever had in a land-bound vehicle. During the speed of sound run he was to be subjected to an estimated 4gs of force, or four times his body weight, pulling a further g at over 600mph when he hit the Sidewinder.

After spending almost 30 minutes inspecting the car and talking with its owner, Hal Needham, Barrett climbed into the tiny cockpit. Crew chief Kirk Swanson buckled him in and Bill Fredrick asked Stan to pray for God's blessing, gave the thumbs up to the working crew and engineering support team, and the canopy was closed.

There was an ominous silence and after a wave from Kirk Swanson, the process of arming the rocket commenced. After actuating the proper sequence of switches transmitted to the vehicle's radio by Bill Fredrick, who was kneeling on the course close by, Barrett increased the pressure in the rocket engine's combustion chamber, blasting clouds of hydrogen peroxide vapour from the exhaust outlet. 'She's ready to go, Stan,' called Fredrick, who then commenced the countdown, '. . . 3, 2, 1'. Barrett depressed the accelerator with his right foot, igniting the engine. The rocket car blasted away from the line with a menacing roar and disappeared in a stream of white smoke, scorching a path across the dusty dry lake toward the unknown.

The rocket engine burned for about 16–20 seconds (the thrust and length of burn were calculated by computer to achieve the desired speeds) with about another 50 seconds required to bring the car to a halt. The car skipped at times on the first part of the run – as a result of the tremendous acceleration which left wheel rotation catching up with the vehicle's speed.

Stan Barrett in the tiny cockpit of the Budweiser Rocket *car after becoming the first man to surpass the speed of sound on land at Rogers Dry Lake, Edwards Air Force Base. Inverviewing Barrett is Chuck Yeager, the first man to break the sound barrier 'upstairs' in the legendary Bell X-1 rocket plane in 1947. (Author's collection)*

'I could hardly see as the vibration was so great. The ½ mile markers looked like telephone poles due to the buffeting as the car roared down the course. I was afraid I wouldn't be able to distinguish where to fire the Sidewinder from all the jostling around, and felt some real hard thrust.' Barrett ignited the Sidewinder, yelling only one word, 'Wow!' as the rocket car hurtled through the timing traps with the rear wheels literally off the ground. 'The acceleration was phenomenal with that boost of power,' Barrett recalls. 'Some 5 seconds later, I surpassed the speed of sound.' Chuck Yeager was among the first to reach Barrett at the end of the course.

The 36-year-old father of three pulled himself out of the car with the help of his friend, Hal Needham, amidst a crowd of onlookers, family friends and working crew. He hugged Needham, now in tears, then embraced his wife and children. An Air Force Northrop T-38 chase plane flew over at 100ft as a salute from one mach-buster to another. Although Barrett had become the first man to break the sound barrier on land, the historical event was not accepted by the Fédération Internationale de l'Automobile as a new World Land Speed Record. In order to be official, a record has to be set by averaging the speed of two runs through a 1-mile timed course. However, the objective of Project Speed of Sound was to surpass the sound barrier, not set a supersonic land speed record.

Stan Barrett had to wait nearly ten hours for his speed to be confirmed. In a telegram to Hal Needham, Colonel Pete Knight of the US Air Force broke the news. The car had exceeded Mach 1. It was official. Stan Barrett had indeed become the first man to break the sound barrier on land. Barrett offered thanks to God – and celebrated with a large bowl of strawberry ice cream.

Watching the run with this author was Chuck Yeager, who thirty-two years earlier broke the sound barrier in a rocket plane to earn his place in history. Yeager, now USAF Brigadier General (retired), who interviewed Barrett during the warm-up runs, pointed out, 'It's far more dangerous than what I did back in '47. At that time, nobody knew what would happen should a plane go faster than sound. I had 42,000 feet of space between me and the ground to play with . . . something goes wrong here, and Barrett's gone.'

Stan Barrett and Chuck Yeager, now Brigadier General (retired), who thirty-two years earlier became the first man to break the sound barrier at Edwards Air Force Base, when he flew the experimental Bell X-1 rocket plane Glamorous Glennis. *(Author's collection)*

Barrett's supersonic run was sanctioned by the International Hot Rod Association, scrutinized by Earl Flanders. Flanders set up three sets of timing traps set at 52.8ft. (1/100 of a mile) apart, with special sensors accurate to a millionth of a second. The speed of sound run was also monitored by Edwards' state-of-the-art accelerometer, photographic and extrapolation from a radar trace, in addition to the car's own telemetry equipment manned by Earl Williams, Ray Van Aiken and Joe Sargent, seconded to Project Speed of Sound.

In the telegram to Hal Needham, the United States Air Force confirmed that along with engineering personnel from the rocket crew it had 'performed a review of the limited accelerometer, photographic, air speed and radar data taken during the speed of sound land speed attempt at Rogers Dry Lake at Edwards Air Force Base in November–December 1979. Within the accuracy of the speed measuring device used, it is our judgement that the overall object of attaining Mach I (the speed of sound) with a land vehicle was achieved at 7.26 a.m. on December 17, 1979.' The telegram was signed 'very sincerely Yours, Col. Pete Knight, Vice Commander, Air Force Flight Test Center'. Needham said, 'We can't thank the Air Force enough. They have been so supportive and helpful, we couldn't have done it without them.'

Sophisticated telemetry equipment relayed every function of the Budweiser Rocket *back to a mobile computer command post, manned by a team of specialists under the direct management of Earl Williams, the leading US computer consultant seconded to the Project Speed of Sound. Joe Sargent (left) and Ray Van Aiken evaluate the telemetry readout after a successful 'low speed' trial run of the car at Bonneville. (Hal Needham)*

Barrett had reached a terminal speed of 739.666mph (1,190.377kph) or Mach 1.0106 on the Mach meter. He ran out of fuel between 200 and 400ft before the timing lights; he had 734mph on radar, 739 on air speed; they had unquestionably broken the speed of sound. Fredrick and Needham insist 'this was a high-technology, scientific and engineering achievement. We've got a whole stack of data that we'll be using for years on this thing going supersonic on the deck.'

Ken Squier of CBS once asked Barrett about the risks involved in driving the rocket car. He replied, 'I believe that it's a pretty calculated risk. I really believed that we could do it or I wouldn't have got in the car. What may seem like a risk to someone else, may not seem like one to me. I knew where the boundaries were, I had a good sense of what would work and what wouldn't work. With those kind of speeds and that kind of energy that you're developing, if you have an accident I think you are in big trouble. I wasn't afraid of getting hurt, and I certainly wasn't afraid of dying. I was as prepared to die as I was to live.' Then came the critics . . .

A reporter on the *Los Angeles Times* said the team had no intention of abiding by the rules set down by the FIA, stating that any land speed record attempt must be made under them or their appointed agent's watchful eye. Another critic, absent from the supersonic run, led a wave of criticism and investigative journalism, and discovered that the normal

Beyond the sound barrier: the Budweiser Rocket *shortly after completing its controversial run at Rogers Dry Lake, Edwards Air Force Base. Note the shallow depressions left by the light alloy wheels in the dry lake bed. In the distance, Earl Flanders' timing traps can be clearly seen. (Author's collection)*

THE BUDWEISER ROCKET

Length:	39ft 2in	Wheels Dimensions:	
Width:	20in	(front)	30in × 3in dia
Height:	24in (from ground to top of fuselage), rising to 8ft 10in at top of tail fin	(rear)	32in × 3in dia
		Steering:	Self-centering butterfly acting on ¾ turn of the front wheel
Wheelbase:	19ft 2in	Turning Circle:	½ mile
Track (front):	3in	Brakes:	Deist 12ft diameter drag chute for speeds below 800mph, plus 16ft diameter secondary ribbon drogue for speeds below 600mph
(rear)	12ft		
Weight (with fuel):	5,300lb		
Fuel:	Hydrogen peroxide/polybutadiene liquid and solid fuel propellants		
Engine:	Romatec V4 hybrid solid fuel rocket, augmented by AIM–9L Sidewinder missile	Suspension:	Hydroelastic-pneumatic (front) suspension, (rear) torsional flexing of wheel struts
		Suspension Travel:	2.0in (front) 1.5in (rear)
Chassis:	US Steel square and round chromoly nickel-steel spaceframe	Thrust:	24,000lb (Romatec V4) 6,000lb (Sidewinder missile)
Body Shell:	US Steel/Alcoa aluminium (stressed)	Max Output:	48,000hp (Romatec V4) 12,900hp (Sidewinder missile)
Windscreen:	Sierracin (supersonic) 3mm	Max Acceleration:	5.01g at 600mph (965kph)
Wheels:	Three US Steel/Fredrick heat-treated solid forged aluminium		

132ft timing trap was not used. He noted that a 52.8ft (1/100 of a mile) zone was employed, clearly oblivious to the fact that the team was not actually gunning for a new record. Barrett later explained, 'Gary Gabelich holds the record, my run was only in one direction so I wouldn't have posted it as a new record.'

The *Budweiser Rocket* is now in the Smithsonian Institute, Washington DC, the most visited museum in the world. Its collection contains some of the most important craft in history, craft that were designed by men and women who have expanded the frontiers of science, and that museum simply doesn't display bogus cars. Barrett explains, 'We really pushed the envelope up there at Edwards. I guess those guys who have cast doubt on the veracity of our speed resent taking second place. We can all be winners in different races, that is why I spend as much time as I can spreading the good news of Jesus Christ! Mark Twain once wrote, that "Someday, when man can go 700 miles an hour, he'll again long to go seven miles an hour." For some this may not be the case, but then again I have been there and beyond.'

RICHARD NOBLE – MOTIVE FOR A MISSION

Prestige is more than just a word to an Englishman: it is a veritable way of life. It was the driving force behind the motivation of men like John Cobb, Sir Malcolm and Donald Campbell, and a Twickenham businessman called Richard Noble, who risked their lives for the sake of a new land or water speed record.

Richard Noble was born on 6 March 1946 at Comley Bank in Edinburgh. His interest in speed was first sparked in 1952 when he was six years old. One afternoon he was taken for a drive in the family Hillman Minx along the banks of Loch Ness, when his father, a colonel in the army, happened upon a crowd gathered around a sleek silver boat, edged with goldfish red. There, tied alongside the jetty was John Cobb's 31-ft jet-powered, three-pointer hydroplane *Crusader*, being prepared for an attempt on the World Water Speed Record. Noble still recalls the impression this sight made upon his life. 'It was an absolutely beautiful-looking thing: I thought, someday I would really like to do something like that.'

As a boy he would sketch record cars in his school exercise books, and by his tenth birthday he had Eric Burgess's definitive work *Rocket Propulsion*. He was clearly hooked on velocity. He collected all the information he could on the *Crusader* and developed an interest in jet engines. It was the speed element of *Crusader* – the first powerboat to be specifically designed and built for turbojet power – that provided the real inspiration, and throughout his childhood and adolescence a large part of Richard's reading was devoted to anything he could garner on speed records and the brave men who attempted them.

Richard Noble was educated at Winchester College in Hampshire. He didn't do particularly well academically, but admits 'I had an awful lot of fun and made some great friends'. He earned the respect of his friends as a prankster. Sadly, his headmaster was not impressed by his liberated lifestyle – after Noble tear-gassed the headmaster's first parents' cocktail party – and threatened him with expulsion.

While at Winchester College he worked as a gardener for a spell, then joined ICI as a paint salesman. He resigned from this job in 1971 and started work on the nightshift at Nova Jersey Knit in City Road, London, where he fashioned pattern discs for knitting machines. He had always dreamed of becoming a novelist, but this career path proved to be short-lived. While living and working in London he bought a Series II short-wheelbase Land Rover that would come to play a major role in his immediate future. He wanted to see the world. . . .

Noble placed a small ad in *The Times* inviting applicants to join him on a frugal expedition to Africa. The advertisement, which led to him meeting his wife Sally, read, 'London to Cape Town overland. Small expedition, £200'; it was and outstanding success. Noble had 160 replies, but most of them were lotus-eaters seeking some paradise lost. He eventually ended up with a short list of six. In April 1972, Noble and his team of six fellow travellers set off for Cape Town. A second overland expedition took him to India and Pakistan, returning to England via the hippie trail.

Upon his return to England in 1974, Noble began working on plans for a jet-powered car capable of earning him a place in the annals of record-breaking. To finance the all-British initiative he was forced to sell his beloved French-blue Triumph TR6, but he was destined for much greater horsepower, culminating in the most powerful car ever built. By selling his family car Richard was able to raise £1,100 and with it he bought a surplus Rolls-Royce Derwent jet engine from Fred Lewis's renowned Portsmouth Marine Salvage yard in Hampshire. The Derwent centrifugal jet engine was taken from an RAF Gloster Meteor, and developed 3,500lb of thrust. Lewis had some thirty of these Derwents in his yard, and after Noble had spent an afternoon checking them all, he persuaded Lewis to part with one for a princely sum of £200.

Thrust 1 was the first pure-jet car to be designed and built in Britain. 'I had never designed a car before in my life,' Noble recalls, 'so it was a fundamental exercise and when completed it looked like a cathedral on wheels!' *Thrust 1* was built in private garages in Thames Ditton and Turnham Green by Richard in his spare time. He was then working as export manager at GKN Floors in Maidenhead. While the end result may have looked like a 'cathedral on wheels', in demonstrations it established Noble as a determined young man with a larger than life ego-trip ahead of him. Whether or not he was to be taken seriously as a potential land speed record contender was yet to be discovered.

Noble took *Thrust 1* to RAF St Athan in South Wales for its initial trials, attaining modest speeds of between 70 to 80mph. Nevertheless, the BBC were there and, with the distinguished endorsement of Raymond Baxter, the car soon appeared on the Corporation's *Tomorrow's World*.

Richard and Sally were married on 30 July 1976, and bought a house in Rivermeads Avenue, Twickenham – the home of Project Thrust.

On 7 March 1977, the day after Noble's thirty-first birthday, *Thrust 1* was taken to RAF Fairford in Gloucestershire, which had a 10,000ft runway. However, during a run, a wheel bearing seized and *Thrust 1* did a triple airborne roll at 140mph. Noble was able to climb out unscathed but *Thrust 1* was a total write-off. That same evening he decided to push ahead with *Thrust 2*. The wrecked car was sold to a scrap merchant in Feltham for £175 and this became the total working capital for the planned *Thrust 2*. It never occurred to Noble to abandon his LSR project, cut his losses and retire gracefully from the land speed record scene. 'I'd learned a lot from *Thrust 1*, he wrote in a letter to this author in 1979. 'I knew that the next car would have to be professionally designed and I realized that the funding would have to come from sponsorship, for to do the job properly would cost very large sums of money.'

That the ill-fated *Thrust 1* had given Richard and his ambitions a high degree of credibility was soon made evident. Invited to give a lecture to a gathering of junior ranking RAF officers, and asked exactly what he would need to give his next car a chance of bringing back the World Land Speed Record, he replied, 'An Avon engine from a Lightning fighter!' After the young officers consulted their superiors, he got the engine; a Rolls-Royce Avon 210 from an obsolete F2A Lightning that had been withdrawn from service. The price to Richard was 'nominal'.

More, however, was needed now than just an engine and some credibility. He required a very competent engineer who could translate his dreams into reality. Unable to afford to advertise, Richard drafted a 'devastatingly simple' press release headed: 'Wanted: 650mph car designer'. This novel and attention-seeking approach gained a lot of media exposure, particularly in the *Daily Telegraph*, and attracted an enormous number of equally eccentric applicants. On the learned recommendation of Ken Norris, who designed Donald Campbell's *Bluebird-Proteus CN7*, John Ackroyd was selected. John was at that time working as a contract designer with Porsche in Germany, and had behind him a career that spanned aircraft and hovercraft, as well as automotive design. These were ideal qualifications for the job ahead but at that time there were insufficient funds in the sponsorship kitty to employ him full time. However, such was Ackroyd's enthusiasm for the project that he put in long hours of his spare time at the drawing board getting the initial design concept together in addition to maintaining his demanding full-time employment with Porsche.

In 1977, a piece of very good luck came Richard's way with the offer by the *Daily Express* of a 1,000 sq ft stand space free of charge at the Motorfair it was organizing at London's Earl's Court. Though the stand space itself was free, Richard still had to find contractors' fees for its construction, amounting to some £5,000, so he sold advertising space on the stand in order to pay for it. 'It was a tremendous gamble; if we didn't succeed in getting the stand together our credibility would have been back at zero and the project dead,' he says. It was a close run thing to get the display off the ground but public response at the exhibition was incredible.

Of the many thousands of visitors to the first-floor stand, one set was to prove very important indeed. A group of executives from Tube Investments, one of the firms that had taken out advertising space with Noble, paid a visit. Richard explains, 'The team and I pooled what little money we had left – it mounted to some £65 – and we blew the lot on taking them to lunch.' It proved to be money well spent, for the company responded with an offer to build, free of charge, the massive spaceframe of *Thrust 2* – the biggest such chassis ever built in Britain at that time. Tube Investments assigned Ken Sprayson to the project.

By May 1978, John Ackroyd had become a full-time member of the project team, Initial Services and Loctite UK having by this time responded to Richard's approaches and provided cash sponsorship for what they saw as a very exciting enterprise. By now in schools across the country the talk among classrooms was of a new *Boy's Own*-type hero who had emerged with a dream that was gaining momentum as a reality.

Within a year, the spaceframe had been completed and the Rolls-Royce Avon 210 jet engine installed, at which point the entire building programme was transferred to the Ranalagh Works in Fishbourne, on the banks of Wootton Creek on the Isle of Wight, a location chosen because it offered relatively cheap workshop facilities and contained a wealth of aircraft engineering expertise and skilled labour. John Ackroyd came from the Isle of Wight and by taking him on as designer, Noble knew he would be able to tap into the island's manpower infrastructure. Ackroyd always joked that his trusty old Hercules push-bike was his company car.

There were now five full-time members on the Project Thrust team. In addition to Richard and John Ackroyd these were operations manager Eddie Elsom and development engineers Ron Benton and Gordon Flux. A further team of eight part-timers included an RAF Lightning engine specialist and an electronics engineer. Others handled the accounts, publicity and transport and Sally, Richard's devoted wife, ran the Thrust Supporters Club, membership of which was now growing towards thousands.

The original Project Thrust concept had been that it would be a three-stage operation with *Thrust 2* being built and run in demonstrations purely as a fund raiser for the planned *Thrust 3*, which would be the actual land speed record vehicle. It soon became apparent, however, that the potential of *Thrust 2* was such that it would be able to exceed 650mph and from that moment the elusive record came within sight.

In May 1980, *Thrust 2* was given its first static engine test at RAF Coningsby, Lincolnshire, prior to the first running trials at Leconfield, just north of Humberside, a former active airbase, now operating as an army training centre run by Colonel Pat Reger. Noble had trouble attaining any sort of meaningful speed at Leconfield, averaging little more than 180mph on the bumpy runway. This test was soon followed by *Thrust 2*'s first public exhibition run at HMS *Daedalus*, Lee-on-the-Solent in Hampshire, where Noble attained a more acceptable 200mph.

Then, over the weekend of 24 and 25 September 1980, Richard Noble and the bodyless jet car claimed no fewer than six new British land speed records at RAF Greenham Common. Among them, Barry Bowles's 218.71mph (351.03kph) flying quarter-mile mark set in his rocket-powered dragster the *Blonde Bombshell* at Elvington airfield in Yorkshire in October 1977. Noble demolished Bowles's record at 259.74mph

Driving Thrust 2 *on its aluminium wheels across the hallowed Bonneville Salt Flats proved to be an 'utter nightmare' for the indefatigable Richard Noble. However, on 10 October 1981 he attained a respectable 418.118mph (672.03kph) average through the kilometre, despite a faulty battery connection which cut off the fuel supply halfway through the measured distance. It was the fastest speed ever achieved by a British car and driver. (Author's collection)*

(418kph), but the most satisfying record was a new 248.87mph (400.32kph) figure for the flying mile.

Within a year, Noble had gone back to the RAF and negotiated the purchase of a more powerful Rolls-Royce Avon 302 series engine from a Lightning F6 supersonic fighter. This 17,000lb thrust jet power unit provided 20 per cent more power than the 210 series it replaced.

The vehicle, 27ft 2in long, 4ft 6in high at the top of the streamlined body and rising to 7ft 2in at the top of the two stabilizing fins at the rear, weighed 8,000lb dry – some 5,000lb heavier than the *Budweiser Rocket* – and rode on hand-forged L77 solid alloy wheels. Each wheel had a diameter of 30in and was 4in wide, with a rolling radius of 14.8in. Suspension was independent all round.

To accommodate the new 302 engine *Thrust 2* was modified at the Ranalagh Works, and Noble brought in a team of expert panel beaters, including Brian Ball, to join Ron Benton in fabricating the body panels. The spaceframe chassis was clad in a smooth aluminium, flush-rivetted bodyshell, while Westland moulded the fibreglass engine intake nacelle. The new 302's first static engine test soon followed at RAF Wattisham in Suffolk.

Richard Noble launched the modified *Thrust 2* on 8 September 1981 in Birmingham's Metropole Hotel, clinching an attractive £40,000 sponsorship deal with Fabergé soon after. By the end of September, with the team full of hope and optimism, the gold, white and red machine was shipped out to the hallowed Bonneville Salt Flats. Noble was intent on breaking Gary Gabelich's long-standing record.

Driving *Thrust 2* on its aluminium wheels across the salt proved to be an 'utter nightmare' for the indefatigable Noble. Initial tests were conducted without reheat, attaining little more than 270mph. The car that had been running so smoothly and with stability on wheels shod with Dunlop rubber in Britain, developed a tendency to yaw to the right. Gradually, Noble progressed to speeds in the low 300mph regime, but again *Thrust 2* veered to the right. On one 400mph sortie across the salt flats, Richard was joined in the passenger cockpit by car designer John Ackroyd, riding on the other side of the mighty Rolls-Royce jet engine – something of a progression from his trusty old Hercules push-bike.

Then, on 10 October, Noble, now alone in the cockpit attained a respectable 672.03kph (418.118mph) average through the kilometre, despite a faulty battery connection which cut off the fuel supply halfway through the measured distance. It was the fastest speed ever achieved by a British car and driver, but it was a long way from Gabelich's record.

Within days the salt flats were under 4in of water. Without further ado the *Thrust 2* entourage crated up and returned to England, vowing to return for another shot in 1982. But Richard Noble's abortive attempts to regain the World Land Speed Record for the United Kingdom never really got off the ground at Bonneville: the weather was against the Project Thrust team in 1981 and the following year. No sooner had the team arrived back at the Bonneville course in 1982, than the salt flats disappeared under 4ft of water. Freak weather conditions had again flooded the saline plain and even Salt Lake City, some 120 miles away, saw its citizens fleeing from their homes to escape the floods. With no positive fall-back plan for the record attempt and their dwindling sponsorship budget being eaten away, the Project Thrust team had very little time for choosing an alternative site.

Noble immediately initiated a search of the western United States yielding two potential alternative sites to Bonneville – the immense Alvord Desert in Oregon, a dry lake bed that was selected by Bill Fredrick for

Above: *Unlike Walt Arfons' free-wheeling, rocket-powered* Wingfoot Express II, *the jet-powered* Wingfoot Express *was driven to a new World Land Speed Record at Bonneville in 1964. Walt Arfons kneels before his creation, exposing the great maw of the business-end of the jet prior to the fitting of the vertical tail fin. (Author's collection)*

Right: *The Westinghouse J46 10,000hp triple-jet powered* Wingfoot Express *driven by Tom Green during the record breaking run at Bonneville. Green averaged 413.02mph (664.95kph) through the mile on the afternoon of Friday 2 October 1964. It was a tremendous victory for thirty-year-old Green and the car's owner, Walt Arfons, and it came as the lowering sun warned that time on the salt was running out for the duo. (Author's collection)*

Above: *Walt Arfons (standing) offers last minute advice to Bobby Tatroe before the record attempt in the* Wingfoot Express II.
Left: *The rocket-powered* Wingfoot Express II *arrived at Bonneville in October 1965 with its team of experimentalists, Walt Arfons and driver Bobby Tatroe (left), and within two hours the delta-shaped car was ready for its assault on the sound barrier. (Author's collection)*

Right: *Designed and built by Walt Arfons, the* Wingfoot Express II *by all accounts should have exceeded the speed of sound at Bonneville. The final version had twenty-five 1,000lb Aerojet (JATO) solid fuel rockets, fifteen mounted in the tail supplemented by five more bolted on each side of the fuselage. Driver Bobby Tatroe approached 510mph (821kph) but again was robbed of sufficient thrust to surpass the official mile and indeed the sound barrier. (Author's collection)*

Below: *A striking rear view of the* Wingfoot Express II *shows Walt Arfons' endeavours to increase high-speed stability of the car. The rear wheels extend beyond the rear of the vehicle and have a wide track for roll stability. (Author's collection)*

In August 1962, the $250,000 Spirit of America *was loaded on a trailer and brought to the desolate Bonneville Salt Flats. Accompanying the vehicle was an expert working crew of more than twenty men and women, seen here shortly after their arrival on the salt, equipped with everything from a complete machine shop to spare parts. (Author's collection)*

Opposite: *A rare colour photograph of Craig Breedlove's* Spirit of America *cutting an almost surreal outline against the Bonneville skyline in July 1963. Numerous test runs and minor adjustments were made and after a week of teething problems the car was ready. (Author's collection)*

Right: *Craig Breedlove and his* Spirit of America *jet car, in which he set the World Land Speed Record at 407.45mph (655.696kph) at Bonneville on 5 August 1963. As far back as 1954, Captain George E.T. Eyston had predicted that the next holder of the record would be an American hot rodder who learned his craft during the Bonneville National Speed Trials. Below: Following the black sighting strip marked in the salt, Craig Breedlove hurtles the* Spirit of America *into the start of the measured mile marked by timing equipment each side of the 100ft wide course. (Author's collection)*

Against a mountainous backdrop, the Spirit of America *roars through the measured mile at Bonneville on the first run on the morning of 15 October 1964. Breedlove's speed: 513.33mph (826.12kph). (Author's collection)*

In 1965, Craig Breedlove showed up on the salt stage with a new car, the 4½-ton Spirit of America – Sonic I, *at first thought to be capable of travelling faster than the speed of sound. The new* Spirit *was powered by a General Electric J79 thrust jet engine and had four wheels to satisfy the FIA. (Author's collection)*

Craig Breedlove prepares to regain his record from Art Arfons on 15 November 1965. This frontal aspect of the Spirit of America – Sonic I *shows Breedlove's wide, tinted screen and the snug cockpit below the vast intake for the turbojet engine. (Author's collection)*

Craig Breedlove emerges from the cockpit of Spirit of America – Sonic I *after cementing a new record of 555.483mph (893.921kph). The vehicle's waisted centre later earned it the nick-name 'the Coca-Cola bottle', regardless of its superior engineering and otherwise streamlined appearance. (Author's collection)*

Kitty O'Neil's 1976 sortie in the *SMI Motivator*, and the Black Rock Desert, Nevada. On the advice of British *Thrust* follower, Peter Moore, they settled for the Black Rock Desert, a relatively unknown alkali playa, once part of prehistoric Lake Lahontan, near the little town of Gerlach (population: 350) on the far edge of the desert, some 600 miles west of Bonneville. Incredibly, Richard Noble relocated his team to the Black Rock Desert in just six short days – an outstanding feat without precedent in record history.

Dry lakes are the flattest of all geological land forms. The Black Rock Desert is a playa, a pluvial lake, one of 120 dating from the Pleistocene epoch, about 1.5 billion years ago. Glacial activity dropped temperatures and increased precipitation, creating hundreds of pluvial lakes, which fluctuate between wet and dry phases. They appear in arid regions in the lowest areas of basins and contain great quantities of sediment. Black Rock originally received its water from overflow of rivers in the Calico Mountains to the north-west. In time, the water sources disappeared, the lake dried and the arid Nevada Desert now keeps it that way except for the briefest of periods when rain floods its surface to a depth of a few inches.

The desert winds blow the water (and suspended sediment) back and forth across the lake surface, filling cracks and smoothing the silt. When the water evaporates, the lake is perfectly flat and smooth. Once dry, Black Rock is also hard; the water and winds remove dissolved salts from the sediment, which dries to a hard crust – from 19 to 45 centimetres (7½ to 13½ inches) deep at Black Rock. The Sierra Nevada has a great number of lakes like Black Rock and the nearby Hualapai Flats, names well known to all involved in drag racing and land speed – El Mirage,

In 1982, freak weather conditions had again flooded the Bonneville Salt Flats for Thrust 2. *Incredibly, Richard Noble relocated his team to the vast Black Rock Desert, Nevada, in just six short days – an outstanding feat without precedent in record history. (Castrol International)*

China Lake, Lucerne, Carson Sink, Searles, Cuddeback, Harper, Koehn, Winnemucca; Rogers, the largest dry lake in the world, is clearly visible to the traveller flying into Los Angeles from the east. This author's wife, Rosemary found the spectacle of this vast desert region an awe-inspiring experience as we flew to LA on a recent vacation to Southern California.

Before *Thrust 2* could run on the prehistoric mud lake, Noble had to acquire a permit from the Bureau of Land Management (BLM), which is responsible for maintaining the environment and natural habitat of the region. Initial objections to the record attempt were thwarted when the citizens of Gerlach and Empire lobbied the BLM; Noble and the enthusiastic townsfolk were given the 'green light'. It was go. . . .

In wintry conditions, with the thermometer reading around 43°F and with rain threatening, Richard Noble made an attempt at the World Land Speed Record on Thursday 3 November at 11.59 a.m. Unfortunately, poor surface conditions did not allow *Thrust 2* to be taken far enough back for a proper run-in to the measured mile. Nevertheless, the two-way average speeds were 575.489mph (926.09kph) and 575.652mph (926.88kph) respectively. Noble had once again upped the British car and driver mark. An earlier pass on the valley floor had yielded 463.683mph (746.57kph) through the mile and 754.62kph (468.972mph) in the kilometre.

Friday 4 November was to be the big day at Black Rock, the day Richard Noble would end an eight-year struggle to realize his dream of exceeding the existing record of 622.407mph (1,001.664kph) set by Gary Gabelich on 23 October 1970 in the exquisite 35,000hp, rocket-powered *The Blue Flame*. Before Noble could commence his assault on the record, the USAC timekeepers moved the timing traps 1 mile further north because of adverse weather conditions.

After spending almost an hour inspecting the car and talking with the designer John Ackroyd, Noble, looking like a middle-weight wrestler in his black racing suit and face mask, climbed into the now familiar cockpit of *Thrust 2*. After running through a carefully typed check-list and actuating a sequence of switches and associated valves, Noble gave the thumbs up and the cockpit canopy was sealed. Operations manager, Eddie Elsom announced 5 minutes to the start of the first run. The red Palouste turbine starting unit was connected to its socket adjacent to the offside front wheel, and whined into life, flames darting from its exhaust as it began to spin *Thrust 2*'s Avon turbine. A muffled thunder and a stream of heat from the engine's exhaust signalled that the ex-Lightning fighter unit had ignited and as Noble built up the power against the brakes the Palouste was hurriedly disconnected and the panel covering its socket replaced. The turbine now reached a crescendo that sent vibrations into the chest of Noble, strapped into the sweltering cockpit. Suddenly, *Thrust 2* lurched forward with a crackling roar. Blasting clouds of dust into the air, the car roared away from the line – the earth trembled as the 4-ton leviathan gathered momentum, trailing the distinctive rooster tail of flying dust from the mud lake. Within 10 seconds the car was lost to the eye as the reflective morning haze cast a watery sheen on the dry, sun-baked desert course. A voice crackled over the radio from control. 'It's a beautiful run . . . 596.421mph [959.03kph] through the mile, 596.412mph [959.01kph] through the kilo.' *Thrust 2* pulled up at the 8½ mile marker, the course was declared clear and the mad rush began as the crew converged on the car at the end of the course for the turnaround. Noble, jubilant at the result, got out of the cockpit and declared, 'I'm still alive.' If Noble could make a return run in excess of 650mph he would achieve the project objective, but there were problems. On the first run the car registered an incredible 20° yaw angle on occasions.

Tension was high, but controlled. Noble's brain was like a blowlamp: it went straight to the point and ignored everything else. Two minutes later he kitted up again and climbed back into the cockpit to begin what he must have known was likely to be his very last attempt to regain the record. The bowser pulled away having replenished the fuel tanks with Jet-A spirit. A short countdown commenced and *Thrust 2* was once more blasting its way toward the distant measured mile and Noble's dream.

The performance was poor and all hopes were soon dashed as the car sped on its course. Even before the run was over everyone knew the attempt to beat Gary Gabelich's record had failed. The voice of the USAC timekeeper crackled once again over the radio from control, 'Return run: 584.795mph [941.00kph] through the mile, 587.121mph [945.01kph] through the kilo.' *Thrust 2* had peaked at 615mph, averaging 590.551mph (950.54kph) in the mile and 590.843mph (951kph) in the kilometre, raising Noble's own British car and driver record in the process. Emerging from the cockpit of *Thrust 2*, Richard Noble hugged his wife, Sally, both obviously reflecting in silence . . . So near, and yet so far.

Conditions at Black Rock on 4 November could barely have been more favourable, despite the pressures from the local environmentalists to have his earlier attempts temporarily banned. The vehicle, however, simply couldn't produce the required thrust to exceed the existing record.

Initial design considerations for the vehicle had not led to an aerodynamic configuration that fell in the range from high subsonic to low supersonic. The lower surface of the vehicle was flat, which, at high subsonic speeds would not dissipate the swell of pressure and boundary layer build-up approaching low supersonic speeds. The centre of pressure was located forward of the centre of gravity, alleviating the necessary counteraction against yaw tendencies, through the emplacement of two, short vertical stabilizing fins at the rear instead of a more appropriate single sharply raked stabilizing fin, which would have significantly reduced the 20° yaw angle registered on occasions. It must have been painfully obvious to John Ackroyd that, having overcome earlier mechanical and aerodynamic setbacks at Bonneville, he was now faced with a design concept which fell well below the required standard to capture the World Land Speed Record for the United Kingdom.

That evening in Bruno's Country Club in downtown Gerlach, the board of Thrust Cars Limited decided unanimously to abandon their assault on the record and project objective. Looking strained under the subsequent pressure from his sponsors, Richard Noble pledged he would return to England to raise the necessary funds to return to the Black Rock Desert in 1983.

In 1983 the *Thrust 2* team came back to Gerlach; this time vital modifications had been made to the underside of the car, and the team had a realistic organisational strategy . . . they meant business! But *Thrust 2* refused to start . . . Richard Noble sat patiently in the cockpit and tried again. Nine years is a long time to wait – nine years to spend just 5½ seconds covering one mile of hard sun-baked desert. Attempting the culmination of a lifelong ambition, one could be forgiven for being nervous. Richard Noble could not afford nerves. . . . He tried again. . . . *Thrust 2* still refused to start.

Everything else was perfect. The car had been polished. The wind sock on the mast of the Project Thrust base camp hung limply; the vast Black Rock Desert was almost wind free. Memories of the almost monsoon conditions at Bonneville 12 months before were forgotten. It was just before 2 p.m. on Tuesday 4 October 1983, the hottest time of the day. The ambient temperature was 75°F; near perfect land speed weather and better

THRUST 2

Length:	27ft 2in
Width:	8ft 4in
Height:	4ft 6in, rising to 7ft 2in at top of tail fins
Wheelbase:	20ft 10in
Track (front):	76in
(rear)	90in
Weight:	8,000lb (dry)
	8,500lb (with fuel and driver)
Ground Clearance:	5in
Engine:	Rolls-Royce RG 146 Avon Mk 302C
Engine Weight:	2,938lb
Fuel:	Avtur A-1 Capacity: 124 gallons. Consumption at max reheat: 50 gallons per minute
Lubricants:	Engine Oil: OX-38 12 pints
	Turbo Pump Oil: OX-38 500 cc
	Air Starter; OX-38 50 cc
Wheel Hubs:	Kluber Isoflex Topaz NB52-12 cc per bearing
Chassis:	Tubular steel – Reynolds 531 spaceframe and 28 SWG stainless steel firewalls with 277 Rockwool sandwich
Body Shell:	Aluminium panels flush riveted with GRP 8 layers of .011in Resin 199 over nose intake
Wheels:	Four hand forged L77 aluminium
Wheel Dimensions:	
(front):	30 O/D × 4 in wide. Rolling radius: 14.8in
(rear):	30 O/D × 4 in wide. Rolling radius: 14.8in
Suspension:	4 wheels, independent all round
	Front: Nearly parallel wishbones 1.5in travel
	Rear: Trailing A Frames 1.5in travel
	Springs: Hollow rubber compression and rebound
	Dampers: 2 per wheel, gas/hydraulic
	Hubs: Timken taper roller bearings
Steering:	Rack and Pinion (Adwest) ratio 25:1
Braking:	600mph (24,000lb drag) 7ft 6in diameter Irvin transonic parachute: 375mph (24,000lb drag) Cluster of three 7ft 6in in diameter Irvin parachutes: 125mph; Lucas Girling wheel disc brakes
Thrust:	17,000lb

than the conditions at Bonneville in 1981, better than Black Rock the previous year. Morale was high. So was the temperature in the cockpit of *Thrust 2* as Noble, dreaming of a place in the annals of record-breaking waited for the verdict. A fuse had blown!

An ambition of a lifetime was held up by a blown igniter fuse. Changing it was simple; the problem was that the service van was 15 miles away at the other end of the projected run, ready to turn *Thrust 2* round within the permitted time limit of one hour. The radio buzzed, Noble waited, the fuse arrived and was fitted, the service van sped back across the mud flats for the 15-mile return journey. The wind sock had not moved, the temperature had not dropped. Richard Noble took his chance.

Hands firmly on the yoke steering wheel, left foot ready on the brake pedal, the other on the accelerator, Noble began to depress the pedal under his right foot. The high-pressure cock was opened and fuel from the 124 gallon tank began to enter the mighty Rolls-Royce Avon 302 engine.

The noise and the spectacle were matters of which Noble was oblivious. After all, he had driven this car before. He continued progressively to push down the accelerator pedal to full throttle to begin the most important 59 seconds of his life. That was the moment when Noble applied *Thrust 2*'s kick-down to instigate the afterburner. The trick, as he puts it, is to hold the throttle to the floor for as long as possible on full thrust – in this case, 34,000hp for 59 seconds.

The instruments showed that *Thrust 2* was running perfectly; Noble had pulled his heavy machine away from the line and concentrated on the distant marker buoys. Up to 350mph *Thrust 2* is steered, after that she will run straight unaided. The difficulty is making sure the vehicle is pointing in the correct direction; from then on it's basically a question of aiming. Noble had had problems seeing the marker buoys during previous runs, but now they were more visible and he kept the nose of the car 11ft away from them, running parallel.

At 2.38 p.m. *Thrust 2* broke the timing beam just over 5 miles away from the starting point. The first flying mile took 5.767 seconds at a peak speed of 632mph (1,017kph) and an average of 624.241mph (1004.616kph). The team turned *Thrust 2* around, refuelled her and prepared for the return run. From south to north there was a slightly longer run-up over six miles, and the mud was harder baked, which meant that there would be less drag on the wheels and on paper this should produce a quicker run.

For the second time Noble was catapulted across the Nevada Desert, the nose of *Thrust 2* breaking the timing light at 24 minutes 38.724 seconds past 3 o'clock. A mere 5.599 seconds later, Noble had covered one mile. With his right foot flat to the boards, the Rolls-Royce engine had consumed the Avtur fuel at a rate of just under one gallon per second, and the average speed for the mile was 642.971mph (1,034.758kph), with a peak reading of just over 650mph (1,046kph).

Richard Noble hit the right-hand button on the steering yoke and the 7ft 6in Irvin transonic braking parachute opened and began to slow the 8,500lb vehicle and its intrepid passenger. The 24,000lb of drag brought the speed down to around 375mph before Noble hit the second button, a cluster of three more chutes opened and *Thrust 2* coasted to a leisurely 125mph. Noble applied his left foot braking technique and the Girling disc brakes brought the machine to a halt. On hearing USAC timekeeper Dave Petrali announce the return speed for the mile, Noble reported, 'My God, I thought, that's bloody fast!'

Long before, it seemed, the timing computer had confirmed that history had been made; the official average speed was 633.468mph (1,019.465kph). Dave Petrali would sign the timing certificate. Richard Noble's remarkable Project Thrust had begun nine years before and now Britain once again held the World Land Speed Record.

Richard Noble is a formidable disciplinarian who attained a peak of perfection against daunting odds. Fame is spread by images such as his, which eventually become legendary. In the late 1990s, as a gripping Anglo-American match race began to create the world's first supersonic land speed record, he was determined to achieve this world first for Britain . . . the proudest of all nations in the competition for the World Land Speed Record.

NINE

THE DRAMA IN THE DESERT

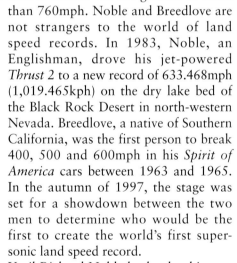

Richard Noble is a formidable disciplinarian who attained a peak of perfection against daunting odds. Fame is spread by images such as this, which eventually become legendary. In the late 1990s, as a gripping Anglo-American match race began to create the supersonic land speed record, he was determined to achieve this world first for Britain. (Author's collection)

It is now over fifty years since Chuck Yeager and the Bell X-1 first whiplashed the Mojave Desert with a supersonic boom. What was at the time considered impossible, or at best difficult, became commonplace twenty-five years later, and now does not seem remarkable at all. For over forty years, supersonic jet fighters have routinely exceeded Mach 1 in level flight and for over twenty years a supersonic jet transport, the BAC-Aerospatiale Concorde, has plied the skies.

Just as the world witnessed Chuck Yeager breaking the 'sound barrier' in the Bell X-1 fifty years ago, in 1997 it focused on two high priests of high speed, Richard Noble and Craig Breedlove, as each of their teams attempted to blast through that elusive barrier on the ground at more than 760mph. Noble and Breedlove are not strangers to the world of land speed records. In 1983, Noble, an Englishman, drove his jet-powered *Thrust 2* to a new record of 633.468mph (1,019.465kph) on the dry lake bed of the Black Rock Desert in north-western Nevada. Breedlove, a native of Southern California, was the first person to break 400, 500 and 600mph in his *Spirit of America* cars between 1963 and 1965. In the autumn of 1997, the stage was set for a showdown between the two men to determine who would be the first to create the world's first supersonic land speed record.

Until Richard Noble broke the thirteen-year-old World Land Speed Record in 1983 American interest in the mark had lain largely dormant, but that changed with the introduction of a new contender, Craig Breedlove's latest $3 million reincarnation of his legendary *Spirit of America* thoroughbreds: a 47ft, 8,500lb projectile financed by corporate America – the *Spirit of America – Sonic Arrow*.

The new, third-generation *Spirit* is an all-composite structure powered by a modified General Electric J79 GE-8D-11B-17 jet engine from a US Navy F-4 Phantom, developing an awesome thrust output of 22,650lb, 48,000hp, with a maximum afterburn thrust of around 24,000lb. The engine is fuelled by 92 octane unleaded Formula Shell Premium from an 118 gallon capacity fuel chamber located behind the front wheels, forward of the powerplant. The vehicle's fuselage, wings and fairings are engineered around a spaceframe of Ryerson-Rystar steel tubing with a stressed Alcoa aluminium bodyshell and bulkheads. The vehicle, 47ft in length, 8ft 4in wide and 5ft 10in high at the top of the tail fin, weighs 9,000lb with fuel and driver, and rides on five 36.5in Center Line/Alcoa heat-treated alloy wheels, banded with narrow strands of Hercules filament-wound carbon fibre with a rubberized Goodyear epoxy matrix tread, consisting of three close-coupled front wheels on a single axle, and two outrigged rear wheels mounted on the end of sharply swept torsional flexing wheel struts. Longitudinal stability is provided by aerodynamic fairings over fully enclosed, outrigged rear wheels on a 7ft 4in wide track extended beyond the rear of the vehicle, and pitch stability is controlled by the driver from a form-fitting cockpit through the emplacement of two canard foreplanes and rear wing strut trim tails.

Steering is through the front wheels and controlled by a 'self-centering yoke system', invented by Breedlove, which, thanks to a gentle rocking motion, prevents the wheels from digging into a potentially fatal edge, and interlinked to an aerodynamic pivotal dorsal fin on top of the fuselage above the front wheel housing. The cockpit capsule, a complete monocoque unit, is constructed of Hercules/Kevlar carbon fibre and the driver is protected by a carved-billet bulkhead. Inside, there are two pedals: go and stop. There are two thumb switches, for the mortar-deployed Syndex Aerospace parachute braking system and its back-up drogue. Braking is completed by a friction ski system mounted on the underside of the vehicle for speeds below the 200mph regime. Breedlove calls this his 'Fred Flintstone' brake! He designed the car from 'a blank piece of paper'. Conceiving every minute detail of a land speed record car and then realizing the results is, according to the inventor, 'like building an F-16 in your garage with six people to help you'.

Shell Oil Products is the primary sponsor of the *Spirit of America – Sonic Arrow*. Formal announcement of Shell's continuing support was made in a press conference at the Petersen Automotive Museum in Los Angeles on 15 November 1995 – the thirtieth anniversary of Breedlove becoming the first man to officially drive a car 600mph. That pinnacle of fame assured him a place in history. For a time, that was enough. Then, about 15 years ago, Breedlove lost his first wife, Peggy. In one of the profoundly cruel ironies that life sometimes concocts, she, not he, was killed in a car accident, by a drunk driver. 'For many years I was lost, I had no purpose,' he remembers. 'I needed to fill that empty space with a goal. I turned to what I knew best . . . ultimate speed on land.'

Breedlove's dream of resurrecting the *Spirit of America* was stalled until, out of nowhere, Hollywood actor Craig T. Nelson, himself a race car driver, appeared and stepped in with the money and connections to help his idol write the *Spirit of America*'s final chapter. Nelson and his celebrated Screaming Eagles Racing World Sports Car team support the entire all-American initiative. Nelson recently purchased the movie rights for Breedlove's dramatic life story.

After Richard Noble set the land speed record in 1983, he designed, built and certified a new light aircraft, the ARV Super 2, with which he intended to challenge the American monopoly of the market. This was followed in 1988 by an involvement with Adrian Hamilton's transatlantic record bid with the *Atlantic Sprinter*, but the Blue Riband challengers were unable to attract a sponsor.

Noble's supersonic dream began in 1992, when he went down to the Bournemouth Flying Club to see Ken Norris, who had been team manager with *Thrust 2* from 1982 onwards. Norris introduced him to Ron Ayers, who had been doing a spot of research into the history of land speed record-breaking at the Brooklands Museum in Weybridge. Ron Ayers had been Head of Operations Research and Deputy Head of Management Services for the British Aircraft Corporation Guided Weapons Division at Bristol, and was chief aerodynamicist on the Bloodhound 2 anti-aircraft missile. Bloodhound 2 was developed by the Bristol Aeroplane Co. and Ferranti in 1958 as the RAF's SAM for home defence under the code name Red Duster.

Noble told Ayers of his plans for a supersonic car and tentative research commenced. First they needed backing. Confident of success, the indefatigable Noble went to British industry. On 6 August 1993 Noble received a letter from Dr Brian Ridgewell, Castrol International's marketing and technology director, offering £40,000 to fund the supersonic car's detailed research and development, and *Thrust SSC* was born.

Their immediate problem was finding a method of gathering aerodynamic data. For this they turned to computational fluid dynamics (CFD) – an aerodynamic study first used in the development of a land speed record by Ray Van Aiken in 1976 for Kitty O'Neil's *SMI Motivator*. Noble and Ayers turned to a company called CDR, which was integrated with Swansea University and which, with Imperial College, London, had developed a pioneering computer analysis programme called 'Flite'. After several days on the computer at CDR, the computational fluid dynamics results on the likely performance of *Thrust SSC* were now ready for experimentation.

By the end of August they had their first composite model of *Thrust SSC*, and this was taken to the supersonic rocket sled facility at the Proof and Experimental Establishment at Pendine in South Wales for CFD verification. The model, developed by a company called G Force, accelerated from 0 to 850mph in 0.8 seconds – Mach 1.1 – then retro rockets were fired to slow it down for the deceleration phase. By studying frame by frame footage of the Pendine tests, Ayers was able to prepare an analysis of the airflow and draw up an accurate prediction of the car's behaviour. By the end of May 1994 they had completed all of the scheduled runs on the test track and compared the readings from the rocket sled with the readings from the CFD.

Construction of *Thrust SSC* began in February 1995 in Q Shed at the Defence Evaluation Research Agency, Farnborough. Noble had always envisaged *Thrust SSC* (the initials stand for supersonic car) as a research vehicle, progressing to Mach 1 in incremental steps.

It was powered by two Rolls-Royce Spey 202 Phantom fighter jet engines producing 110,000hp, and yielding a combined afterburn thrust of around 50,000lb – more powerful than two Royal Navy Leander class frigates or 1,060 Ford Escorts – making it the largest and most powerful LSR car ever built. The vehicle, 54ft in length, 12ft wide and approximately 7ft high at the top of the tailplane (dependant on suspension), weighed a staggering 10.5 tons, and was fabricated around a spaceframe of welded T45 steel tubing, while the two engine nacelles and central nose moulding were of a carbon fibre composite, with the remainder of the body a mix of carbon, aluminium stainless steel and titanium. The actual shape of *Thrust SSC* was arrived at through extensive Cray computer analysis at Pendine using a 1:25 scale model covered with delicate load sensors.

The engines were slung well forward of a central monocoque fuselage, housing the cockpit. Designed by Glynne Bowsher, the two wide-based, 34 × 10in HDA solid-forged alloy front wheels were housed in the outboard sides of the engine nacelles, forward of the powerplants, while the offset 34 × 6in alloy rear wheels were set on a narrow track in the central fuselage, behind the engines, creating a unique reverse tricycle layout. The centre of gravity was located forward of the fuel tank. Two engines were incorporated for stability characteristics simultaneously in pitch, yaw and roll, not for performance. Longitudinal and pitch stability was provided by a graduated fin and T-tail mounted on a long moment arm at the rear of the vehicle. In order to counteract the potentially huge aerodynamic forces on the large platform, Ayers incorporated an active suspension system to adjust the pitch attitude.

Thrust SSC had another land speed record innovation: rear-wheel steering, also developed by Glynne Bowsher. Noble was sceptical of Bowsher's pioneering steering concept initially. To convince him and other doubters, Bowsher converted an abandoned 1300cc BMC Mini to rear-wheel steering set in the same 'tandem offset' configuration he envisaged for the full-size LSR car. After initial trials at the Motor Industry Research Association's Leicester test track facility, Noble was convinced, hailing the designer 'a bloody genius'.

Noble surrounded himself with a team of automotive and aerospace engineering specialists: Glynne Bowsher, who designed the structure and the mechanical components incorporated within the shape of *Thrust SSC*, had also designed the brakes for *Thrust 2*; and Jeremy Bliss, an ingenious systems designer, created all the electronic and hydraulic systems, including the vehicle's computer-controlled active suspension system; and Ron Ayers was the team's brilliant aerodynamicist.

The *Thrust SSC* project was launched in June 1994 at the London headquarters of the Society of Motor Manufacturers and Traders, off Belgrave Square. Then Noble made one of the hardest decisions of his distinguished career – to step down and let somebody else drive the car. He turned to the power of advertising to select a candidate for the programme. After an exhaustive six-month selection procedure a suitable candidate was found.

Noble called a press conference at Brooklands on 2 February 1995 and it was announced that 32-year-old ice-cool RAF Squadron Leader Andy Green would be the driver of *Thrust SSC*. Green's CV was most impressive: he read Mathematics at Worcester College, Oxford, with sponsorship from the RAF's University Cadet Scheme, graduating with first class honours in 1983. When Richard Noble broke the land speed record in 1983, Green had just finished university and was starting officer training with the Royal Air Force. As a Squadron Leader, he is a key member of the Joust programme at the Defence Evaluation Research Agency. He was also an accomplished competitor on the Cresta Run.

In September 1996, *Thrust SSC* made its first run under power on Runway 25 at Farnborough, momentarily touching 200mph on one run. The vehicle and driver were now ready for interim

Andy Green, the first man to establish a supersonic land speed record. As an RAF Squadron Leader, he is a key member of the Joust programme at the Defence Research Agency at Farnborough. He is also an accomplished competitor on the Cresta Run. (Castrol International)

trials on the Al Jafr Desert in the Hashemite Kingdom of Jordan. The team had heard about Al Jafr from Ken Waughman who had surveyed the desert with the Royal Engineers shortly after the war, noting that 'the surface was as smooth as a billiard table'. Their intention from the outset was to push *Thrust SSC* up to the 600mph regime at Al Jafr, then take the car to the Black Rock Desert, Nevada, for the supersonic record.

Craig Breedlove, meanwhile, had originally planned to run the *Spirit* on the 5-mile Space Shuttle runway on Rogers Dry Lake at the Edwards Air Force Base, California, but there were a number of logistic problems, leaving the team no option but to head for more familiar ground . . . the Bonneville Salt Flats. Breedlove arrived at Bonneville in August 1996, attaining a reported 360mph (580kph) soon after. The limits of the salt had clearly been reached and he retired following a number of technical and personal problems. Breedlove, a passionate animal lover, was devastated after his faithful German Shepherd, Star, was run over and killed. He returned to Rio Vista, California, for checking and de-salting and took advantage of a lapsed permit to run the car on the Black Rock Desert.

Despite overnight rain, Breedlove made his first run on the desert late on Wednesday 23 October, attaining a timed speed of 448mph (721.01kph), before the great playa was swept by storms, threatening to pound the vulnerable car. On Sunday 27 October the storm passed and at exactly 1.22 p.m. Breedlove blasted away from the line toward the measured mile. The timekeeper announced a speed of 563mph (907.03kph). It was a radical ride for Breedlove. He was set to gun for Noble's long-standing record, but further storms robbed him of a return run at the mile.

Shortly before dawn on Monday 28 October, Breedlove was strapped into his exquisite stiletto of a car and set the afterburn. Moments later, the J79 turbine whined into a menacing crescendo and the *Spirit* roared towards the measured mile. The timed speed: a disappointing 470mph (757kph). The car was turned around, and, with a 4-mile run-up to the start of the measured mile, the car roared toward the horizon. Seconds later, Breedlove emerged through the mirage at incredible speed, when, at an estimated 675mph (1,103kph) the *Spirit of America – Sonic Arrow*'s left rear wheel suddenly lifted, turning the car on to its left side, scribing a 180° arc across the desert floor, before coming to a rest. Miraculously, Breedlove emerged from his battered lance unscathed. The American attempt was over for 1996, but Breedlove vowed to return for another assault on the sound barrier in 1997.

Richard Noble had arrived at the Al Jafr Desert air base on 26 October and quickly set up camp. Initially, *Thrust SSC* had to be loaded on and off its trailer each day. It was a time-consuming effort, so Noble sourced an immediate alternative. Within forty-eight hours, Richard Bailey of the Huddersfield-based company Aireshelta arranged to freight out a giant yellow inflatable hangar, enabling the team to set up a workshop on the Jordanian desert.

After initial problems with the fuel system Andy Green was able to make his first run at 230mph (371kph) on 12 November. The surface of the desert proved much harder than anything the team had experienced with *Thrust 2*. On the first run, the rear of *Thrust SSC* sustained an impact loading of more than 20 tons after Green crossed a series of inch-deep ruts cut across the 10-mile course bypassing Bedouin. Green hit one of these ruts and was airborne for 70ft or more. For the next run, four days later, Jeremy Bliss softened the gas dampers in the suspension and Green achieved 325mph (524kph). *Thrust SSC* made just one more run in

Shortly before dawn on Monday 28 October 1996, Craig Breedlove climbs into the cockpit of Spirit of America – Sonic Arrow. *On the return run, at an estimated 675mph (1,103kph), the* Spirit's *left rear wheel suddenly lifted, turning the car on to its left side, scribing a 180° arc across the desert floor, before coming to a rest. Miraculously, Breedlove emerged from his battered lance unscathed. (Peter Brock)*

Jordan that year before bad weather forced the team to abandon its plans. From now on *Thrust SSC* would be in the spotlight wherever she went. Noble's vision was now public property.

By May 1997, Noble was ready to return to Jordan, and this time he was determined to 'come back with something worthwhile'. On 25 May Andy Green made his first run at Al Jafr, with a peak speed of 136mph (219kph), before climbing to 300mph (483kph). By 4 June he attained his fastest speed yet – 479mph (771.02kph), followed soon after by an impressive 540mph (870kph), but there were problems with the course, causing the suspension to fail when a mounting bracket sheared at over 500mph. Noble knew he had a car capable of achieving his goal, but with rising midsummer temperatures the prospect of reaching the 600mph target speed was looking remote. Reluctantly, he returned the team to

SPIRIT OF AMERICA – SONIC ARROW

Length:	47ft
Width:	8ft 4in
Height:	5ft 10in at top of tail fin
Wheelbase:	27ft 6in
Track (front):	1 ft 4in
(rear):	7ft 4in
Weight (with fuel):	9,000lb
Fuel:	92 Octane, unleaded Formula Shell Premium
Fuel Tank:	118 gallon capacity. Consumption: 10 gallons per mile
Engine:	General Electric J79 GE-8D-11B-17 jet engine with afterburner
Chassis:	Ryerson-Rystar steel-tubed spaceframe
Body Shell:	Alcoa aluminium (stressed) and carbon fibre
Wheels:	Five Center Line/Alcoa heat-treated solid forged aluminium, banded with narrow strands of Hercules filament-wound carbon fibre
Wheel Dimensions:	36in × 5in dia (front and rear)
Tyres:	Goodyear rubberized epoxy matrix tread
Steering:	Self-centering yoke acting on the front wheels
Brakes:	Syndex Aerospace braking chute and back-up drogue, plus friction ski mounted on the underside of the vehicle for speeds below 200mph
Suspension:	Coil over hydraulic shock (front) suspension, (rear) variable deflection beam
Thrust:	24,000lb
Max Output:	48,000hp

Farnborough to prepare for an all-out assault on Mach 1 on the Black Rock Desert later in the year.

Until then, Noble had never really discussed the funding of the project with anyone, save perhaps for his wife, Sally. The reality of his situation was that to get his team to America, he had to raise close to £600,000 in forty-three working days. Noble sent out a distress call to the 231 companies that had supported them, and the funds began to trickle in. Then Castrol came up with a loan of around £70,000 and also took out a £20,000 logo space on the nose of the car.

Craig Breedlove, meanwhile, had arrived on the Black Rock Desert with the *Spirit of America* crew, and set up camp at the Gerlach end of the great playa below the Selenite Range. He began testing his car on 4 September. Two days later, the British team arrived on the desert.

Andy Green made his first run on 8 September, with a leisurely 148mph (219kph) pass, working up to 517mph (849kph) over five consecutive runs. On 11 September Green reached 550mph (886.kph), and then surpassed the 600mph mark for the first time, equalling Richard Noble's average from his 1983 record run, with a peak of 624mph (1,006kph).

On Thursday 25 September Green took Noble's thirteen-year-old record from 633.468mph (1,019.465kph) to a staggering 714.144mph (1,150kph), consuming fuel at the rate of 4 gallons per second. He also shattered Gary Gabelich's 630.388mph kilometre record, which Noble had just missed with *Thrust 2*. Craig Breedlove was now forced to aim for Andy Green's new World Land Speed Record.

Thrust SSC had been designed with its active suspension as an intrinsic part of the system, but after a 560mph sortie on 3 October,

Within its inflatable Aireshelta, Thrust SSC *is prepared for another day of trials on the playa. The vehicle had been designed with its active suspension as an intrinsic part of the system, but after a 560mph sortie on 3 October 1997, when the car became divergent in yaw, the design team decided* Thrust SSC *should be run with the tailplane in the fully up position, removing the active-suspension element that controlled its pitch angle. (Author's collection)*

A study in attention . . . Richard Noble's Thrust SSC *shortly after cementing the first supersonic land speed record on the immense alkali playa of the Black Rock Desert, Nevada, in 1997. The speed was an astonishing 763.035mph (1,227.985kph) or Mach 1.0175. (Castrol International)*

THRUST SSC

Length:	54ft
Width:	12ft
Height:	7ft
Wheelbase:	28ft
Track (front):	9.75ft
(rear)	1ft
Weight (with fuel):	10.5 tons
Fuel Weight:	1 ton
Engines:	Two Rolls-Royce Spey 202s
Chassis:	Welded T45 steel tube spaceframe
Body Shell:	Aluminium, carbon fibre and titanium
Steering:	Worm drive acting on the rear wheels
Wheels:	Four HDA solid forged aluminium, rear pair in staggered formation
Wheel Dimensions: (front)	34in × 10in dia (0.87 dia × 0.25 metre)
(rear)	34in × 6in dia (0.87 dia × 0.15 metre)
Braking Chute:	7ft 6in (2.28 metres) ribbon drogue plus reverse
Disc Brakes:	17in dia (0.43 metre) dia. Two on each front wheel, one on each rear wheel, two calipers acting on each disc
Peak Speed Achieved	771mph (1,241kph)
Thrust Per Engine:	9 tons
Max Output (two engines)	110,000hp (80 mw)
Afterburn Thrust:	25 tons (combined yield)
Max Acceleration:	1.05g at 600mph (965kph)

when the car became divergent in yaw, the design team decided *Thrust SSC* should be run with the tailplane in the fully up position, removing the active-suspension element that controlled its pitch angle. Emotions were high, but Green continued to edge the Mach number up point by point.

On 6 October, Breedlove ran the *Spirit of America* at 531mph (855kph) before it was Green's turn again. *Thrust SSC* averaged 714mph (1,150kph) and 727mph (1,170kph) respectively. Then, on the morning of Tuesday 7 October *Thrust SSC* went supersonic for the first time. However, the run was untimed.

On Monday 13 October Green set out to make the record official, timed by USAC. Green's petite girlfriend, Jayne Millington, *Thrust SSC*'s controller, gave the all clear over the radio, 'SSC, you are cleared supersonic. Your discretion.'

On his first run Green achieved an unbelievable speed of 749.876mph (1,206.022kph), on the second, 764.168mph (1,230kph) – Mach 1.007. *Thrust SSC* had again gone supersonic, and this time it *was* official, but Green had missed the required 1 hour turnaround for two runs by 49.6 seconds. In a fabulous, sporting gesture Craig Breedlove had given Noble his allocated time on the course.

Two days later, just before 9 o'clock, Jayne Millington began the countdown for Andy Green's most crucial run to date, and at eight minutes past the hour she announced that *Thrust SSC* was rolling. Green

thundered through the mile at 759.333mph (1,222.01kph) – Mach 1.015, sending the double clap of a sonic boom across the Nevada desert. He was halfway there. The return run was equally spectacular, peaking at 771mph (1,241.01kph) – Mach 1.03. USAC timekeeper, Dave Petrali announced the speed for both runs: 763.035mph (1,227.985kph) or Mach 1.0175. Andy Green had set the world's first official supersonic land speed record. The previous day, 14 October 1997, had been the fiftieth anniversary of Chuck Yeager's first penetration of the sound barrier in the Bell X-1, and now Andy Green had earned his place in history too. Craig Breedlove was among the first to congratulate the *Thrust SSC* team after they went supersonic, vowing to return for the record himself in 1999.

Thrust SSC was an absolute triumph of British engineering and technology. Noble had beaten the Americans in their own backyard. Few gave it a chance and even fewer gave it support, but on that final run on 15 October 1997, Andy Green proved he also had 'The Right Stuff'.

EPILOGUE

The golden era of land speed record-breaking came to a halt in 1970, but the pool of technical knowledge became greater and greater, and it was this that gave birth to the jet and rocket dragsters of the early seventies. It is now over two years since the World Land Speed Record was last broken and almost three decades since the Americans held the coveted timing slip; world interest in the record has lain largely dormant. Now the

Thrust SSC scorches a path across the great playa below the Selenite Range, achieving an unbelievable speed of 764.168mph (1,230kph) – Mach 1.007. Thrust SSC had gone supersonic and this time it was official, but Green had missed the required 1 hour turnaround for two runs by 49.6 seconds. (Castrol International)

SPEED OF SOUND, AND MACH NUMBER

In 1887, Dr Ernst Mach, an Austrian physicist, wrote a lengthy scientific paper entitled 'Photographic Registration of the Phenomena in the Air Produced by a Projectile'. This paper described experiments with artillery shells travelling at supersonic speeds through the air. The photographic registration system was called 'Schieren apparatus' (Schieren in German meaning 'shadow').

A parameter of great importance in high-speed flight is the speed of sound, the rate at which small pressure disturbances will spread through the air. As an aircraft moves through the air, velocity and pressure changes create pressure disturbances in the airflow surrounding the aircraft. If the aircraft is travelling at low speed, the pressure disturbances spread through the air ahead of the aircraft, much like the bow wave of a boat.

To understand the problem, the nature of air itself must be understood. Although invisible, the air is composed of countless extremely small atoms and molecules of nitrogen, oxygen and other gases. Each atom or molecule is so tiny that some 400 billion of them can be found in every cubic inch of the air at sea level. Sound waves can be likened to the ripples created by the dropping of a stone or pebble into still water. Travelling outward, the sound waves eventually pulsate against the ear drums, much as water pulsates when agitated.

Generally speaking, sound travels at 1,100ft per second, but this varies with altitude, air density and temperature. At 59°F (15°C) at sea level, sound travels at a speed of about 760mph (661.48knots). Between 50,000ft and 60,000ft, where the temperature averages minus 70°F (57°C), it is 660mph (573.02knots). It varies in fact with the square root of absolute temperature (absolute zero is minus 459.4°F (273°C) thus the freezing point of water is 273° Kelvin and its boiling point 373°K).

At subsonic speeds the airflow ahead of an aircraft or land-bound vehicle is relatively stable, but when the vehicle travels faster than the speed of sound, a different airflow pattern results. At such speeds, the air is compressed into a cone-like pattern called a shock or 'compression' wave. This extreme disturbance accumulates in a narrow region just ahead of the travelling vehicle or aircraft. The shock wave travels to the ground at the speed of sound, follows the path of the vehicle, and becomes audible as a sonic boom.

Thus, the aircraft or land-bound vehicle will experience compressibility effects at speeds below the speed of sound because the subsonic and supersonic flow might exist over different portions of the craft at various times during high-speed travel. The local areas of supersonic flow that occur on a land-bound vehicle travelling at speeds above the critical Mach number are accompanied by the formation of shock waves.

The airflow accelerates easily from subsonic to supersonic over a smooth airflow surface; however, when the flow is decelerated from supersonic back to subsonic without any direction change, a shock wave will form. The shock wave forms a boundary between the two regions of flow. Sharp increases in both static pressure and density, and a loss in energy to the airstream, occur across the shock waves. This energy loss might be accompanied by separation of the flow. The strength of a given wave and the magnitude of the changes across it increase with increasing Mach number.

Mach number is defined as the ratio of true airspeed (TAS) to the speed of sound. If the aircraft TAS is used to compute the Mach number, it is called the airplane Mach number. If a velocity at some point on an aircraft or land-bound vehicle is used, the resultant value is referred to as a local Mach number.

pendulum is beginning to swing back with no fewer than five competitors, including Craig Breedlove, gunning for Andy Green's record of 763.035mph (1,227.985kph) or Mach 1.0175.

AUSSIE INVADER 3

Australian record holder, Rosco McGlashan hit 498.6mph (802.01kph) at Lake Gairdner, Australia, on 27 March 1994, raising his own record to 597.165mph (951.03kph) soon after. Theoretically, McGlashan's car *Aussie Invader 2*, had a potential top speed of 670mph. That was enough to claim the Australian record, but nowhere near Mach 1.

Since setting the Australian land speed record with *Aussie Invader 2*, McGlashan has been busy building *Aussie Invader 3* in a small garage near Perth, Australia. *Aussie Invader 3* is designed around a single SNECMA 9K-50 afterburning turbojet engine, capable of producing 19,000lb of thrust, 36,000hp. The vehicle, engineered around a chassis of 4130 chrome moly tubing, is just 27ft long, 4ft high and 7ft wide, and rides on four solid forged L77 aluminium wheels.

McGlashan is sponsored by an Australian television network, 7 Sport, so whatever happens to *Aussie Invader 3* will be broadcast for the world to see. He plans his assault on Lake Gairdner, a vast salt lake 400 miles north of Adelaide in South Australia, in December 1999. Paula Elstrek, a prominent Australian race car driver, will be joining McGlashan and his team on Lake Gairdner in an attempt on Kitty O'Neil's long-standing women's record of 512.71mph (825.126kph), set on 3 December 1976.

Access to Lake Gairdner requires a drive of over 75 miles on dirt roads across the Eyre Peninsula to the last cattle station and the last services, then another 25 miles of primitive road to the lakebed. Lake Gairdner is over 100 miles long and 20 miles across with salt over 4ft thick in places. There is no shortage of flies and venomous snakes, but the greatest danger on the track is an occasional kangaroo. McGlashan says the salt is 'perfect'. But one thing is for certain: if you plan to watch McGlashan and Elstrek live you have to take everything you will ever want during your stay or expect a long drive back to collect whatever it was you forgot.

NORTH AMERICAN EAGLE

In the United States, Ed Shadle's *North American Eagle* team is planning its assault on the record in a converted military Lockheed F-104A-10 Starfighter jet, shod with four solid aluminium billet wheels, machined by Steve Green of Abbotsford BC, Canada, at a cost of $20,000. Green also performed the expensive finite element analysis to verify structural integrity.

The 52ft long, 10,000lb *North American Eagle* is powered by a modified General Electric J79 15,000lb thrust turbojet engine, consuming approximately 10 gallons of JP4 aviation fuel per second.

Similar to Craig Breedlove's General Electric J79 GE-8D-11B-17, the *North American Eagle*'s powerplant is a monster of an engine. It is just over 17ft long, and slightly more than 3ft in diameter, and weighs around 3,600lb. It is a single-shaft engine whose later high-pressure compressor stages incorporated variable-incidence stator blades. These movable components are linked together mechanically so that their position can be controlled by the fuel supply. The compressor has seventeen stages and is driven by a three-stage turbine.

The F-104A-10 is an aircraft designed for sustained Mach 2 flight, and the team envisage a joint research and development agreement with the United States Air Force at Edwards Air Force Base, California. Shadle and his team have already run the *North American Eagle* on the 5-mile Space Shuttle runway at Edwards, and plan to use the facility for the record attempt in 2000.

SONIC WIND

Waldo Stakes, from Sacramento, California, has turned to rocket propulsion for his assault. His *Sonic Wind* is powered by a mighty Reaction Motors XLR-11 engine. This four-chambered rocket motor developing 3.63 tonnes of thrust was developed for the North American X-15 hypersonic research aircraft. Stakes is fuelling his vehicle with alcohol and liquid oxygen. The driver will lie in the supine position in the nose of the vehicle. The *Sonic Wind* is of a complete monocoque design of ballistic carbon fibre composite, and, like the X-15, will ride on skis.

The *Sonic Wind* has been designed to run on a frozen lakebed, which will be graded especially for the record attempt in 2000. It is estimated the vehicle will accelerate at a constant 50mph second to 900mph. Stakes and the *Sonic Wind* team is currently conducting low speed tests on a frozen lakebed north of Oshkosh, Wisconsin.

MAVERICK

In England, meanwhile, the McLaren Formula One team has also been working in great secrecy on a supersonic car, based on a design concept similar to Craig Breedlove's *Spirit of America – Sonic Arrow*.

McLaren Advanced Vehicle's (MAV's) contender is still in the planning stages. To be called *Maverick*, it measures 46ft long, 17ft wide and 11ft high at the top of the tail fin. There is a wheel at the end of each wing, plus two alloy wheels set side by side on a common axle under the nose of the vehicle. A third of its estimated 6,600lb weight is a Turbo Union RB199 Mk 104 gas-turbine engine rated at 38,000hp, which should push the *Maverick* from 0 to 850mph in less than 40 seconds.

The vehicle is made of Kevlar carbon fibre. Much like a fighter pilot, the driver will be strapped into a gyro-controlled ejection seat programmed to blast him free if, as Mclaren's managing director, Ron Dennis delicately explains, 'the angles experienced by the computer are inconsistent with the wheels being on the ground'. Much like *Thrust SSC*, the McLaren *Maverick* has a computerized active suspension that's derived from Formula One racers. The engineers hope this will allow the vehicle to smoothly traverse the Mach 1 'speed bump.' The McLaren team plans to make its LSR attempt by the summer of 2000.

☆   ☆   ☆

For many years it was generally felt that crossing the 'sound barrier', even in today's technological age, was far from possible, yet alone safe. Now, the military jet, and indeed Concorde, fly supersonic speeds on a daily basis. As the layman might say, 'in a jet you have plenty of room for manoeuvre', but it was thought that a car travelling at such speeds would simply disintegrate within its own shock waves.

Writing in the early seventeenth century, Sir Francis Bacon said in *The Advancement of Learning*: 'By far the greatest obstacle to the progress of science and to the undertaking of new tasks and provinces therein, is found in this – that men despair and think things impossible.' The men who designed, maintained and drove the *Budweiser Rocket* and *Thrust SSC* did not despair and did not think their task impossible. Through them, automotive engineering crossed the invisible threshold to drive faster than sound.

The author is pictured here at the Bonneville Salt Flats in October 1981, shortly after Richard Noble in Thrust 2 *attained the fastest speed ever achieved by a British car and driver. Within days the famed salt flats were under 4in of water. (Author's collection)*

EVOLUTION OF THE LANI

Date	Place	Country	Driver	Nationality	Car
8.12.1898	Achères	F	Gaston de Chasseloup-Laubat	F	Jeantaud Electric
17.1.1899	Achères	F	Camille Jenatzy	B	CITA
17.1.1899	Achères	F	Gaston de Chasseloup-Laubat	F	Jeantaud Electric
27.1.1899	Achères	F	Camille Jenatzy	B	CITA
4.3.1899	Achères	F	Gaston de Chasseloup-Laubat	F	Jeantaud Electric Profilée
29.4.1899	Achères	F	Camille Jenatzy	B	CITA No. 25 La Jamais Contente
13.4.1902	Nice	F	Léon Serpollet	F	Gardner-Serpollet Oeuf de Pâques
5.8.1902	Ablis	F	William K. Vanderbilt	USA	Mors Z Paris—Vienna
5.11.1902	Dourdan	F	Henri Fournier	F	Mors Z Paris—Vienna
17.11.1902	Dourdan	F	M. Augieres	F	Mors Z Paris—Vienna
7.3.1903	Clipstone	GB	Charles S. Rolls	GB	Mors Z Paris—Vienna
17.7.1903	Ostend	B	Arthur Duray	B	Gobron-Brillié Paris—Madrid
7.1903	Dublin	IRL	Baron de Forest	F	Mors Dauphine Paris—Madrid
10.1903	Clipstone	GB	Charles S. Rolls	GB	Mors Dauphine Paris—Madrid
5.11.1903	Dourdan	F	Arthur Duray	B	Gobron-Brillié Paris—Madrid
12.1.1904	Lake St Clair	USA	Henry Ford	USA	Ford The Arrow (New 999)
27.1.1904	Daytona	USA	William K. Vanderbilt	USA	Mercedes-Simplex 90
31.3.1904	Nice	F	Arthur Duray	B	Gobron-Brillié Paris—Madrid
31.3.1904	Nice	F	Louis Rigolly	F	Gobron-Brillié 'Gordon Bennett'
31.3.1904	Nice	F	Louis Rigolly	F	Gobron-Brillié 'Gordon Bennett'
25.5.1904	Ostend	B	Pierre de Caters	B	Mercedes-Simplex 90
21.7.1904	Ostend	B	Paul Baras	F	Darracq 'Gordon Bennett'
21.7.1904	Ostend	B	Louis Rigolly	F	Gobron-Brillié 'Gordon Bennett'
13.11.1904	Ostend	B	Paul Baras	F	Darracq 'Gordon Bennett'
24.1.1905	Daytona	USA	Arther E. Macdonald	GB	Napier L48
25.1.1905	Daytona	USA	Herbert L. Bowden	USA	A Mercedes Flying Dutchman II
31.1.1905	Daytona	USA	Herbert L. Bowden	USA	B Mercedes Flying Dutchman II
15.11.1905	Arles	F	Frédéric Dufaux	CH	Dufaux Brighton
30.12.1905	Arles	F	Victor Hémery	F	Darracq V8
23.1.1906	Daytona	USA	Victor Hémery	F	Darracq V8
25.1.1906	Daytona	USA	Louis Chevrolet	USA	Darracq V8
26.1.1906	Daytona	USA	Fred H. Marriott	USA	Stanley Steamer Rocket
8.11.1909	Brooklands	GB	Victor Hémery	F	Benz No. 1
16.3.1910	Daytona	USA	Barney Oldfield	USA	Benz No. 1 Blitzen Benz
23.3.1910	Daytona	USA	Barney Oldfield	USA	Benz No. 1 Blitzen Benz
23.4.1911	Daytona	USA	Robert Burman	USA	Benz No. 1 Blitzen Benz
24.6.1914	Brooklands	GB	L.G. Hornsted	GB	Benz No. 3
12.2.1919	Daytona	USA	Ralph De Palma	USA	Packard '905' (Liberty Racer)
27.4.1920	Daytona	USA	Tommy Milton	USA	Twin Duesenberg Double Duesey
6.4.1922	Daytona	USA	Sigmund Haugdahl	USA	Wisconsin Special
17.5.1922	Brooklands	GB	Kenelm Lee Guinness	GB	Sunbeam
23.6.1923	Fano	DK	Malcolm Campbell	GB	Sunbeam Bluebird
19.6.1924	Saltburn	GB	Malcolm Campbell	GB	Sunbeam Bluebird
26.6.1924	Arpajon	F	J.G. Parry Thomas	GB	Leyland-Thomas No. 1

Engine(s)	Flying kilometres			Flying mile		
	Time(s)	kph	mph	Time(s)	kph	mph
1 × Fulmen 40bhp, electric	57.0	63.158	39.245			
1 × Fulmen 40bhp, electric	54.0	66.667	41.425			
1 × Fulmen 40bhp, electric	51.2	70.312	43.690			
1 × Fulmen 40bhp, electric	44.8	80.357	49.932			
1 × Fulmen 40bhp, electric	38.8	92.783	57.653			
2 × Fulmen-Jenatzy 60bhp, electric	34.0	105.882	65.792			
1 × Serpollet 2.95 × 3.54in, 4 cyl, electric 106bhp (S)	29.8	120.805	75.065			
1 × Mors 4 cyl, 9.2l, 60bhp	29.4	122.449	76.086			
1 × Mors 4 cyl, 9.2l, 60bhp	29.2	123.287	76.607			
1 × Mors 4 cyl, 9.2l, 60bhp	29.0	124.138	77.136			
1 × Mors 4 cyl, 9.2l, 60bhp	27.0	133.333	82.849			
1 × Gobron-Brillié 4 cyl, 13.5l, 110bhp	26.8	134.328	83.468			
1 × Mors 70bhp	26.6	135.338	84.095			
1 × Mors 70bhp	26.4	136.363	84.732			
1 × Gobron-Brillié 4 cyl, 13.5l, 110bhp	26.4	136.363	84.732			
1 × Ford 4 cyl, 16.7l, 72bhp				39.4	147.047	91.371
1 × Mercedes 4 cyl, 11.9l, 90bhp				39.0	148.555	92.308
1 × Gobron-Brillié 4 cyl, 13.5l, 110bhp	25.2	142.857	88.767			
1 × Gobron-Brillié 4 cyl, 13.6l, 130bhp	24.0	150.000	93.206			
1 × Gobron-Brillié 4 cyl, 13.6l, 130bhp	23.6	152.542	94.785			
1 × Mercedes 4 cyl, 11.9l, 90bhp	23.0	156.522	97.258			
1 × Darracq 4 cyl, 11.3l, 100bhp	22.0	163.636	101.679			
1 × Gobron-Brillié 4 cyl, 13.6l, 130bhp	21.6	166.666	103.561			
1 × Darracq 4 cyl, 11.3l, 100bhp	21.4	168.224	104.530			
1 × Napier 6 cyl, 15l, 90bhp				34.4	168.419	104.651
2 × Mercedes '60' 4 cyl, 9.2l, 60bhp				32.8	176.635	109.756
2 × Mercedes '60' 4 cyl, 9.2l, 60bhp	20.6	174.757	108.589			
1 × Dufaux 4 cyl, 26l, 150bhp	23.0	156.522	97.258			
1 × Darracq V8 ohv, 22.5l, 200bhp	20.6	174.757	108.589			
1 × Darracq V8 ohv, 22.5l, 200bhp	19.4	185.567	115.306			
1 × Darracq V8 ohv, 22.5l, 200bhp				30.6	189.334	117.647
1 × Stanley 2 cyl, horizontal 900–1,000lb psi 120bhp (S)	18.4	195.652	121.573	28.2	205.448	127.659
1 × Benz 4 cyl, ohv, 21.5l, 200bhp	17.761	202.691	125.946			
1 × Benz 4 cyl, ohv, 21.5l, 200bhp				27.33	211.988	131.723
1 × Benz 4 cyl, ohv, 21.5l, 200bhp	17.04	211.267	131.275			
1 × Benz 4 cyl, ohv, 21.5l, 200bhp	15.88	226.700	140.865	25.40	228.096	141.732
1 × Benz 4 cyl, ohv, 21.5l, 200bhp				29.01	199.711	124.095
1 × Packard Liberty V12 ohc, 14.8l, 240bhp @ 2,400rpm	14.86	242.261	150.534	24.02	241.200	149.875
2 × Duesenberg straight-eight ohc, 5l, 92bhp @ 3,800rpm	14.40	250.00	155.343	23.07	251.133	156.047
1 × Wisconsin 6 cyl, single ohc, 12.5l, 250bhp	13.80	260.869	162.097	19.97	290.117	180.270
1 × Sunbeam Manitou 60° V12, single ohc, 18.3l, 350bhp @ 2,100rpm	16.73	215.182	133.708	27.87	207.880	129.171
1 × Sunbeam Manitou 60° V12, single ohc, 18.3l, 350bhp @ 2,100rpm	16.41	219.378	136.315	26.14	221.639	137.720
1 × Sunbeam Manitou 60° V12, single ohc, 18.3l, 350bhp @ 2,100rpm	15.40	233.766	145.255	26.07	222.234	138.090
1 × Leyland Eight, straight-eight, single ohc, 7.3l, 115bhp	16.72	215.311	133.788	26.75	208.780	129.730

Continued

Date	Place	Country	Driver	Nationality	Car
6. 7.1924	Arpajon	F	René Thomas	F	Delage DH La Torpille
12. 7.1924	Arpajon	F	Ernest A.D. Eldridge	GB	Fiat Special Mephistopheles II
25. 9.1924	Pendine	GB	Malcolm Campbell	GB	Sunbeam Bluebird
21. 7.1925	Pendine	GB	Malcolm Campbell	GB	Sunbeam Bluebird
16. 3.1926	Southport	GB	Henry O'Neal de Hane Segrave	GB	Sunbeam Ladybird
27. 4.1926	Pendine	GB	J.G. Parry Thomas	GB	Higham-Thomas Special Babs
28. 4.1926	Pendine	GB	J.G. Parry Thomas	GB	Higham-Thomas Special Babs
4. 2.1927	Pendine	GB	Malcolm Campbell	GB	Napier-Campbell Bluebird
29. 3.1927	Daytona	USA	Henry O'Neal de Hane Segrave	GB	Sunbeam (Slug)
19. 2.1928	Daytona	USA	Malcolm Campbell	GB	Napier-Campbell Bluebird
22. 4.1928	Daytona	USA	Ray Keech	USA	White Triplex (Spirit of Elkdom)
11. 3.1929	Daytona	USA	Henry O'Neal de Hane Segrave	GB	Irving Napier Special Golden Arrow
5. 2.1931	Daytona	USA	Malcolm Campbell	GB	Napier-Campbell Bluebird
24. 2.1932	Daytona	USA	Sir Malcolm Campbell	GB	Napier-Campbell Bluebird
22. 2.1933	Daytona	USA	Sir Malcolm Campbell	GB	Campbell-Rolls-Royce Bluebird
7. 3.1935	Daytona	USA	Sir Malcolm Campbell	GB	Campbell-Rolls-Royce Bluebird
3. 9.1935	Bonneville	USA	Sir Malcolm Campbell	GB	Campbell-Rolls-Royce Bluebird
19.11.1937	Bonneville	USA	George E.T. Eyston	GB	Thunderbolt
27. 8.1938	Bonneville	USA	George E.T. Eyston	GB	Thunderbolt
15. 9.1938	Bonneville	USA	John Rhodes Cobb	GB	Railton
16. 9.1938	Bonneville	USA	George E.T. Eyston	GB	Thunderbolt
23. 8.1939	Bonneville	USA	John Rhodes Cobb	GB	Railton
16. 9.1947	Bonneville	USA	John Rhodes Cobb	GB	Railton-Mobil-Special
9. 9.1960	Bonneville	USA	Mickey Thompson	USA	Challenger
17. 7.1964	Lake Eyre	AUS	Donald Campbell	GB	Campbell-Norris Bluebird-Proteus CN7
12.11.1965	Bonneville	USA	Robert S. Summers	USA	Goldenrod

Unlimited Records

Date	Place	Country	Driver	Nationality	Car
5. 8.1963	Bonneville	USA	Norman Craig Breedlove	USA	Spirit of America
2.10.1964	Bonneville	USA	Tom Green	USA	The Wingfoot Express
5.10.1964	Bonneville	USA	Arthur Eugene Arfons	USA	Green Monster
13.10.1964	Bonneville	USA	Norman Craig Breedlove	USA	Spirit of America
15.10.1965	Bonneville	USA	Norman Craig Breedlove	USA	Spirit of America
27.10.1965	Bonneville	USA	Arthur Eugene Arfons	USA	Green Monster
2.11.1965	Bonneville	USA	Norman Craig Breedlove	USA	Spirit of America – Sonic I
7.11.1965	Bonneville	USA	Arthur Eugene Arfons	USA	Green Monster
15.11.1965	Bonneville	USA	Norman Craig Breedlove	USA	Spirit of America – Sonic I
23.10.1970	Bonneville	USA	Gary Gabelich	USA	RDI The Blue Flame
4.10.1983	Black Rock D.	USA	Richard Noble	GB	Thrust 2

The First Vehicle to Exceed the Speed of Sound on Land

Date	Place	Country	Driver	Nationality	Car
17.12.1979 (unofficial)	Edwards AFB	USA	Stan Barrett	USA	Budweiser Rocket

The World's First Supersonic Land Speed Record

Date	Place	Country	Driver	Nationality	Car
15.10.1997	Black Rock D.	USA	Andy Green	GB	Thrust SSC

Note: Unless otherwise stated all engines are of the internal combustion type

(S) = Steam

(R) = Rocket

Engine(s)	Flying kilometres			Flying mile		
	Time(s)	km/h	mph	Time(s)	km/h	mph
1 × Delage 60° V12, ohv, 10.6l, 280bhp @ 3,200rpm	15.62	230.473	143.210	25.12	230.638	143.312
1 × Fiat type A-12, 6 cyl, 24-valve, single ohc, 21.7l, 300bhp	15.32	234.987	146.014	24.675	234.798	145.896
1 × Sunbeam Manitou 60° V12, ohc, 18.3l, 350bhp	15.305	235.217	146.157	24.63	235.226	146.163
1 × Sunbeam Manitou 60° V12, ohc, 18.3l, 350bhp	14.83	242.751	150.838	23.878	242.635	150.766
1 × Sunbeam-Coatalen 75° V12, dohc, 12 cyl, 4l, 306bhp @ 5,300rpm	14.687	245.115	152.307	24.108	240.320	149.328
1 × Packard Liberty 45° V12, ohc, 26.9l, 400bhp	13.213	272.459	169.298	21.419	270.490	168.075
1 × Packard Liberty 45° V12, ohc, 26.9l, 400bhp	13.08	275.229	171.019	21.099	274.593	170.624
1 × Napier Lion 12 cyl, ohc, 'broad arrow', 22.3l, 450bhp	12.791	281.447	174.883	20.663	280.387	174.224
2 × Sunbeam Matabele, 12 cyl, V12, dohc 22.5l, 435bhp	11.02	326.679	202.989	17.665	327.973	203.793
1 × Napier Lion 12 cyl, ohc, 'broad arrow' 22.3l, 450bhp				11.395	333.063	206.956
3 × Packard Liberty V12, ohc, 12 cyl, 26.9l, 400bhp				17.345	334.024	207.553
1 × Napier Lion 12 cyl, ohc, 'broad arrow', 26.9l, 925bhp	9.66	372.671	231.567	15.56	372.341	231.362
1 × Napier Lion supercharged 12 cyl, ohc, 'broad arrow' 26.9l, 1,450bhp	9.09	396.040	246.088	14.65	395.470	245.733
1 × Napier Lion supercharged 12 cyl, ohc, 'broad arrow' 26.9l, 1,450bhp	8.90	404.494	251.341	14.175	408.722	253.968
1 × Rolls-Royce 'R' supercharged V12, ohc, 36.5l, 2,300bhp	8.21	438.489	272.465	13.23	437.916	272.109
1 × Rolls-Royce 'R' supercharged V12, ohc, 36.5l, 2,300bhp	8.10	444.444	276.165	13.01	445.322	276.710
1 × Rolls-Royce 'R' supercharged V12, ohc, 36.5l, 2,300bhp				11.955	484.620	301.129
2 × Rolls-Royce 'R' supercharged V12, ohc, 36.5l, 2,350bhp	7.165	502.444	312.203	11.56	501.179	311.418
2 × Rolls-Royce 'R' supercharged V12, ohc, 36.5l, 2,350bhp	6.48	555.555	345.206	10.42	556.011	345.489
2 × Napier Lion supercharged 12 cyl, ohc, 'broad arrow' 26.9l, 1,250bhp	6.39	563.380	350.068	10.28	563.583	350.194
2 × Rolls-Royce 'R' supercharged V12, ohc, 36.5l, 2,350bhp	6.26	575.080	357.338	10.07	575.336	357.497
2 × Napier Lion supercharged 12 cyl, ohc, 'broad arrow' 26.9l, 1,250bhp	6.05	595.041	369.741	9.785	592.094	367.910
2 × Napier Lion supercharged 12 cyl, ohc, 'broad arrow' 26.9l, 1,250bhp	5.68	633.803	393.827	9.132	634.398	394.196
4 × Pontiac V8 pushrod, ohv, 6.7l, 700bhp					654.359	406.60
1 × Bristol-Siddeley Proteus 4,100hp gas turbine	5.67	634.920	394.521	8.93	648.783	403.135
4 × Chrysler Hemi 426, V8, ohv, 6.9l, 608bhp	5.46	659.341	409.695	8.796	658.667	409.277
1 × General Electric J47-GE-15 5,200lb thrust jet	5.4785	657.114	408.312	8.8355	655.722	407.447
1 × Westinghouse J46-WE-8 6,200lb triple jet	5.389	668.027	415.093	8.7125	664.980	413.199
1 × General Electric J79-GE-3A 15,000lb thrust jet	5.15	699.029	434.356	8.2945	698.491	434.022
1 × General Electric J47-GE-17 5,200lb thrust jet				7.6905	754.331	468.719
1 × General Electric J47-GE-17 5,200lb thrust jet				6.8405	846.961	526.277
1 × General Electric J79-GE-3A 15,000lb thrust jet	4.111	875.699	544.134	6.7075	863.755	536.712
1 × General Electric J79-GE-3A 15,000lb thrust jet	4.027	893.966	555.485	6.485	893.391	555.127
1 × General Electric J79-GE-3A 15,000lb thrust jet	3.907	921.423	572.546	6.244	927.873	576.553
1 × General Electric J79-GE-3A 15,000lb thrust jet	3.723	966.962	600.842	5.994	996.573	600.601
1 × RD HP-LNG 22,000-V liquid fuel rocket 13,000lb thrust (R)	3.5485	1014.513	630.389	5.784	1001.666	622.407
1 × Rolls-Royce RG 146 Avon MK. 302C, 17,000lb thrust jet	3.528	1020.408	634.052	5.683	1019.468	633.468
1 × Romatec V4 bio-propellant rocket, 24,000lb thrust & Sidewinder missile 4—6,000lb thrust, 48,000bhp (R)		1190.377	739.666 (equals Mach 1.0106)			
2 × Rolls-Royce Spey 202 25,000lb thrust jet		1227.985	763.035 (Mach 1.0175)			

Ab Jenkins and the Mormon Meteor III *record car at Bonneville. Powered by a Curtiss Wright Conqueror, V-type 12 cylinder, water-colled engine developing 700hp, the car was one of the greatest engineering triumphs in racing history (see pages 54–60). (Author's collection)*

BIBLIOGRAPHY

Baker, David, *The Rocket – The History and Development of Rocket & Missile Technology*, New Cavendish Books, London, 1978.

Beckh, H.J. von, 'Technical Note AFMDC 58–11'. US Air Force Missile Development Center, Holloman, New Mexico, 1958.

Bochroch, Albert R., *American Automobile Racing*, Patrick Stephens Ltd, Cambridge, 1974.

Boddy, William, *The Story of Brooklands*, Grenville, London, 1948.

Breedlove, Craig, *Spirit of America*, Henry Regnery Company, Chicago, 1971.

Campbell, Sir Malcolm, *My Thirty Years of Speed*, Hutchinson, London, 1935.

——, *Speed on Wheels*, Sampson Low, Marston & Co. Ltd, London, 1949.

Clark, John D., *Ignition*, Rutgers University Press, New Brunswick, 1972.

Clifton, Paul, *The Fastest Men on Earth*, Herbert Jenkins Ltd, London, 1964.

Davis, S.H.C., *The John Cobb Story*, G.T. Foulis & Co. Limited, London, 1953.

Day, J. Wentworth, *The Life of Sir Henry Segrave*, Hutchinson, London, 1931.

Eyston, George E.T., *Speed on Salt*, Floyd Clymer, Los Angeles, 1939.

Goddard, Robert, *Rocket Development*, Prentice-Hall, New York, 1948.

Hardcastle, David and Jones, Peter, *Drive it! The Complete Book of British Drag Racing*, Haynes Publishing Group, Sparkford, Nr Yeovil, 1981.

Holthusen, Peter J.R., *The Land Speed Record*, Haynes Publishing Group, Sparkford, Nr Yeovil, 1986.

Horsley, Fred, *The World's Fastest Cars*, Trend Books, Los Angeles, 1955.

Houlgate, Deke, *The Fastest Men in the World-on-Wheels*, The World Publishing Co., New York, 1971.

Isenberg, Hans G., *Raketen auf Rädern* (Rockets on Wheels), Falken-Verlag GmbH, Niedernhausen/Ts, 1981.

Jenkins, Ab and Ashton, Wendell J., *The Salt of the Earth*, Clymer Motors, Los Angeles, 1945.

Käsmann, Ferdinand C.W., *Weltrekord-fahrzeuge 1898 bis heute*, Verlag W. Kohlhammer GmbH, Stuttgart, 1984.

Katz, Frederic, *Art Arfons: Fastest Man on Wheels* Rutledge, London, New York, Toronto, 1965.

Knudson, Richard L., *Land Speed Record Breakers*, Lerner, Minneapolis, 1981.

Montagu, Lord E.J., *The Gordon Bennett Races*, Cassell, London, 1963.

Noble, Richard, *Thrust*, Transworld Publishers Ltd, London, 1998.

Pearson, John, *Bluebird and the Dead Lake*, Collins Publishers, London, 1965.

Pearson, John, *The Last Hero. The Gallant Story of Donald Campbell and the Land Speed Record*, Davis McKay Company, New York, 1966.

Pershing, Bernard, *Aerodynamics and Racing Cars*, AIAA, Los Angeles, 1974.

Posthumus, Cyril, *Land Speed Record*, Osprey Publishing Ltd, London, 1971.

Shapiro, Harvey, *Faster Than Sound*, A.S. Barnes & Co. Inc, New Jersey, NY, 1975.

Sox, Ronnie and Martin, Buddy, *The Sox & Martin Book of Drag Racing*, Henry Regnery Company, Chicago, 1974.

Stambler, Irwin, *The Supercars and the Men Who Race Them*, Putnam's & Sons, New York, 1975.

Sutton, George P., *Rocket Propulsion Elements*, John Wiley & Sons, New York, 1963.

Thompson, Mickey, *Challenger*, Prentice-Hall, New Jersey, NY, 1964.

Tours, Hugh, *Parry Thomas – Designer – Driver*, Batsford, London, 1959.

Villa, Leo, *The Record Breakers, Sir Malcolm & Donald Campbell, Land and Water Speed Kings of the 20th Century*, Paul Hamlyn, London, New York, Sydney, Toronto, 1969.

Wentworth Day, J., *Speed. The Authentic Life of Malcolm Campbell*, Hutchinson, London, 1931.

Wolfe, Tom, *The Right Stuff*, Jonathan Cape, New York, 1979.

Zarem, Lewis, *New Dimensions of Flight*, E.P. Dutton & Co., New York, 1959.

FILMOGRAPHY

(Recommended Viewing)

The Fastest Man on Earth, IPC Video/Cygnet Films, Bushey, Herts, 1977.

One Second From Eternity, Pickwick Video Ltd, London, 1981.

Speed King, The Donald Campbell Story, Castle Communications Plc, London, 1994.

Thrust SSC, Clear Vision Video, Enfield, Middlesex, 1997.

Thrust SSC Supersonic Dream, Clear Vision Video, Enfield, Middlesex. 1998.

Brooklands Speed, Duke Marketing Ltd, Douglas, Isle of Man. 1999.

INDEX